DELIBERATION DAY

DELIBERATION

DAY————————————————

Bruce Ackerman and
James S. Fishkin

Yale University Press
New Haven & London

Published with assistance from the foundation established in memory of Philip Hamilton McMillan of the Class of 1894, Yale College.

Designed by Nancy Ovedovitz. Set in Galliard Old Style with Copperplate 33BC type by Achorn Graphic Services. Printed in the United States of America by Vail-Ballou Press.

Library of Congress Cataloging-in-Publication Data
Ackerman, Bruce A.
Deliberation Day / Bruce Ackerman and James S. Fishkin.
   p. cm.
Includes bibliographical references and index.
ISBN 0-300-10101-5 (cloth : alk. paper)
1. Political participation — United States. 2. Democracy — United States. 3. Elections — United States. 4. Legitimacy of governments — United States. 5. Forums (Discussion and debate) I. Fishkin, James S. II. Title.
JK1764.A27 2004
324.6′0973 — dc22   2003019490

A catalogue record for this book is available from the British Library.

The paper in this book meets the guidelines for permanence and durability of the Committee on Production Guidelines for Book Longevity of the Council on Library Resources.

10 9 8 7 6 5 4 3 2 1

FOR ROBERT DAHL

DEMOCRATIC VISIONARY

CONTENTS

PREFACE

We have been friends for almost thirty years. And looking back, this book builds on conversations that began in the good old days when we were young Yale professors in search of truth and light. But the disparate threads all came together in 1999 on a walk around Jim Fishkin's house in Austin, Texas. Within the space of an hour, we began to see how Deliberation Day might unify our separate efforts to imagine new forms of legitimacy that might sustain democratic government in the twenty-first century.

The next four years involved the exploration of many bright ideas that turned out to be dead ends. As time marched on, the clouds began to clear amid the ceaseless exchange of e-mails between Ackerman in New Haven and Fishkin in Austin.

But there is nothing like face-to-face conversation to get things really moving—and the book made great progress during the spring of 2002, when both of us were fellows at the Center for Advanced Study in the Behavioral Sciences in Palo Alto, California. Many thanks to Doug McAdam, Mark Turner, and the entire staff for sustaining this oasis.

During the long hard slog, Ackerman's ongoing work was given unstinting support by Dean Anthony Kronman of the Yale Law School. Ackerman was also given the priceless opportunity to undertake a systematic revision by the Center for Advanced Study in Budapest, where he served as a fellow during the fall of 2003. His work was also greatly enriched by some fabulous Yale graduate students from the law school, the political science department, and the economics department: Rebekka Bonner, Michael Durham, Ethan Leib, Luis Madrazo, Jon Michaels, and Julie Chi-hye Suk. Eric Tam's work on the costs of implementing Deliberation Day was so sustained and ingenious that we mark him out as a coauthor of the appendix that summarizes our findings.

Fishkin would like to single out his principal empirical collaborator Bob Luskin for innumerable insights that inform this book throughout. He would also like to thank all the members of the Special Project on Deliberative Public Opinion at the Center for Advanced Study, 2002–3. In addition to Bruce Ackerman these include Henry Brady, Jane J. Mansbridge, Shanto Iyengar, Paul Sniderman, Kasper Hansen, David Brady, Norman Bradburn, Roger Jowell, Christian List, Richard Brody, Larry Lessig, Russell Hardin, Roberto D'Alimonte, and Guillermo O'Donnell. Pam Ryan, Director of Issues Deliberation Australia, also offered key insights. Special thanks to Neil Smelser, then director of the center, who first suggested the special project, and to Bob Scott, then associate director, who helped bring it to realization at the center.

Thanks are due to the William and Flora Hewlett Foundation, its president, Paul Brest, and Senior Fellow Smita Singh, for their support of several of the projects discussed here. Fishkin is also grateful to the Renee B. Fisher Foundation for support that allowed him to bring some of the scholars together at the center, and to the University Research Institute at the University of Texas, for support of his ongoing work.

Finally Fishkin would like to thank two senior advisers who have long served the Center for Deliberative Polling at the University of Texas, and, more recently, the new Center for Deliberative Democracy at Stanford. Dan Werner, president of MacNeil/Lehrer Productions, and Dr. Charls E. Walker, a former deputy secretary of the treasury, provided the essential insights and encouragement that transformed an academic idea into a reality.

An early version of this argument was published in article form, both in *Philosophy, Politics, and Society,* volume 7, *Debating Deliberative Democracy* (Blackwell, 2003) and in the *Journal of Political Philosophy* (June 2002). The authors are grateful to both publications and especially to the late Peter Laslett and to Robert Goodin for their thoughtful reactions.

PART

I

THINK IT OVER

1

IMAGINE

Deliberation Day—a new national holiday. It will be held two weeks before major national elections. Registered voters will be called together in neighborhood meeting places, in small groups of fifteen, and larger groups of five hundred, to discuss the central issues raised by the campaign. Each deliberator will be paid $150 for the day's work of citizenship. To allow the rest of the workaday world to proceed, the holiday will be a two-day affair, and every citizen will have the right to take one day off to deliberate on the choices facing the nation.

If Deliberation Day succeeded, everything else would change: the candidates, the media, the activists, the interest groups, the spin doctors, the advertisers, the pollsters, the fund raisers, the lobbyists, and the political parties. All would have no choice but to adapt to a more attentive and informed public. When the election arrived, the people would speak with a better chance of knowing what they wanted and which candidates were more likely to pursue the popular mandate.

Deliberation Day is a new idea, but it builds on a host of smaller experiments involving ordinary citizens deliberating on public issues. In many different forums, in different cities and countries around the world, citizens have gathered together for experiments in serious and balanced public discussion. Many of these experiments have proved remarkably successful,[1] but we will focus on one particular method of citizen consultation, the Deliberative Poll. Because the Deliberative Poll is designed as a social science experiment,[2] it provides the best evidence for the viability of our proposal. Since one of us, Jim Fishkin, has spent the past decade of his professional life designing and observing Deliberative Polls on a wide variety of issues, we can use these social scientific experiments with a solid understanding of their strengths and limitations. We are also in a position to make cautious generalizations of Deliberative Poll results to the rest of the population. In most other citizen forums, it is far less clear how the participants are selected and how their individual opinions are affected by the process.[3]

A Deliberative Poll is a survey of a random sample of citizens before and after the group has had a chance to deliberate seriously on an issue. The process begins by selecting a representative sample from the population and asking each person a set of questions on the issue raised at the Deliberative Poll. This initial survey is the standard sort conducted by social scientists doing public opinion research. The respondents are then invited to a specified place for a weekend of discussion. A small honorarium and travel expenses are paid to recruit a representative sample.

In preparation for the event, the participants receive briefing materials to lay the groundwork for the discussion. These materials are typically supervised for balance and accuracy by an advisory board of relevant experts and stakeholders. On arrival, the participants are randomly assigned to small groups with trained moderators. When they meet, they not only discuss the general issue but try to identify key questions that merit further exploration. They then bring these questions to balanced panels of competing experts or policymakers in larger plenary sessions. The small groups and plenary sessions alternate throughout the weekend. At the end of the process, the respondents take the same questionnaire they were given on first contact.

These typically reveal big changes in the distribution of citizen opinion. When ordinary people have the chance seriously to consider competing sides of an issue, they take the opportunity to become far more informed. Their considered judgments demonstrate higher levels of knowledge and greater consistency with their basic values and assumptions. These experiments demonstrate that the public has the capacity to deal with complex public issues; the difficulty is that it normally lacks an institutional context that will effectively motivate it to do so.

Our design for Deliberation Day builds upon the practical experience developed at these polls. Our new holiday will require important changes in these time-tested formats. The participation of tens of millions of citizens will require a rethinking of the deliberative process from the ground up. Nevertheless, the experience gained through the polls provides a precious source of guidance for Deliberation Day, as does statistical analysis of the data generated at these experiments.

Deliberative Polls and other microprojects in deliberative democracy provide us with some confidence in the basic feasibility of our proposal. Time and again these real-world exercises have defeated cynics who deny that ordinary citizens have what it takes to think through complex public issues. These sessions don't degenerate into shouting matches or slug-fests. They reveal that ordinary citizens are remarkably good at productive interchange — hearing out spokespersons for different sides, and changing their minds on the basis of new arguments and evidence. Ordinary men and women *can* function successfully as citizens. The challenge is to design institutional contexts in which they are effectively motivated to exercise this competence in productive collaboration with their peers.

But why can't people simply organize themselves, without the assistance of a new civic holiday and its associated social engineering? After all, we don't live in a civic vacuum. Sustained conversations do take place in countless settings — from the breakfast table to the coffee break at the office to the meeting at the neighborhood church or union hall. And their intensity and frequency do increase during election campaigns. But the social context that motivates public deliberation is usually lacking, and the resulting levels of public information are disappointing.

Facts are facts. If six decades of modern public opinion research establish anything, it is that the general public's political ignorance is appalling by any standard. As one influential researcher concludes, "the political ignorance of the American voter is one of the best-documented features of contemporary politics."[4] And another: "The verdict is stunningly, depressingly clear: most people know very little about politics, and the distribution behind that statement has changed very little if at all over the survey era."[5]

To pick just a few examples: At the height of the Cold War, a majority of the American public could not correctly answer whether the Soviet

Union was in NATO.[6] While the public reliably supported efforts to protect West Berlin during the Cold War, most Americans did not know that West Berlin was surrounded by East Germany! And as the country considered possible war with Iraq in January 2003, half the public thought that Iraqis were among the 9/11 hijackers.[7]

Other recent work makes the same point. In its comprehensive study of voter involvement in the 2000 election, Harvard's Shorenstein Center quizzed a random sample on their knowledge of the issues just before they went to the polls: "[We] asked respondents to agree or disagree with twelve issue statements—six that addressed Gore's positions and six that concerned Bush's. On the average issue, 38 percent correctly identified the candidate's position, 16 percent incorrectly identified it (an indicator that a third or more of the correct answers were also mere guesses), and 46 percent said they did not know."[8] A majority was able to identify *only one* of each candidate's stands correctly—with 58 percent saying that Gore favored a prescription drug benefit and 52 percent saying that Bush favored "a large cut in income taxes" (and some of these people were only guessing).[9] These dismal results are not restricted to the United States. To take just one example, when the British public was recently asked whether Britain had a written or an unwritten Constitution, a quarter said "unwritten," a quarter said "written," and half said "don't know."[10]

In a systematic overview of survey questions asking factual questions about politics of the American public, Michael Delli Carpini and Scott Keeter found that

> Only 13 percent of the more than 2,000 political questions examined could be answered correctly by 75 percent or more of those asked, and only 41 percent could be answered by more than half the public. Many of the facts known by relatively small percentages of the public seem critical to understanding—let alone effectively acting in—the political world: fundamental rules of the game; classic civil liberties; key concepts of political economy; the names of key representatives; many important policy positions of presidential candidates or the political parties; basic social indicators and significant public policies.[11]

This is not to say that the mass public is clueless or that it is incapable of dealing with complex political matters. Our position is quite the contrary. When the public is given good reason to pay attention and focus on the issues, it is more than capable of living up to demanding democratic aspirations. And even when it is not paying much attention, it does have some crucial information bearing on its voting decisions[12] and it is resourceful at making use of limited information.[13] Nevertheless, this information is very limited indeed, leading to large mistakes in mass assessments of the basic problems facing the nation and the nature of the solutions offered by competing candidates.

There is a further problem. Data reported by conventional public opinion polls often exaggerate the public levels of awareness. As Philip Converse of the University of Michigan demonstrated years ago, many of the opinions reported in polls probably do not exist.[14] Phantom opinions or "non-attitudes" are reported by polls because respondents almost never wish to admit that they do not know, even when offered elaborate opportunities for saying so. Hence they pick an alternative, virtually at random.

George Bishop and his colleagues at the University of Cincinnati dramatized this point in their study of attitudes toward the so-called "Public Affairs Act of 1975." Large percentages of the public offered an opinion even though the act was fictional. The *Washington Post* more recently celebrated the "twentieth unanniversary" of the nonexistent "Public Affairs Act of 1975" by asking respondents about its "repeal." The sample was split, with half told that President Clinton wanted to repeal the act and half that the "Republican Congress" wanted its repeal. The respondents apparently used these latter cues to guide their answers, without recognizing the fictional character of the entire episode.[15]

Even when respondents have actual opinions, they are often "top of the head," merely reflecting an impression of sound bites and headlines, and highly unstable.[16] The "public opinion" described by the standard poll is rendered even more problematic by the refusal of many people to respond to the pollsters' inquiries. Nonrespondents may be disproportionately less well-informed — so the surveys of respondents present a misleadingly optimistic picture, even as they reveal widespread ignorance about the elementary facts of political life.[17]

Some argue that citizens can function effectively without the kinds of specific knowledge called for by most survey questions. What is really important is for voters to place candidates or political parties in the broader framework of a basic liberal-conservative dimension. Yet Robert Luskin has shown that the American public does a terrible job on this task as well. Once corrections for guessing and nonresponses are introduced, surveys show that the American public does slightly worse in locating the parties' positions than it would do if it proceeded by flipping a coin.[18]

None of this is really controversial. Indeed, the past generation of political economists has gone to great lengths to explain why voter ignorance is only to be expected.[19] Acquiring and analyzing information is a time-consuming business. Time spent on public affairs competes with time acquiring information on more personal matters — like the price and quality of cars or houses. In these cases, each of us suffers a direct cost for ignorant decisions — I may buy a lemon unless I am careful to analyze options ahead of time. In contrast, nobody pays a price for voting ignorantly since the outcome of a major election never hinges on a single ballot. (Even Bush v. Gore isn't an exception!) As a consequence, it may well be "rational" for individual voters to remain ignorant about public matters. They can then reserve all their time analyzing information on cars, houses, and other matters of personal consumption — where the sanction for ignorant decisions is felt directly. This point doesn't depend on whether voters are public-spirited citizens. Even if they are deeply concerned about the nation's future, their individual votes still don't make a difference, and so there isn't an instrumental reason to make their choice a well-informed one.

We do not endorse the cynical conception of instrumental rationality that often motivates the expositors of the theory of "rational ignorance." Most residents of Western democracies recognize that they have a responsibility as citizens to take the public good seriously. Nonetheless, the political economists are on the right track in explaining why Westerners do such a terrible job fulfilling these responsibilities.

And things are getting worse, not better. Most Americans continue to rely principally on television to follow the campaign, and yet the networks increasingly treat politics as a marginal matter. In 1992 nightly newscasts carried 728 campaign stories during the general elections, averaging 8.2 minutes per show; in 2000 there were 462 stories, averaging 4.2 minutes.[20] More broadly, the proportion of news coverage devoted to public affairs has diminished from 70 percent in 1980 to 50 percent in 2000.[21]

Despite our present infatuation with the Internet, the rising forces of technology threaten to exacerbate the consequences of civic privatism. We have a public dialogue that is ever more efficiently segmented in its audiences and morselized in its sound bites. We have an increasingly tabloid news agenda that dulls the sensitivities of an increasingly inattentive citizenry. And we have mechanisms of feedback from the public, from viewer call-ins to self-selected Internet polls, that emphasize the intense commitments of narrow constituencies, unrepresentative of the public at large.

Add to this the powerful new forces unleashed by modern polling techniques, and we are confronting a serious problem indeed. Earlier generations of politicians might have wished to exploit the ignorance and selfishness of voters, but they labored under certain technical disadvantages. They were free to read newspapers, talk to cronies, attend community functions, weigh letters from constituents, and canvass opinion informally through local political organizations.[22] But without scientific random sampling and the modern art of survey design, they had a hard time getting an accurate picture of public opinion. They could not penetrate the hearts and minds of ordinary Americans to learn *precisely* which combinations of myth and greed might work to generate support from key voting groups. In the absence of good data, even the most cynical politicians sometimes were obliged to consider the good of the country.

But over the past few decades, this uncertainty has been dissolved by the scientific study of public opinion. The entire point of "focus group" and public opinion research conducted during campaigns is to discover the power of different images and slogans to motivate voters. These studies proceed in an exceedingly fine-grained fashion. Politicians "pretest" their positions with focus groups, constantly modifying them to increase their appeal to marginal voters. Within this high-tech environment, James Madison's great hope that legislators would filter out ignorant and selfish impulses seems hopelessly old-fashioned. Campaigns can now aim to spin a precise message that will snare a majority.

Focus group research is followed up with the scientific marketing of candidates by sound-bite specialists. Sloganeering and flag-waving have been important in American politics from the beginning. Nevertheless, we have been making a great leap forward into a brave new world. Candidates nowadays really are being sold like commodities. Commercial norms have completely colonized the norms for political "advertisements." Techniques for selling a Lexus or a pack of Marlboros are simply carried over to sell the president. The idea that principles of deliberative democracy might require, for example, that no "advertisement" last for less than five minutes would be dismissed out of hand by the highly paid consultants who take their cue from Madison Avenue. The search is on for ten-second sound bites that hit "hot-button" issues discovered through focus group research.

Matters are made worse by the failure of campaign finance reform.[23] The new techniques cost lots of money. Given the current financial imbalance, the invisible hand of the political marketplace is leading us to the plutocratic management of democratic forms. But the basic problem would not go away even if we managed to equalize the financial playing field. This might lead to the redistribution of sound bites and hot-button issues, not the creation of a deliberative democracy.

Our anxiety is not new. Eighty years ago, Walter Lippmann was already remarking upon the phantom character of public opinion in the modern world and despairing at its consequences for democratic life:[24]

> The private citizen today has come to feel rather like a deaf spectator in the back row. . . . He does not know for certain what is going on, or who is doing it, or where he is being carried. No newspaper reports his environment so that he can grasp it; no school has taught him how to imagine it; his ideals, often, do not fit with it; listening to speeches, uttering opinions and voting do not, he finds, enable him to govern it. He lives in a world which he cannot see, does not understand and is unable to direct.[25]

Lippmann's response to this dilemma also turned out to be prophetic. He did not call for a reconstruction of institutions to encourage more active and informed citizenship. He counseled us to lower expectations about democracy, and learn to live with the status quo.

The canonical case for lowered expectations was provided by Joseph Schumpeter in *Capitalism, Socialism, and Democracy*.[26] As the Nazis rose to power in Germany, Schumpeter moved to America, but he was understandably skeptical about the democratic majority's capacity to engage in an ongoing process of public reason. He continued to endorse democracy, but for more humble reasons — its capacity to disrupt political elites and thereby prevent tyranny. However ignorant it may be, the democratic majority is a notoriously fickle beast: it may well place Tweedledum into the presidency as a result of the brilliance of his smile or his passion for apple pie, but the next election may find the majority backing Tweedledee for equally frivolous reasons. So long as the Ins are randomly ousted by the Outs, the powerful will find it far harder to oppress the rest of us. Although the disruption of tyranny is a worthy goal, it is a far cry from the democratic vision of ordinary Americans taking control of their own fate after due deliberation.[27]

The mainline of democratic theory has, in any event, moved beyond Schumpeterianism to embrace a pluralist conception of American democracy that seems downright optimistic, if only by comparison. On this pluralist view, the secret of the system is the wide variety of interest groups constantly pressuring politicians to achieve satisfactory public outcomes. Though individual voters may be ignorant, their organized groups are looking out for their interests — bargaining with one another, and with politicians, to get the results that roughly correspond to the public interest. Rather than merely exposing elites to almost random electoral shocks, American democracy achieves a certain form of popular responsiveness through relentless interest group pressure.[28]

This is hardly enough to satisfy the partisan of deliberative democracy. Interests don't count under pluralism unless they can organize, and many groups find this difficult — especially those with broad concerns dealing with matters like environmental integrity and social justice. Even more fundamentally, citizens don't get much of a chance to criticize and redefine the interests asserted in their name by group leaders. Serious democrats should insist on something more than a system of elite wheeling and dealing. Ordinary citizens have the fundamental right to determine the broad direction of public policy through electoral decisions made on the basis of popular deliberation.

But this democratic dream seems to shatter against the hard facts with which we began. Given the notorious failure of Americans to take the time and trouble for the hard work of citizenship, isn't talk of popular sovereignty so much hot air?

Not necessarily. As we shall see, Deliberative Polls and other microexperiments establish that ordinary people *are* perfectly willing to take up the task of citizenship within appropriate settings. Perhaps the problem lies not so much in each individual's failings but in a collective failure to organize our elections appropriately.

Speaking broadly, we have been passive as the massive technological forces of the late twentieth century have transformed our electoral practices before our eyes. This contrasts sharply with nineteenth-century attitudes toward election reform. During the declining decades of the 1800s, American elections were conducted in a way that also made talk of popular sovereignty into a joke. In those days voters did not cast secret ballots but marked their preferences in plain view of party bosses — who paid off the faithful in cash and kind, and meted out retribution for any show of independence. It was the introduction of the secret ballot from Australia, not any sudden burst of civic virtue, that served to remedy this sorry situation. Once each voter went behind a curtain, it was no longer possible for leaders to identify who should be rewarded with a turkey for his loyalty and who should be denied all further patronage for his independence. A system that seemed hopelessly corrupt achieved a more credible democratic standing through intelligent institutional reform.

Deliberation Day raises a similar possibility. By all means, let us take citizens as they are, and not as starry-eyed versions of democratic theory wish them to be. It still isn't obvious that the invisible hand of the political marketplace has encouraged ordinary people to make good use of whatever civic virtue they possess. Is the time ripe for another innovation, like the secret ballot, that channels the invisible hand of political interests in a more productive direction?

Maybe not. The secret ballot promised a neat technological fix to the problem of vote buying then afflicting American democracy. Simply by drawing a curtain around the booth, each citizen managed to insulate himself from a host of corrupt incentives. Our current problem isn't amenable to a magical technological solution. Granted that a majority of voters are woefully ignorant and readily manipulated, is there any guarantee that Deliberation Day won't make the problem worse? What is to prevent the new holiday from degenerating into a prototctalitarian system forcing Americans into "political education" centers to hear spokesmen for the government brainwash them into "the truth"?

Even without the dreadful experiences of the twentieth century, it would be silly to make light of such fears. Nevertheless, we don't really think that creeping totalitarianism is a serious problem in the contemporary West, and it won't be hard to create safeguards that make such extreme fears entirely unrealistic. The real challenge is to design a format that has a reasonable prospect of enabling millions of ordinary people to engage in constructive dialogue rather than destructive shouting matches. We hope to convince you that this too is a manageable problem, and that the collective effort is well worth the distinctive contribution that Deliberation Day would make to our democratic life. In making the case, we emphasize problems as well as solutions, and we are careful not to claim too much for our proposal. Even if successful, it would constrain, but not eliminate, the dangers posed by civic privatism.

The question is not whether Deliberation Day measures up to some unattainable ideal but whether it deserves serious consideration as a constructive response to the sound-bite politics that will otherwise overwhelm us. This question cannot be answered until we develop our proposal in a sustained way. We shall be presenting you with a reasonably detailed framework, but in a distinctive spirit. If anything like Deliberation Day were to come into being a decade or two from now, it would look quite different from the holiday described in this book. But only by confronting a host of real-world design issues can we give you a sense of the practical promise and moral choices involved in the project. We shall succeed if our own sketch prompts counterproposals, leading to further improvements in the format. The ongoing dialogue would give further substance to our basic claim: Deliberation Day is no mere pipe dream, but a realistic response to a serious problem.

This is an essay in realistic utopianism. We do not underestimate the serious political obstacles that block acceptance of anything like Deliberation Day. As the sorry story of campaign finance reform teaches, these roadblocks will be substantial. But their existence should not be allowed to deflect us from a deeper problem. Though liberal ideals of democracy are currently ascendant, triumphalism has provoked self-congratulation, not political imagination. Westerners have been content to offer up present practice as if it were an adequate model for the world.

This is a serious mistake. Liberal democracy is a relative newcomer on the historical stage — very much a work in progress even in those few countries with established traditions. Short-term roadblocks should not prevent vigorous exploration of the horizon of realistic possibilities.

So join us in a thought-experiment, and let us see where it leads.

Perhaps a roadmap will prove useful. In Part I we aim to convince you that DDay is an entirely practical idea; if we fail here, there is no need to read further. But if we succeed, it makes sense to move on to Part II, where we explore DDay's relation to democratic theory in general, and to the American tradition in particular.

The next two chapters go together. In Chapter 2 we describe the new holiday: Is there a future for civic celebration in the twenty-first century? If so, how should DDay be organized to make democratic deliberation a social reality in the lives of ordinary citizens? In Chapter 3 we compare our proposed format for DDay with the real-world experience accumulated in the Deliberative Polls. The DP data show that ordinary citizens are willing and able to engage in constructive dialogue, and that deliberation makes a very real difference in citizens' understanding and in their ultimate decisions on the merits. In shaping our concrete proposal for DDay, we have relied heavily on the protocols developed at the DPs. But for a variety of reasons, our proposal departs significantly in some respects. We consider the most important differences in turn and conclude that they do not seriously undermine the hopeful implications of the DP studies.

Chapter 4 opens the next stage in the larger argument. There we show how DDay will revolutionize the methods of governing and campaigning that increasingly dominate the democratic world. Once sitting presidents and prime ministers have to face the voters on DDay, they will no longer rely on the latest poll when making key decisions. Pollsters who measure "top of the head" opinion can no longer serve as reliable guides to the judgments reached by voters after a full day's discussion. *Government by pollster* will be replaced with *government by responsible politician* — a representative whose motivations are a bit closer to those postulated by Madison and other creators of the modern system of democratic government.

Campaigning will also be different. While ten-second sound bites will remain on the airwaves, they will now compete with longer "infomercials" designed to anticipate the case the candidates will make on Deliberation Day. A politician who relies solely on TV sound bites risks losing millions of voters on DDay. He will also lose precious momentum as the campaign moves down the homestretch from DDay to Election Day. No sensible politician would accept such a risk.

There is no need to exaggerate. DDay won't end the politics of charisma or demagogic appeals to fear and hate; but it will keep in check some of the darker forces facilitated by our present technologies of communication and shift the balance toward a more deliberative politics. And that is not nothing.

In Chapter 4 we make the systemic case for DDay by considering how the new holiday would change the incentives confronting candidates as they run for the presidency and as they govern from the White House. In Chapter 5 we extend this presidentialist paradigm to a variety of other electoral contests — including the distinctive modifications required to adapt DDay to multiparty contests characteristic of parliamentary systems throughout the world. We also consider how rising Internet technologies will open up new DDay possibilities over the next generation or two.

But we conclude Part I on a less visionary note. Without indulging futuristic fantasies, how much would it really cost to implement DDay in the here and now? In Chapter 6 (and an accompanying appendix) we consider both the big-ticket items and the variety of other expenses required to run and administer Deliberation Day. When citizens are called to do jury duty, they receive a modest daily stipend. Should DDay participants receive more, or less, or nothing? How costly would it be to prepare schools and other civic centers for citizen deliberation? And so forth.

Our estimates suggest that DDay is entirely affordable — in terms of real economic resources, it would be one of the least significant programs in the federal budget. But in terms of democratic values, the gain will be inestimable. We can't provide any assurance, of course, that our experiment will succeed. But without continuing experiments, it is hard to see how democracy will remain a flourishing enterprise in the twenty-first century.

Or so we will argue in Part II.

2

THE HOLIDAY

Deliberation Day will be a serious holiday. We will reserve two days for the deliberative exercise, with half the citizenry invited each day. This will allow the other half to continue working—permitting basic services to continue while maintaining the civic focus essential to a serious collective conversation. Some employers may compel their labor force to ignore their civic obligations, but they will do so at their peril—any such demand will be subjected to heavy penalties.[1] This won't deter all violations, but it will suffice to make them exceptional.

While citizens are guaranteed a day off, nobody will force them to participate in Deliberation Day activities. They are perfectly free to catch up on their sleep or go to the movies. But if a citizen chooses to spend the day in a civic discussion on the issues raised by the forthcoming election, he or she will receive a stipend of $150 as compensation.

As we shall show, all this is perfectly doable. The question is whether it is worth the effort.

An answer requires us to reflect on the present state of our national holidays. Speaking broadly, they have disintegrated into occasions for shopping sprees, ski weekends and sunbathing rituals. Is there still a place for civic celebration in America?

A thoughtful answer depends in part upon the design of the new holiday. How to create a format for collective deliberation that can make a serious contribution to democratic life? As we shall explain in succeeding chapters, our concrete proposal builds on existing experience with Deliberative Polling and other microexperiments in political conversation. But this experience takes us only so far. It is one thing to organize an exercise for five hundred citizens in a Deliberative Poll, quite another to create a plausible framework for tens of millions to engage in the thoughtful practice of self-government. A host of fascinating questions arise, and we expect others to resolve them differently.

Nevertheless, it is important to aim for a concrete proposal. If we are to convince you that Deliberation Day is not merely a utopian dream, we must confront the series of midsized trade-offs required to translate democratic ideals into political realities. Our efforts to resolve these practical trade-offs are ultimately less important than our effort to define them. This will not only provoke others to propose better formats. It will make some progress toward defining the ultimate questions: Is Deliberation Day sufficiently valuable and practical to warrant serious consideration as the next generation defines its political agenda? Or does this exercise in institutional design suggest that Deliberation Day can't work and that we should resign ourselves to a politics of media hype based on the Madison Avenue manipulation of focus groups?

Do Civic Holidays Have a Future?

Broadly speaking, our secular holidays are generated by four logics. Some honor great men: Washington, Lincoln, and Martin Luther King Jr. Some, great events: the discovery of America, the declaration of independence, the sacrifices of war. Still others, great causes: Labor Day is an obvious example, but Martin Luther King Day is a tribute to the triumphs of the civil rights movement. And finally there are holidays that serve as signals for celebratory rituals: Thanksgiving Day signals an occasion for families to gather for celebration, and New Year's Day for friends to come together and look forward to better times ahead.

Different holidays have suffered different fates over time. Great men lose much of their inspirational quality as their concrete historical struggles become lost in the mists. During the early decades of the Republic, Washington's Birthday was a day of great rejoicing — exceeded only by the Fourth of July.[2] Now it has been merged with Lincoln's Birthday into a generic Presidents Day, principally celebrated by massive bargains offered at malls throughout the nation. Great events suffer similar disintegration: the struggle that we call World War I was originally known as "the Great War," and the participants marked its ending by creating Armistice Day as a national holiday. But other great wars have put the first one into perspective, and the original holiday has been transformed from a celebration of peace into a celebration of Veterans Day. Memorial Day, originally created to honor the Civil War dead, has fared better, since it can readily be generalized to remember soldiers killed in all wars. Nevertheless, its civic meaning has greatly declined in national life. Independence Day has fared a bit better—fireworks still blaze, and some may take a moment to reflect on the meaning of Jefferson's Declaration, but it's fun in the sun that matters most to most. The movement holidays have also sustained themselves to a degree, thanks to the continuing interest of concrete social groups in celebrating their achievements. (The conversion of Armistice Day to Veterans Day exploits a similar logic.)

Martin Luther King Day is still a youngster, but all the others suffered terrible erosion over the twentieth century—and not only because of the ravages of time. At the root of their decline are two forces: the rise of mass-marketing and the transportation revolution.[3] During the nineteenth century, many Americans' idea of a good time was simply to take a day off and listen to local orators celebrate Independence Day while enjoying the music of a local band and the glory of a military drill.[4] But this prospect pales in comparison to the pleasures of a day at the beach. Though it is a bare shadow of its former self, Independence Day has not suffered as badly as some others. At least it is still celebrated each year on July 4, while the dates of others shift about from year to year to create three-day weekends for the convenience of the skiing or swimming public.

Lest one suppose that this process is inexorable, consider the different fate of holidays of the fourth type—the ones that mark out concrete communal rituals, notably Thanksgiving and New Year's. Thanksgiving provides an especially revealing example because, unlike New Year's, the celebration does not invite a great deal of commercial activity. Americans may find it difficult to believe but, except for Canada, this holiday is unknown elsewhere. Families throughout the world gather together from time to time, but not for a common day of thanksgiving that sets the day apart as a communal event. While the holiday is rooted in the nation's religious traditions, it has long since taken on a secular aspect—Americans of all beliefs sit around the table, eat their turkey, and share the mixed blessings of life amongst their extended families. If anything, the transportation industry has tended to encourage this holiday rather than to undermine it: millions take to autos and airplanes to join the get-together with far-flung family members. Why has this holiday resisted the lures of the shopping mall and vacation industry?

Because it marks out a concrete ritual that everybody can share. The other holidays commemorate something distant from ordinary life—a name, an event, a cause. It is then up to ordinary people to figure out how to express their commitment to the distant ideal: shall we hold a commemorative march, visit a cemetery, or organize an oral rendition of the Declaration of Independence? Given this gap between commemorative ideal and concrete realization, it is tempting to leave the task of organizing an appropriate ritual of remembrance to the next guy, and to succumb to the lure of shopping mall or ski weekend. The temptation is all the greater since one may watch a televised broadcast of the Labor Day march or Memorial Day wreath-laying and thereby participate vicariously in a moment of commemoration.

In contrast, something quite specific attaches to the holidays that mark concrete rituals. If you don't engage in the expected behavior, you feel—and are—left out. Your family will wonder why you weren't with them on Thanksgiving, your friends will remark on your absence from the New Year's party.

Deliberation Day is more like Thanksgiving than Washington's Birthday. Its point is not to honor a distant hero but to do your concrete bit for democracy. Just as you share the turkey with your family, and share the bubbly with your friends, you will be discussing the issues with your neighbors as you ponder your forthcoming decision on Election Day. This hardly implies that everybody will heed the call. But it does suggest that you may well feel left out if you take advantage of the holiday to catch up on your sleep or go fishing with a few buddies.

The contrast with other holidays is especially important as we turn to consider the first key policy question raised by our proposal. It is all well and good to urge the creation of new civic holidays, but when assessed in dollars and cents, this step actually represents the most expensive part of our initiative. Most of the economic costs of an extra holiday don't show up in public budgets, but they will be paid in lost production in the private sector. While estimating this loss is a tricky business, it would be sizable — tens of billions of dollars might be lost for every day of civic discussion.[5]

This economic cost is especially heavy since one day won't be enough to carry out our project. Consider the problem posed by essential workers. Police, fire, hospital, transit, and many other essential activities must operate 365 days a year. It would be terribly wrong to exclude these workers from Deliberation Day and thereby deny their equal standing as citizens. The only way to accommodate these Americans is by extending the holiday over a two-day period and requiring all enterprises to provide one day off. A one-day holiday also poses a problem for religious observance — at least if the holiday is on Friday, Saturday, or Sunday. We certainly shouldn't require anybody to choose between obligations to religion and duties to country. A two-day holiday will also ease the strain on facilities — America's schools, colleges and other civic centers can accommodate tens of millions comfortably, but things could get tight if a particularly controversial election drives turn-out into the stratosphere.[6]

Two days would cost an awful lot in terms of lost economic production — but only if we create Deliberation Day by appropriating two working days. There is another and better choice. Given the sorry condition of most civic holidays, we could simply shift one or more of them to the election season and rededicate the old holiday to democratic deliberation. Our first choice is Presidents Day. This holiday has been completely hollowed of its civic meaning. Its real function — if it has any — is to enable the nation's shopping malls to eliminate their excess inventories by announcing special sales. Even if deprived of this opportunity, advertisers will undoubtedly invent another gimmick to attract the public to their Fabulous February sales event. The only real losers will be the skiers and ski resort operators deprived of a three-day winter weekend.

We have communed with the spirits of Washington and Lincoln, and we are happy to report that they enthusiastically endorse a conversion of "their" holiday into a day of deliberation. Surely there can be no serious objection to the calendar change from February to October. Presidents Day has already been uprooted from either president's actual birthday — the present law decrees that the holiday fall on the third Monday in February so as to serve the greater glory of the vacation industry. We need not even change the name: Presidents Day is perfect for a day spent deliberating over the candidate best qualified to serve in the White House. We would also prominently display the portraits of Washington and Lincoln at each deliberative site, encouraging Americans to measure the contending candidates against the highest standards of the past. These two great men would gain much more respectful attention at DDay than they presently receive at the current Presidents Day sales.

Presidents Day comes once a year, but we elect a president only once in four. Allocating two days for presidential election years still leaves us with two free days on a quadrennial basis. If Presidents Day proves successful, we would dedicate these "free days" to a comparable event during the midterm elections: call it Congress Day.

It would be a mistake to introduce this second holiday immediately. Voter turnout at midterm elections is less than 40 percent, and we fear that the sudden introduction of a two-day holiday might yield demoralizingly low attendance levels. Better to launch the experiment in its most congenial setting—the presidential election, when public engagement is already higher. As a transitional device, we would be content to share Presidents Day with the skiers and the shoppers during the first two presidential cycles, introducing Congress Day only after a significant fraction of the citizenry has established a habit of attendance.

Despite this go-slow strategy, Congress Day is important.[7] The American system is based on the separation of powers between president and Congress, and it would distort the constitutional order if we placed only one of these branches in the spotlight. Congress Day will provide a much needed mechanism for local voters to monitor their senators and representatives in a serious fashion.

But aren't we putting the cart before the horse? America is one of the few advanced democracies that don't make Election Day an official holiday: shouldn't we first correct this mistake before considering the creation of brand new holidays?

We don't think so. Making Election Day into a holiday will marginally increase turnout—though it is unclear by how much.[8] But it will do nothing to create a more informed electorate. Our proposal focuses on the quality, not the quantity, of citizen participation in democratic life. If it is successful, it will enable a critical mass of citizens to transform the very character of their relationship to the process of self-government. Deliberation Day may even generate more of an increase in voter turnout than would an official holiday on Election Day. The conversations begun on DDay will cascade through the next two weeks and reach tens of millions who did not themselves attend. Once those citizens are enmeshed within the conversational net, they may well decide to vote on Election Day as a result.[9]

We would be happy to join a larger coalition interested in creating national holidays for both Deliberation Day and Election Day. A special commission headed by Presidents Carter and Ford recently called for a national holiday on Election Day. Rather than reducing the work year by another day, they propose to trade Veterans Day for their new electoral holiday.[10]

We have focused on Presidents Day because it strikes us as a particularly degraded civic holiday. Rather than honoring Washington and Lincoln, we are disgracing their great contributions to the Republic by commercializing their memories in such a grotesque fashion. But we agree with the Carter-Ford commission that there are other holidays ripe for the picking. Combining Veterans Day and Presidents Day would give us enough free time to propose a two-stage plan. During the first phase, we could use Presidents Day to create a two-day deliberative holiday during presidential elections and use the other two free days to make a national holiday of every federal Election Day. After the first two presidential election cycles, we would transform Veterans Day into Election Day on an annual basis, thereby including state and local elections — at the same time creating Congress Day for deliberation during federal midterm elections.

We propose, in short, to reclaim two holidays for a revived civic purpose. As citizens of the twenty-first century look at their calendar, they will be regularly invited to carve out a special period for the serious discharge of their civic responsibilities — Deliberation Day beginning the period; Election Day ending it.

The Basic Format

Turn next to the task of providing Deliberation Day with a concrete structure. We begin by proposing a particular format, and then slowly unpack its organizing assumptions. There is nothing sacrosanct about our set-up, but it will fix ideas to enable a more textured assessment. Consideration of operational realities will also give substance to our exploration of the larger political, institutional, and human issues in later chapters.

Our thought-experiment divides the holiday into a series of large-group and small-group sessions. After arriving at neighborhood schools and community centers between 8 and 9 A.M., deliberators will be randomly assigned to groups of fifteen for the first event, at which they will sit together to watch a live television debate on the leading issues between the principal national candidates.

The organization of this National Issues Debate requires a lot of care. The formal process should start one month before the main event, with the debate organizers asking each major candidate to answer one simple question: What are the one or two most important issues presently confronting the nation?

Within a two-party framework, this query will generate two to four themes that will structure the conversational run-up to Deliberation Day.[11] The candidates' major issues will drive lots of talk around the dinner table and on the Internet, among the television pundits and in the newspapers. They will also attract a great deal of campaign money. We expect competing "infomercials" devoted to rival presentations of the central facts and values, capped perhaps by a national address from each of the candidates the night before Deliberation Day.

Candidates will predictably rely on media merchandisers during the run-up, but they are on their own during the National Issues Debate. We adapt the town meeting format that is already a familiar part of television debates between presidential contenders.[12] Each candidate will be given a couple of minutes to answer questions posed by members of an audience composed of "ordinary people."

But we propose putting real substance into the town meeting metaphor. In the current format, citizens at "town meetings" are selected in an ad hoc fashion from one or another locale. In contrast, we will be using scientific random samples as employed in Deliberative Polls to generate a representative cross-section of the nation to serve as the "town meeting" for the televised debate. This assembly of five hundred citizens will convene two days before the debate and consider the major national issues designated by the contenders. They will conduct their inquiry in the way that has become standard in Deliberative Polls, where participants meet in small groups to define questions that are then debated by leading experts and policymakers in plenary sessions. As a consequence, the candidates on Deliberation Day will not only confront a "town meeting" representative of the nation but will debate questions that have been refined through thoughtful dialogue.

The televised debate will last for seventy-five minutes. The first hour of the show will be divided into two- to four-issue segments, depending on the number of major national issues specified by the candidates. As in the existing format, contenders can't give long speeches but must respond succinctly to the questions raised by the national "town meeting." The show will conclude with a fifteen-minute segment that gives each candidate a chance to elaborate on any of his earlier answers and address themes left undeveloped by the earlier Q and A.

Each candidate can also supplement his or her televised presentation with a written statement emphasizing key points. Each side can say anything it likes on the major issues, but the statements must be succinct— no more than 1,500 words. These statements will be distributed to citizens as they arrive on Deliberation Day, allowing for ready reference.

The TV debate begins at 9 and ends at 10:15 in the morning: "And now it is your turn, our fellow Americans, to take up the debate. But first, let's all take a fifteen-minute break, during which small group members can introduce themselves to those they haven't had a chance to meet before the National Issues Debate began."

During the break, each small group selects a foreman by lot—but those who don't want to serve are free to opt out. The group is now prepared for the day's business. We do not envision a free-floating dialogue that can readily degenerate into boring irrelevance or angry confrontation. The small group begins deliberation with a clearly defined task. After one hour of discussion, small-group members will meet with other citizens in a larger assembly of five hundred. Each citizen assembly, as we shall call this larger body, will have a nonpartisan community leader as its presiding officer: call him or her the moderator. Sharing the podium will be local representatives of the two political parties. During the assembly, the moderator will ask party representatives a series of questions compiled from lists prepared by the small groups in their previous discussions. The citizen assembly will, in short, be a real-life continuation of the National Issues Debate that began on television. Only this time, it won't be a "representative town meeting" asking the questions; local citizens will be doing the job themselves, and local party representatives will be trying to respond on behalf of their candidates.

We will soon describe these citizen assemblies in greater detail. But we have said enough to define the task confronting small groups as they begin deliberation at 10:30 in the morning. They have just heard the two candidates debate the major issues before the nation; their job is to continue this debate and set the agenda for the citizen assembly. Given their time constraints, the national candidates have inevitably left large questions unanswered as they struggled to perform credibly before the national audience. The small group's aim is to frame some of these unanswered questions in the hope that, by the end of the day's give-and-take, the engaged citizenry gain a better sense of the issues at stake in the election.

This task not only provides a clear focus for the group; it is framed to elicit cooperation, not confrontation. Their job isn't to argue over which candidate represents the forces of good or evil. It is to frame questions that will provoke further deliberation after the party representatives give their answers. When a group member suggests that the citizen assembly be asked a particular question, he need not claim that he is asking the only question worth asking. He can simply present it as one of many that deserve attention. So when another group member suggests a different query, the different questioners are not contradicting or competing with one another. They are engaged in a collaborative effort, searching for the most profitable ways of moving the conversation forward.

The small group's task does not require participants to pretend to greater knowledge about the issues than they possess. They have all just heard the same National Issues Debate. Their job is not to elaborate on the candidates' responses, but to ask what was left out. There is no embarrassment involved in confessing ignorance and expressing the hope that clarification will come from the local party representatives during the next hour. By emphasizing the process of discovery, the set-up discourages deliberators from playing the part of know-it-all. Such a posture is premature when the matter will be discussed further in the citizen assembly and the rest of the day.

Since everybody has just seen the same debate on television, the candidates' definition of the leading issues will serve as a natural starting point for discussion. But the television show need not determine the scope of the conversation. Citizens are perfectly free to raise concerns that both candidates have found it convenient to ignore: "I know that the candidates say that the big issues are war and the economy, but as far as I'm concerned, it is global warming or abortion that is the number one concern. Let's ask the party reps where their candidates stand on this issue."

The foreman's job is to call on participants in the order they ask for recognition. He has no power to rule any of the discussant's remarks or questions out of order. But he will have authority to enforce a time limit of ninety seconds on each speaker. To make this effective, the foreman will have a large electric timer that he will set at ninety seconds when calling on a speaker. When the timer hits zero, the foreman calls the speaker to order. No speaker can talk a second time before all are given the opportunity to make some remarks. Since there are fifteen participants, this guarantees each participant the right to speak two times during the first forty-five minutes of discussion.[13] If some remain silent, the others can begin a third round—but those who have been silent previously can claim a preferred place in the queue.

Each citizen will be provided with a few question forms so that he may write out his proposed questions for submission to the group. As the conversation proceeds, participants pass the forms to the foreman. Some participants will also use their speaking time to state their questions explicitly for group consideration. Others may take the floor simply to express their agreement with a prior speaker or to address more general concerns and urge others to shape them into more focused questions. In short, participants are free to use their time any way they see fit. If others find a particular speaker boring or irrelevant, they don't have the right to interrupt him. They must simply wait for the ninety-second clock to run its course.

When the forty-five-minute discussion period has elapsed, the foreman moves to the next phase and reads out each question she has received, assigning each a number. Distributing a voting form to each participant, she asks each to identify those questions worth asking before the larger citizen assembly. Each small-group member votes in secret and can vote Yes for any number of questions. The foreman then counts the ballots in public and identifies the two questions that have gained the most Yes votes, ranking them in the order of the group's preference. (Ties are resolved by lot.) As the members adjourn to the citizen assembly, the foreman transmits the small group's two top choices to the moderator of the larger group. She also gives copies of questions to the small-group members who originally proposed them. When the time comes, they will personally rise and ask their questions in the name of the group.

Consider how this system of balloting shapes the incentives of small-group members during the discussion phase. If speakers want their question to emerge as one of the top two, they cannot appeal to the narrow interests of a few partisans who are already convinced of its importance. The voting system encourages them to reach out to the relatively uncommitted — if they fail to vote Yes, their abstentions may prove very costly on the final ballot. While a particular issue may generate the passionate commitment of a few, the system doesn't reward raw intensity. It searches out areas that attract broad citizen interest: a question that attracts the moderate interest of almost all participants may attract thirteen or fourteen votes, while a question that engages the intense concern of a bare majority is unlikely to get onto the agenda.[14]

If all goes well, this system will encourage each participant to frame questions in ways that elicit broad group interest. Even more important, it encourages citizens to treat each other with respect. The best way to lose a vote is to belittle a voter. Perhaps somebody's contribution to the discussion will suggest that he holds beliefs at variance with majority opinion. But the voting system cautions against treating him as a no-account. His decision to abstain on a question favored by a majority may well deprive it of the support needed to send the issue onward to the citizen assembly.

But of course, institutional engineering will hardly suffice to erase all tensions or prevent all flare-ups. Some speakers will not restrain themselves, and they may dedicate their ninety seconds to a stream of insults or obscenities. The foreman should begin the session by urging group members to ignore inflammatory remarks, rather than dignify them with a further reply.

This will prove difficult at times. Nonetheless, an effort to silence a speaker virtually guarantees an escalation of the conflict, making it almost impossible for the group to return to civil discourse within the short space of forty-five minutes. A clear guarantee of an absolute right to speak, and an unconditional obligation on others to listen, provides the best promise of civil peace and broad-ranging discussion.

It also serves to reduce another potential source of conflict — the temptation by some foremen to abuse their momentary power and play the petty tyrant. By limiting the time for each speech, we make it plain that the foreman cannot allow his favorites to blab on interminably. The foreman must also keep a list of speakers in the order they request recognition, and follow the list without exception. These simple rules should suffice to keep the conversation moving in the typical case.

But everyone won't play by the rules. Some foremen may play favorites by allowing friends to jump the queue or permitting some to keep on talking after the clock has run out. Others will react with rage to one or another conversational provocation, and try to shout down a speaker. Speakers may refuse to stop when their time runs out and ignore the foreman's request to let others participate on equal terms. What happens next?

The rules of order should provide an extraordinary mechanism allowing a supermajority of citizens to exclude a nonconforming participant. Each member shall have the peremptory right to move for exclusion; without any further debate, the matter will be taken up in a secret ballot, and an affirmative vote of twelve out of fifteen members will serve to bar the offending member. If the target of the motion tries to disrupt the vote, any member can leave immediately to call the police.

Some citizens may be excluded unjustly, but an elaborate appeals process doesn't seem worthwhile. The best way to resolve these disputes is by drastically limiting the stakes involved. As we have already suggested, participants will be paid a stipend of $150 for their participation on Deliberation Day.[15] Exclusion means that they will not get this stipend; exclusion from a second Deliberation Day will bar the disruptive citizen from participation at all future events. But no other sanctions should be imposed unless somebody commits a physical assault—in which case they should be prosecuted under the criminal law and provided with the safeguards of due process.

All this, of course, raises a big question. The disruption of some small group meetings is inevitable, but our entire proposal will fail if the overwhelming majority of Americans can't conduct their conversations in a civil manner. How frequently will the meetings break down into shouting matches or worse?

There are suggestive data on this question, and in the next chapter we provide reason for cautious optimism. But for now, we simply note the importance of a simple measure for damage control. Even if some particularly obnoxious person completely disrupts the small-group session, he can destroy only an hour's worth of collective effort. When the clock strikes 11:30, the other group members may be very upset by the initial shouting match. But they may begin to recoup their losses at the citizen assembly, containing about five hundred citizens from all thirty-three small groups.

Suppose that one or two small groups have suffered grave disruption, spending most of their time excluding a disruptive member, calling the police, and seeking to reestablish a semblance of order. When the call comes for the citizen assembly, these groups haven't had a fair chance to identify two issues for further discussion. This is unfortunate, but it will not impede the large group's forward momentum if the remaining 450-plus citizens have been more successful. So long as the moderator receives a substantial number of questions that explore the leading issues, she will have no trouble fashioning an agenda at the next stage of the process.

It is now 11:40, and the moderator opens the citizen assembly for an hour's debate by local party representatives. During the next sixty minutes, she will raise ten or so questions for discussion and give each side two and a half minutes for a response. To fill her agenda, she draws ten lists of questions at random, and calls the name of the small-group representative who proposed the first-choice question from her first list. Then, as the party reps respond, she looks at the second list she has drawn at random. If the first-choice question essentially repeats the one she has asked, she chooses the second question instead and asks the contributing small-group representative to read it out for collective consideration. Moderators must exercise some common sense in making these judgment calls about overlapping questions. But each moderator will be a community leader with experience in running meetings and a reputation for impartiality—say, a local judge or president of a nonprofit organization. Few will be tempted to abuse their limited discretion.

In any event, it would be counterproductive to allow any appeal from their decisions: the point is to have an intelligent debate, not to engage in procedural wrangling. If one of the party representatives, or a group of fifty citizens, believes that a moderator has abused her discretion, they can request that a Board of Review convene on some later day to compare the questions asked with the lists submitted and consider whether the moderator should be barred from playing a similar role at future Deliberation Days.

As the Q and A proceeds, the moderator will begin to encounter a different problem. She may find that both questions raised by a particular group have been fairly answered by the preceding discussion. When this happens, she simply draws at random from the remaining twenty-odd group lists until she locates a useful area of inquiry. Thirty-plus lists should be more than enough to fill the hour many times over.[16]

Indeed, the moderator probably won't reach most of the lists. But this hardly implies that the small-group members were wasting their time. Their efforts to define questions for further deliberation were valuable in themselves, enabling each participant to hear the others' concerns and explore different frameworks for understanding the election. Even if their questions fail to gain expression in the citizen assembly, the small-group conversation will shape the subsequent deliberations of the fifteen group members—as well as all the other people with whom they speak about the election.

There is also good reason to predict that many of these groups' concerns—if not their precise questions—will be voiced at the citizen assembly. Local citizens will be randomly assigned to small groups as they arrive for Deliberation Day. As a consequence, there is likely to be a significant overlap between the concerns of each group. If a significant number give an issue high priority, at least one of their lists is likely to be picked by the moderator. Each small group's decisions on priority questions affects the probability that a particular issue will be debated before the citizen assembly. If several groups rank the issue high, it is almost certain to get on the agenda.

So much for the distribution of Q's; what about the A's? One of the great virtues of Deliberation Day is its promise of reintegrating local political leaders into presidential elections. National campaigns have increasingly excluded local elites from any significant role. Candidates send advance men to stage-manage local media events for maximum impact. But this is only one of many means they use to gain direct media access to the voters' living rooms. Rather than relying on local leaders, the national campaigns shout over their heads through carefully controlled mass advertising.

A need still remains for locally based organizations on Election Day itself. But at this late stage, it is a waste of time for party loyalists to persuade voters on the issues. Their job is to identify true believers, and to drive as many as possible to the polling place.

Deliberation Day changes this picture. For the first time in a long time, it will no longer make sense for presidential campaigns to operate independently of local party organizations. How else will they be able to find tens of thousands of respected local leaders to represent the national candidate at the citizen assemblies?

The need to provide these representatives will give new life and direction to state and local politics. Quite suddenly, local party organizations will have a vital interest in locating the most articulate and thoughtful opinion leaders for their team on Deliberation Day. At the same time, issue activists will have greater interest in involving themselves in local party matters, so as to influence the selection of campaign representatives at citizen assemblies throughout the land. All this cannot help but generate a vast increase in the practical involvement of local elites in national politics.

To fix ideas, assume that the first Deliberation Day is received rather skeptically by ordinary Americans, and that "only" a third of the voting public takes the trouble to show up at the new holiday.[17] Since one hundred million Americans have been voting in presidential elections, this still means that thirty million to thirty-five million deliberators will be attending sixty thousand or seventy thousand citizen assemblies in their communities. Each and every assembly will require the active engagement of two party spokespersons prepared to address a broad range of questions in an informed way.

Since the holiday will extend over two days, some representatives might speak at two sessions, but even assuming that this happens sometimes, each party will require more than thirty thousand well-informed spokespersons! The number may seem staggering, but the human resources already exist. They simply remain untapped by the present system. There are about ninety-three thousand elected officeholders at the local, state, and national levels.[18] The overwhelming majority will find it in their interest to appear before a citizen assembly — as will hundreds of thousands with future office-holding ambitions. Add to that pool the active participants in one or another group with links to the major parties — from labor unions to religious activists — and there are millions of potential party representatives to draw on. Rather than suffering from scarcity, each party will have a problem discouraging zealots and selecting spokespersons who will appeal to a broad cross-section of their particular communities.

But the mobilization and selection of party spokespersons will not be enough. Each national campaign will have powerful new incentives to enter into a serious political dialogue with local elites. During the run-up to Deliberation Day, the parties will prepare briefing books for their spokespersons and hold issue workshops where party positions may be thoroughly discussed. This is the only way to field a team of opinion leaders who can plausibly defend their candidate on Deliberation Day. If one side fails to make the most of its human resources, it may pay a steep price at the voting booth.

This nationwide recruitment effort will have ramifying effects — local leaders talk to lots of other people, and they will be using these conversations as sounding boards as they prepare themselves for debate on Deliberation Day. When the two party representatives square off at their first citizen assembly at 11:40 in the morning, there will be a lot more going on than meets the eye. Their answers might seem spontaneous, but they won't be. They will be the product of a healthy give-and-take between national campaigns, local elites, and ordinary citizens. After gauging the preliminary reactions of ordinary citizens, local leaders will be pressuring national campaigns to reshape their initial positions so that their stands on the issues will make sense to "the folks back home." The national campaigns, in turn, will be seeking to enlarge the political vision of local elites and explain why they have framed their proposed solutions to national problems in ways that may appeal to a national majority. It will then be up to local opinion leaders to find ways to make their candidate's case credible to their neighbors.

In short, the debate before the citizen assembly will help shape the larger political dialogue as well as express it. Once again, an issue need not actually be discussed during the citizen assembly for this broader conversation to take place — the need to prepare briefing books and workshops will suffice to enmesh national and local leaders in a new and fundamental dialogue. Nevertheless, ten questions will make it to the surface of the agenda, and the local citizenry should have a good deal to ponder as they look forward to the next event of the day: LUNCH![19]

Deliberation Day, we remind you, is a holiday. While the food won't be great, we've allocated enough money to make sure that it will be better than your memories of your standard high school meal. But there is more at stake than chicken à la king. We envision a bustle of friendly activity in the lunchroom. A host of community groups will set up tables around the hall, and try to gain the interest and support of deliberators for their larger activities. Casual connections made during DDay will deepen and grow in countless directions over extended periods.

While the participants are munching and mulling and networking, they are also pondering their next task. Come 2 P.M. they will return to their small groups — containing the same people as before — to develop the agenda for a second citizen assembly that will meet one hour later.

Their conversational procedure will be different this time around. Each citizen now has a rough sense of the concerns of the other group members, and is in a better position to anticipate their reactions. As a consequence, each person will be invited — but not required! — to spend a few minutes of the one-and-a-quarter-hour lunch period to write a couple of questions for consideration by the small group. Call the first a "clarifying question." The aim here is to reflect on the recent debate at the citizen assembly: undoubtedly, many of the answers provided by the debaters have failed to confront crucial aspects of the question raised. After all, each side only had two and a half minutes.

What is more, many public speakers are tempted to evade embarrassing questions by deflecting them with canned statements. Each debater may, of course, pay a price for blatant evasive tactics—his conversational opponent can point out the bluster to the audience, which will begin to resent obvious efforts to throw sand in its eyes.

But it is important for ordinary citizens to have a means for taking the matter into their own hands. Not only will clarifying questions give citizens a more genuine sense of participation, but the option of follow-up will encourage more responsive answers in the first place. It is one thing to expect a debating opponent to remark upon evasive tactics, quite another to be required to return to the issue and spend some more time clarifying one's stand at the risk of further alienating the audience. Isn't it better to respond in a (relatively) straightforward fashion the first time around?

The second part of the conversational agenda will involve "supplementary questions." Recall that, a month before Deliberation Day, the candidates will have specified two to four major issues to serve as the prime focus for debate. Since only ten questions were put on the agenda during the first assembly, one or another of these issues might well have been slighted. At the end of the session, the moderator will assess the situation and reserve an appropriate period of time—up to half an hour—for discussion, during the second meeting, of the neglected issues. Even if all four major issues were fairly introduced during the initial session, there may still be a problem. Since Deliberation Day is focused on a particular election, it is only right and proper that the format allows candidates to have a large role in defining the key issues.

But Deliberation Day is much more than an occasion for top-down leadership, and we have emphasized that citizens are entirely free to raise their own concerns, which their small groups will submit if they gain sufficient support on the final ballot. But of course, these "citizens' issues" may or may not have survived the luck of the draw at the first session. If none have made it to the Q and A agenda the first time around, the moderator should reserve fifteen minutes for expansionary questions even if the candidates' issue agenda has been fairly represented at the initial assembly.[20]

In short, the course of afternoon deliberation in the small groups will depend on the morning's developments. If the first citizen assembly canvassed all of the candidates' issues, and at least one raised by citizens, the small group will be invited to focus its energies on issue clarification. But if this didn't happen, they will be asked to draw up some expansionary questions as well.

It is now 2 P.M. Group members hand the foreman their questions, which are displayed on an overhead projector. As talk begins, group members already confront a set of options. From the first speaker, they can talk about which items are more important, and how much each issue has already been clarified. As the conversation proceeds—in ninety-second segments, as before—participants are free to add further questions of clarification or expansion. But beginning with a list should facilitate a more organized conversation than in the morning. A second factor should also make for smoother sailing: the participants are now acquainted with one another. Even though they have gotten together for only a morning of TV and talk, this is typically enough to encourage them to relax and talk more freely with one another.[21] And of course, most of the really disruptive types have already been excluded during the morning session. As a consequence, participants will generally come out of the second small-group session with a sense of accomplishment. After their second hour of talking and voting, many will come away with a sense that it *is* possible, after all, to do a half-decent job as a citizen.

We don't have anything more to say about the second citizen assembly, so let us move immediately to the final session of the day: at 4:15 or so, participants return to their small groups for a concluding forty-five minutes. No questions this time; citizens will each have a chance to sum up their impressions: What questions remain unanswered? Which of the party debaters did a better job? Has the experience changed their minds or confirmed their previous commitments?

This is, perhaps, the riskiest moment: people are getting tired after a long day and flare-ups between opposing ideologues may occur. But if things have gone reasonably well, the group has built up a certain camaraderie, and it will seem pretty pointless to get angry when there's less than an hour to go.

Moreover, and this is crucial, there will be no voting at the end of this discussion—after all, Election Day is still two weeks away. The point is not to come to final decisions, but to think about what is at stake. So it should be productive for group members to hear one another's final reactions in a round-table discussion under the now-familiar ground rules (ninety seconds, at least twice around the table). At the end of the day, there will be nothing left to do but to shake hands, and—last but not least—arrange to get paid.

At 5 P.M., the group's foreman signs all the members' certificates of attendance and hands them over to the representative of the Deliberation Day Authority, a public corporation charged with running the operation. We have already proposed a citizen stipend of $150 for all participants, but we will save a defense of this relatively high amount for a later chapter. It is enough, for now, to assure the deliberators that their checks will soon be in the mail.

For the moment, they will have other things on their mind: How have their kids managed to spend the day? Who has taken up the loose ends left at the workplace? But these private anxieties will mix with reminders of their civic engagement. As they leave the final session, their rush to the exits will be interrupted by exit pollsters from television networks eager to tell their viewers how the day's deliberations have changed the horserace. And as they make their way home, family and friends will want to know what they made of their experience.

The initial round of discussion will broaden further during evening celebrations held throughout the land. Recall that Deliberation Day is actually a two-day event. And during the evening of the first day, cities and towns will conduct a display of fireworks worthy of the Fourth of July. While the first day's participants watch the rockets' red glare, they will contribute to the festivities by telling their friends about their personal experiences. Since half of their conversation partners will attend the second Deliberation Day, they will be especially attentive—perhaps these stories will help them avoid some blunders when they show up the next morning to hear another version of the candidates' debate.

These second-round participants will, in turn, have a lot to say when everybody returns to work on the morning after DDay has concluded.

Mill's Anxiety

There is much more to be said, both pro and con, about our proposal. But it is never too soon to step back and try for a bit of perspective. So follow us on a short trip to the middle of the nineteenth century. This was a time when citizens cast their ballots in public, and no less a thinker than John Stuart Mill wanted to keep it that way.[22] The secret ballot, he predicted, would encourage voters to look upon the ballot as if it were just another commodity for private gratification. Rather than stand up in public to declare which candidate was best for the country, voters would step behind the curtain and choose on the basis of "interest, pleasure or caprice."[23] Politicians would quickly catch on and escalate their appeals to conflicting private interests. Over time, this dialectic would slowly erode the very idea that citizens should be trying to regulate fractional interests on behalf of the common good.

These Millian anxieties were pushed aside in the latter decades of the nineteenth century—but not because they were bogus. They were outweighed by a competing aspect of the democratic ideal—the egalitarian demand for a revolutionary expansion of the franchise. Public balloting might be tolerable in a political world which imposed restrictive property requirements. If the only voters were substantial property owners, they might have sufficient economic independence to state their sincere opinions about the public good on Election Day without fearing reprisals afterward. But as the franchise widened, public voting took on a different appearance. It began to look like a trick by which the rich might retain effective electoral power while formally conceding the right to vote to the unwashed. If the poor could vote only in public, they could not afford to deviate from the political opinions of their economic masters. It was, in fact, John Stuart Mill's father, the philosopher James Mill, who had already made the point: without a secret ballot, ordinary people would only "go through the formalities, the mummery of voting . . . while the whole power of choosing, should be really possessed by other parties."[24] This debate between father and son dramatized the deep functional connection between the expansion of the franchise and the rise of the secret ballot.

In developing our thought experiment, we mean to ask whether it is time to move beyond the Mill-Mill debate and glimpse the best of both worlds. By all means, let us retain the sanctity of the secret ballot. But Deliberation Day will enable Americans to set their electoral choices within a public-regarding framework that makes sense of their claims to citizenship. Instead of permitting Madison Avenue to sell candidates as if they were cereals, the new holiday encourages face-to-face discussion about the public good on the basis of steadily increasing information. Rather than passively receiving a torrent of ten-second sound bites, citizens will actively shape the evolving agenda in the large groups, and will reason with one another about public priorities in the small ones.

If the nineteenth-century practice of open voting was too elitist and coercive, the twentieth-century practice of secret balloting is too ill-informed and privatistic. The twenty-first century can aspire to something more — a two-stage process in which ordinary people speak with their own voices about the great issues of the day in public, and make their final voting decisions about the future of the country in private.

The real-world combination of Deliberation Day and Election Day will, of course, fall short of the impossible ideal of democratic citizens directly determining their own fate after exhaustive and public-spirited debate. But a two-step election process would nevertheless be a great advance over the rituals of the past two centuries. Our next challenge is to suggest that our proposal is no pipe dream but is based upon the lessons of real-world experience. What do Deliberative Polling and similar experiments teach us about the capacities of ordinary people to deal with their citizenship responsibilities?

3

FROM THOUGHT-EXPERIMENTS TO REAL EXPERIMENTS

You have just joined us in imagining a new institution. As our thought-experiment proceeds, we will show how all the main actors in a presidential campaign—candidates, parties, contributors, consultants, advertisers, issue advocates, reporters—will adapt to the new holiday. Our argument may sometimes seem complex, but the basic point is straightforward: Deliberation Day, by informing and engaging the citizenry, will transform public opinion, and in a democracy, public opinion is king. All other political actors will find that they have to adjust to its demands.

Lord Bryce, a discerning British visitor to America in the late nineteenth century, made the point best: "Towering over Presidents and State governors, over Congress and State legislatures, over conventions and the vast machinery of party, *public opinion* stands out, in the United States, as the great source of power, the master of servants who will tremble before it." It is a "key" that will "unlock every door."[1] As subsequent chapters show, a microanalysis of political incentives only serves to emphasize the enduring significance of Bryce's insight.

So if public opinion is the "great source of power," why do we think Deliberation Day would change its character in constructive ways? Indeed, why suppose that a day's discussion will change anything at all?

Our answer builds on two kinds of real-world experience—one familiar, the other less so. We begin with the familiar: over the past generation, nationally televised presidential debates have become a fixture of American political life. Voter response to these debates has important implications for our proposal. We then move to the social science evidence generated by the accumulated experience with Deliberative Polls. These data suggest the potentially profound consequences of enabling citizens to engage in structured conversations about politics and policy.

The Lessons of Experience

For the past quarter-century no presidential campaign has passed without the major candidates engaging in at least one nationally televised debate. The existing system has many weaknesses, but the debates now constitute a high point of the entire campaign for a simple reason. They provide Americans with a window that allows a glimpse of the candidates operating on their own resources, without the distortions of sound-bite journalism and advertising hype. For ninety minutes, the two rivals must speak for themselves on the issues of the day—and tens of millions respond by turning on the tube to watch.

About forty million Americans tuned into each of the three debates between George Bush and Al Gore—40 percent of the total number casting ballots on Election Day.[2] An impressive study from Harvard's Kennedy School permits a quantitative assessment of the debates' impact on public opinion. The researchers made a massive effort throughout the yearlong presidential campaign, interviewing a random sample of one thousand Americans each week to determine their level of engagement. To measure voter knowledge, each interviewee was asked to identify each candidate's position on leading issues. These weekly probes showed that information levels remained roughly constant, and sometimes declined, as the campaign progressed—with the striking exception of presidential-debate weeks.[3] Only then did information significantly increase: "In 2000, Americans' ability to recognize Bush's and Gore's positions on key issues rose by 25 percent during the debate period."[4]

To be sure, respondents remained appallingly ignorant, with the majority failing to identify correctly either candidate's stand on almost all major issues.[5] We shall return shortly to this grim reality, but let us focus first on the more positive findings.

The Kennedy School researchers allow us to glimpse the underlying dynamics that help account for the improvement in voter knowledge.

They report that "a majority of viewers watch the bulk of the ninety-minute telecasts"[6] and that "on the day after the first Bush-Gore debate in 2000, 47 percent—twice the number on an average day—discussed the campaign."[7] The debates also encouraged respondents to widen their range of conversation partners. The Kennedy School study found that most political talk occurs within the family, but this pattern changed in the immediate aftermath of the debates. Suddenly, half of the respondents' political conversations took place with coworkers, friends, and others outside the family.[8] These findings take us one large step down the path toward Deliberation Day. They show that when normal Americans are given an opportunity to penetrate media hype, they seize it in great numbers, and use it as a special conversational opportunity.

At this point, the existing debate mechanism begins to run out of steam. The televised confrontation between the candidates provokes lots of conversation, but it doesn't supply a context within which citizens can expose the candidates' claims to disciplined scrutiny and further exploration. This is, of course, the point of DDay. In its absence, the televised debates generate a marginal increase in information but don't lead to a collective effort to expose this information to critical analysis and reflective discussion. As Jamieson and Birdsell note in their classic discussion:

> Educators and theorists of persuasion would lay down a few simple principles that account for the inability of the presidential debates to change attitudes markedly or drastically raise the knowledge level of the moderately interested or poorly informed. Exposure to any single piece of communication rarely produces attitude change. A more likely consequence is reinforcement of existing beliefs. Those who are best informed to begin with will get the most from exposure to postcards signaling stands on issues. Moreover, learning is a function of motivation . . . and even when motivation spikes attention, new vocabulary needs time to sink in.[9]

There is nothing inevitable about this outcome. The untapped potential of the debate format is suggested by a remarkable initiative that gathers citizens to discuss the television debates in small groups around the country. Debate Watch has organized viewers into hundreds of discussion groups over the past three cycles of presidential debate. The initiative began as a research study with focus groups in 1992 and became, in later presidential cycles, a citizen initiative to set up as many discussion groups as possible following each debate.

The initial wave consisted of sixty focus groups in eighteen cities around the country. They were intended to evaluate the coverage of the issues and the debate formats. But they also demonstrated that the discussions themselves were a powerful learning tool enhancing civic engagement: "In addition to learning from the debates, participants agreed that the discussion provided a learning experience in and of itself. Many focus group members indicated that if it had not been for their participation in the study, they would not have discussed the debates with anyone except for a few brief comments with a spouse."[10]

The focus groups, some of which were randomly selected and most of which had considerable demographic diversity, allowed for conversation across a much broader range of perspectives than people were accustomed to:

> Many focus group participants discovered that they enjoyed talking about politics and admitted that it was the first time that they had engaged in political discussions with someone representing a different political view from their own. They found that they could disagree without becoming disagreeable, and that they discovered a comfort level with the candidates they were not supporting. Many participants indicated that knowing they would discuss the debates forced them to listen more attentively and listen to the opponent they were not supporting with a more open mind.[11]

Many of the effects of Debate Watch could certainly be expected from Deliberation Day—the effects of engaging in dialogue beyond one's immediate family, the heightened level of interest, the increased learning from the discussion, the apparent effects on later participation, and the learning that took place in anticipation of the event.

Debate Watch expanded in 1996 and 2000 into a broader initiative in which hundreds if not thousands of meetings were sponsored by one hundred organizations working in communities around the country. This represents a small but significant step toward Deliberation Day. It makes concrete our vision of decentralized citizen discussion following a presidential debate. And it offers suggestive qualitative evidence that such discussions enhance knowledge and citizen engagement. Unfortunately, but understandably, these exercises have not yet been conducted in ways that permit systematic social science evaluation. In contrast, the study of Deliberative Polls permits a more disciplined assessment of the difference that deliberation can make.

The Poll with a Human Face

For some years now, Jim Fishkin and his colleagues[12] have pursued a research program that engages random samples of the population, under realistic conditions, with a process of deliberation quite similar to Deliberation Day. It assesses the impact of this experience on the participants' attitudes, information, political preferences, and voting intentions. We shall now discuss these findings in more detail.

It requires a deliberate political decision to create a new holiday for an entire nation, but Deliberative Polling aims for something more immediately attainable. It seeks to create a *microcosm* of a nation deliberating, through a social science experiment, and then broadcasts the results to the rest of the country and makes those results available to policymakers. If the conditions are transparent and defensible as methods for facilitating a balanced and informed consideration of the issues, then they deserve a hearing. They should have a recommending force as conclusions the public would reach if it became more informed about the issue.

An ordinary survey provides a snapshot of public opinion as it is, even if it is based on poor information and thin opinions. The Deliberative Poll asks a different question: What *would* the public think about an issue under good conditions for considering it? Suppose the public actually focused on the issue and had good information; what would be its considered judgments? What could the public accept and what might it not be able to accept once it focused on an issue and became better informed?

The connection between the Deliberative Poll and Deliberation Day is simply this: what the poll creates for a microcosm, the day aspires to create for an entire electorate. DDay is designed to expose the whole electorate to something very much like the experimental treatment we have been testing in the Deliberative Poll—the effective opportunity to behave a bit more like ideal citizens. Although there are differences between the design of the day and the poll, they do not undermine the case for cautious optimism generated by the poll's findings. The poll data establish that representative samples of citizens can profit greatly by talking together in small groups and hearing political leaders answer their questions in larger citizen-assemblies. If representative samples can achieve these gains, why not the citizenry as a whole?

We have conducted more than twenty Deliberative Polls—half in the United States and half abroad, in countries ranging from Britain and Denmark to Australia and Bulgaria. DPs have considered a wide range of subjects. Some are quite similar to issues that might be the focus of discussion on DDay. In the National Issues Convention broadcast on PBS in 1996, a national random sample of 459 citizens gathered in Austin, Texas to engage five national politicians in a discussion of three major issues—the economy, America's role in the world, and the current state of the American family. In a second National Issues Convention in 2003, also broadcast on PBS, the topics were four aspects of international affairs—military security and intervention (including Iraq), democratization abroad, the global economy, and humanitarian issues such as world hunger and AIDS. Similarly, the topics in the five British Deliberative Polls were at the top of the political agenda: crime, Britain's future in Europe, reform of the monarchy, the economic issues in the 1997 British general election, and the future of the National Health Service. In Denmark we did a national Deliberative Poll on the euro shortly before the national referendum on joining the European single currency, and in Australia we did two national Deliberative Polls, one before the referendum on whether Australia should become a republic and one on reconciliation with the Aboriginals. These are large issues, with competing sides, sometimes subject to elections or referenda, enmeshing competing values and contested empirical claims. They are the very kinds of issues citizens need to weigh before voting. Since the Deliberative Polls were conducted as contributions to the national debate, sometimes in the midst of intense coverage of those same issues, they constitute realistic field experiments for what random and representative samples of the public can accomplish.

Some other DPs have dealt with subjects further removed from large national concerns. For example, regulated electric utilities in Texas were required by statute to consult the public as part of a process of "Integrated Resource Planning": Were they going to use fossil fuels such as coal or gas, were they going to build renewable energy facilities (wind or solar power), or were they going to invest in conservation (demand-side management) to lessen the need for new power?

These decisions required complex trade-offs that the public was not well informed about. With the active cooperation of the Public Utility Commission, we conducted regional Deliberative Polls for all eight regulated public utilities in 1996. The public's considered judgments led to further investments in natural gas (which was regarded as relatively clean) and in renewable energy. In fact, the decisions resulting from the Deliberative Polls made Texas a national leader in renewable energy — a leadership codified by a Renewable Energy Portfolio written into law by the legislature when it deregulated the industry. The portfolio was justified by the preferences for renewable energy expressed in the Deliberative Polls.[13]

Another distinctive experience, to which we shall return, was provided by a Deliberative Poll in New Haven, Connecticut, in March 2002. This effort employed a random sample of residents of the fifteen towns that make up the greater New Haven region. The dialogue focused on two issues — the future of the airport and regional tax sharing to promote new development (an option recently made available by state law). As in all Deliberative Polls, the sample was given an initial questionnaire on first contact. Then, when the group gathered for the weekend, it was divided into two halves, and each half engaged one of the issues before taking a second round of the same questionnaire. Then the groups switched topics. Those who had discussed the first issue discussed the second and vice versa. In that way, each randomly chosen half of the sample could serve as a control group for the other half, assessing the effects of discussion on opinion change.[14] The experiment clearly demonstrated that discussion is a major engine of change in the Deliberative Poll.

All Deliberative Polls start with a public opinion survey of the standard sort. We reach out to a scientific random sample of the population either through face-to-face interviews (with geographically defined sampling units) or through random-digit dialing. We ask each respondent closed-ended questions. At the conclusion of the interview, we invite the participant to spend a weekend of face-to-face discussions at a central site, with all expenses paid. We recruit vigorously, telling respondents that it will be fun, that their voices will matter, that the proceedings will be covered in the media, that they will be part of a dialogue with public officials. We also provide an honorarium — ranging from $75 to $300 — to encourage participation.

These techniques have sufficed in every case to generate a good microcosm of the population, both attitudinally and demographically. Since the initial survey is completed before the invitations are offered, we can compare participants with nonattenders on every attitudinal and demographic dimension. We can also compare them to the relevant census data. By all these criteria, we have been able to recruit representative microcosms to single sites for a weekend of deliberation.

As the DP participants ready themselves for their weekend trip, a first difference from DDay emerges. A month before DDay, each of the major parties specifies two major issues, and we expect them to flood the airwaves with competing arguments during the run-up to deliberation. In contrast, DP organizers must create their own informational environment if they wish their random sample to prepare themselves for dialogue over the weekend. Since each DP is focused on a small number of issues, the challenge is to create a balanced set of briefing materials that the participants can read in advance. To achieve this aim, we organize an advisory committee of relevant stakeholders who review the document for balance and accuracy. There is obvious danger of bias here, but we have gone out of our way to achieve inclusiveness, and there have been no significant complaints thus far. As a further guarantee of fairness, we make the documents available to the press, who would be quick to criticize any serious departure from balanced argument.

The mix of media is, then, likely to be different in the run-ups to DP and DDay. As they look forward to DDay, many citizens will also be reading print commentaries, but most will rely more on television infomercials and the like.[15] In contrast, DP organizers have had to depend principally on the briefing documents, even though some of the participants won't be comfortable reading text or won't take the trouble to do so. To compensate for this drawback, we have sometimes produced a video version of the briefing document, playing it when the participants first arrive at the site, before the start of the discussions. Unfortunately, we have no data on the difference this makes.

Participants usually arrive on Friday evening for a welcome dinner. The seating typically reflects the composition of the small groups that will be together for the entire weekend. Membership in each group is determined by a random assignment procedure, and there are about fifteen people in each group. As they get acquainted with one another over dinner, participants are also provided with an orientation to the weekend's procedures.

The briefing document is only the beginning of the deliberative process. The key task of each small group is to identify central questions that they wish to ask experts or political leaders in the larger plenary sessions that will include several hundred participants. These questions sometimes probe crucial facts that need clarification before deliberators can make up their minds. Sometimes group members just ask one or another side for a clearer or more complete articulation of its arguments. As in DDay, the DP groups must reach consensus on the questions that should be given highest priority at the plenary sessions. But they reach agreement through a different method. While DDay groups choose their priority questions through a voting procedure, each DP group is guided by a trained moderator, who facilitates the general discussion and encourages members to reach consensus about whether a question is worth asking. Typically, the moderators have the skills and training of focus group leaders. They are careful not to betray their own views, and they try to facilitate everyone's participation while preventing anyone from dominating the discussion. In postevent questions, the participants have always given the moderators high marks in accomplishing these goals.

We shall return to this important difference. For now, it is even more important to note a larger similarity in the function of the small groups. In both DP and DDay, their mission is to prepare the conversational agenda for discussion by opinion leaders at the plenary sessions. But while DDay is merely a thought-experiment, the basic small group–big group format has met the challenges of experience during more than twenty

DPs. On each occasion, the small groups submit their questions to the moderator of the plenary, who vets them for overlap. He then asks the person who originally submitted the question to rise before the plenary assembly and ask it again to the speakers sitting at the podium. The moderator attempts to get through as many questions as possible, allowing time for follow-up if questioners feel the panelists' responses were inadequate or unresponsive. During these sessions, the process of conversational give-and-take has repeatedly proven its viability. If it works for DPs, it should work for DDay as well.

Indeed, there is one important respect in which our hypothetical DDay organizers will have an easier job than the one confronted in real-world DPs. Our thought-experiment relies entirely on the major political parties to recruit their spokespersons at citizen-assemblies throughout the land. It is up to the Democrats and Republicans to select and motivate their leadership teams for DDay. If one party does a worse job fielding a persuasive DDay team, it has only itself to blame.

In contrast, real-world organizers of DPs do not have the luxury of indulging in a laissez-faire approach. We have been obliged to take affirmative action in selecting appropriate groups of competing experts, politicians, or decision makers to discuss the issues at the plenary sessions. The integrity of this selection process is fundamental to our entire enterprise. Our findings on the impact of deliberation will be valueless if we have stacked the deck by selecting especially weak voices for one side of the argument. As a consequence, we have taken special care in constituting our panels, and, thus far at least, our efforts to provide balanced presentations have not been subjected to significant criticism.

Some DPs have allowed us to solve this selection problem in ways that are not too different from DDay. For example, in the Australian referendum on adoption of the republic, there were official Yes and No committees. These committees largely comprised the advisory group for the DP and provided the relevant experts for the event. Similarly, there were publicly recognized Yes and No groups for the Danish referendum on the euro, and these were given representation in the Deliberative Poll agenda for the experts. And in the British general election, each party was asked to provide an expert on each panel. The television network (Britain's Channel Four) then selected a recognized independent expert for each panel who could provide reactions to the experts nominated by each party.

Yet all this work will be unnecessary at DDay for one basic reason. While DPs seek to determine what a nation would think if it *could* deliberate, DDay provides an opportunity for the nation actually to deliberate en masse in the real world. As a consequence, it is no longer necessary for social scientists to select a balanced panel of opinion leaders to simulate the outcome of a national dialogue; we can safely delegate this task to the real-world institutions that we generally rely upon to lead the collective discussion: the national parties and their candidates for the presidency.[16]

We have been focusing on some fine-grained but important differences in the organization of the small groups and plenaries conducted at DPs and DDays. Now is a good time to step back and consider how each small- and large-group session cumulates in a larger whole. In both DP and DDay, citizens don't simply go through the small group–plenary routine a single time. Instead, they can use the first round of meetings as the basis for another round of small-group questions and plenary answers—but this time on the basis of an enriched understanding of the issues. Since DPs involve an entire weekend, and not only a single day, the participants have more chances to exchange questions and answers than we suggest for DDay. After the welcoming dinner on Friday, members get down to business on Saturday morning, with a small-group session lasting at least an hour and a half, followed by a plenary session of comparable length; this three-hour engagement is repeated on Saturday afternoon and Sunday morning.[17] This amounts to nine hours of deliberation for the typical DP, compared with six hours for DDay.[18] Since the DP experience is more intensive, its impact on group opinion may be somewhat larger than that generated by DDay (although data from the New Haven Deliberative Poll indicate that substantial opinion changes can occur after only a morning of discussion).[19]

The intensity of the DP experience is important for another reason. In our many informal discussions about DDay, some skeptical interlocutors have wondered whether normal people will simply rebel at the thought of engaging in six hours of structured discussion with strangers on a single day. But our experience belies these skeptical expectations. We have no reported cases of DP rebellions, but there are many examples of more affirmative responses.

Consider an incident from the DP on Britain's future in Europe in 1995. Jim Fishkin was sitting next to a small-group moderator while one of the plenary sessions was being taped for television broadcast. When the taping ended, a participant raised her hand and said, "Excuse me, but I did not get to ask my question." The television presenter patiently explained that the time had run out. But the questioner insisted on a chance to put her question, and she was eventually given the floor. As the small-group moderator observed this scene, she whispered to Fishkin that, at the beginning of the weekend, the persistent questioner was so shy that she was unwilling to say anything at all. And yet by the end of the weekend she was interrupting the proceedings before television cameras and hundreds of people, politely insisting that she should be heard. She was representing her group, which had approved her question after considerable deliberation. And she felt a responsibility to her fellow members to get their question answered.

This sense of transformed political efficacy is difficult to measure. Nevertheless, we do the best we can to measure all the changes in attitudes and information by concluding the DP with a final questionnaire on Sunday afternoon—which contains the very same questions asked on initial contact. After completing the questionnaire, the participants leave for home. On two occasions (the British crime DP and the American National Issues Convention) respondents have also been surveyed nine or eleven months later. While their attitude changes have moved somewhat in the direction of their initial responses, they also show considerable persistence many months later, approximately splitting the difference between the participants' initial views and their views at the conclusion of the Deliberative Poll weekend.[20] A weekend's discussion appears to have a lasting effect.

The result is a "poll with a human face." Among forms of public consultation, DPs allow for a distinctive marriage of quantitative social science and qualitative insight. On the one hand, the relatively large numbers of participants,[21] along with the care with which they are selected,[22] permits rigorous statistical analysis of the impact of deliberation on the participants' knowledge and preferences. On the other hand, the poll also has much in common with more qualitative forms of opinion research. When these dialogues are taped and edited, they give a human voice to the public's concerns — a voice that can be broadcast to the rest of the mass public as well as to policymakers.

When the Public Deliberates

What have we learned from our study of DPs that might be relevant to the viability of DDay?

First, deliberation makes a difference. When one compares the attitudes and opinions that respondents had at the end of the process with those they had on first contact, there are many large and statistically significant differences. As in the first Deliberative Poll, on crime (broadcast on Britain's Channel Four in 1994), it is not unusual for deliberation to significantly change the balance of opinion on two-thirds of the policy questions.[23] And more than half of the respondents typically change their positions on particular policy items after sustained conversation.[24]

Carmel Meredith, a British participant in the DP on crime, put the point in human terms. Speaking on the TV broadcast, she said that "the questionnaire that I filled in four weeks ago, I might as well rip up now and put it in the bin. It was an absolute waste of time because I didn't know enough about it." After discussions, she had come to seriously reevaluate the top-of-the-head views that she had given to the interviewer in the initial survey. In describing her experience, she was speaking for many other DP participants.

What is going on to produce this kind of change? Some occurs before the event, in anticipation of it. During the British DP on crime, the spouse of one of the respondents came up to thank Jim Fishkin. In thirty years of marriage, her husband had never read a newspaper, but the DP invitation had prompted him to read "every newspaper every day" (and, as a result, he was going to be "much more interesting to live with in retirement"). This encapsulated our aspiration to create incentives to overcome rational ignorance and to motivate people to behave a bit more like ideal citizens.

This example illustrates a general phenomenon. When people anticipate that they will be in a situation where they may have to discuss an issue in public with others, they are far more likely to read materials, to absorb information, and to pay attention to anything they read or hear about the topic. The information has acquired what some researchers have called "communication utility."[25]

While communication utility appears to motivate significant learning in advance, other evidence indicates that learning is more balanced after arrival, when people find themselves in face-to-face discussion with others who may have different points of view. The Danish DP of August 2000 was held before the national referendum on adoption of the euro. We took this opportunity to provide respondents with a second wave of the questionnaire before the face-to-face deliberations began. Some questions elicited information that a supporter of the referendum would tend to cite, some that an opponent would invoke. Even though everyone was sent the same briefing document and everyone was exposed to the public referendum campaign, each person differentially learned the facts more likely to be cited by his own side. But the gap closed by the end of the weekend of face-to-face discussions. The respondents, whether supporters or opponents, now tended to know facts on both sides of the issue.[26]

These results suggest that DP participants are not just learning, they are engaged in more balanced learning. Face-to-face discussions provide different incentives than just reading the materials in isolation or watching the news at home. What's more, DP results demonstrate that the acquisition of information is connected to opinion change. As we have explained, our questionnaires typically test each respondent's information level — both before and after deliberation. Our studies show that those who learn the most are also those whose opinions change the most (and they change in the same direction as the sample as a whole).[27] Hence a second main result emerges from the Deliberative Polls: not only do respondents change their opinions, but they are more informed, and it is the information gain that drives the opinion change.

One small example is illustrative. The 2003 National Issues Convention in Philadelphia focused on America's role in the world. Before deliberation, only 19 percent of the participants could correctly identify the proportion of the U.S. budget that was devoted to foreign aid (about 1 percent). And only 20 percent of the respondents initially wished to increase foreign aid. But after a weekend's discussion, 64 percent knew the right answer, and 53 percent wanted to increase spending levels.

Of course, there is a great deal of learning in the deliberative process that is difficult to measure. At the National Issues Convention broadcast in January 1996, one of the three issues was the current state of the American family. As the discussion began, an eighty-four-year-old white conservative remarked to an African-American respondent, who was on welfare, "You don't have a family." He explained that "a family" required a mother and father with children in the same household. His comment gave many of the participants pause. However, by the end of the weekend, he was heard saying to her, "What are the three most important words in the English language? They are 'I was wrong.'" After extended small group discussion, he had come to understand her situation beyond the impressions received from sound bites and headlines. Obviously, respondents learn a great deal about people from other social positions, about what their lives and perspectives are like. While it is difficult to capture this kind of learning with information questions, it is clearly one of the products of face-to-face discussion with people from different walks of life.

A third main conclusion suggested by DP data is that deliberation makes a difference not only to opinion but also to voting — especially in contexts where the public becomes better informed. In the 1999 Deliberative Poll on whether Australia should become a republic, there was a big increase in the level of knowledge about the referendum proposal and an equally dramatic shift in opinion. The average percentage answering five knowledge questions correctly increased from 39 percent to 70 percent after deliberation. And there was an increase in the support for the Yes position from 57 percent to 73 percent after deliberation.[28] In the 1997 Deliberative Poll in Britain just before the general election, there were also big increases in knowledge and changes in voting intention, particularly with respect to the Liberal Democrats, who increased their share in the Deliberative Poll from 13 to 33 percent. Respondents were also asked to locate the parties and to locate their own views on four policy scales having to do with the economic issues in the campaign. After deliberation, their own views and their placements of the parties had both changed, but in a way that was more closely calibrated with their voting intentions.[29]

Only one DP provides an apparent exception to this tendency. In 2000 we held a Deliberative Poll in Denmark on adoption of the euro soon before the referendum on the issue. After a weekend of discussion, voting intentions did not change significantly. However, this was the sixth national referendum in Denmark on European issues, and the Danes are widely known as the most knowledgeable on such issues (as evidenced by results over the years in the Euro Barometer).[30] Confirming this reputation, the Danes at the DP were distinctive in starting the process at remarkably high levels of information — with many providing correct answers to very difficult questions. But even here the Danes profited from a weekend's deliberation. The final questionnaires showed even higher levels of knowledge, and there were also changes in policy attitudes — just little in the way of shifts in voting intention on the bottom-line question about the euro. Rather than serving as a counterexample, the Danish results suggest the stability of well-informed judgments. While the Australian and British samples radically changed their preferences as they became better informed, the Danes saw no reason to change their already well-considered votes.[31]

A fourth main result of Deliberative Polling is that discussion leads respondents to take some responsibility for the solution of public problems. They look beyond the most narrow and immediate constructions of their self-interest to support the provision of public goods. Consider the series of DPs held in Texas on integrated resource planning for electric utilities. Random samples of Texas consumers were asked to deliberate on such questions as: How should the utilities provide power in the future — through fossil fuels such as coal or natural gas, through conservation (cutting the demand), or through renewable energy (such as wind and solar power)? What should the utilities do about subsidizing poor customers? To make these questions concrete, deliberators were asked whether they would be willing to pay more on their monthly utility bills for these social goods. Eight separate Deliberative Polls confronted these issues, and in a striking series of results, increasing percentages after discussion regularly said they would be willing to pay more. Averaged over all eight DPs, the percentage of participants who were willing to pay more each month for renewable energy rose from 52 to 84 percent at the end of the poll. Respondents were also willing to pay more to support conservation programs and subsidies for low-income customers.[32] As we have noted, these results provided the basis for a permanent commitment to renewable energy in the deregulation legislation.

A regional DP in New Haven, Connecticut, provides another example that suggests public spiritedness. A random sample of the residents of fifteen towns deliberated for a weekend at Yale University on issues of regional development. One issue was whether their towns should share tax revenues to promote new development, taking advantage of a new option in state law. At the beginning of the conversation, there was strong opposition to any revenue sharing by one's own town (80 percent opposed). But at the end, opposition declined to 40 percent, and there were significant increases in support for voluntary tax-sharing arrangements. However, support for the most demanding proposal, mandatory tax sharing, went down, from 42 percent to 28 percent. Deliberation seems to have facilitated a widespread but limited form of public spiritedness. There was less support for requiring tax sharing but far greater support for incentives and voluntary sharing.[33]

In the 2003 National Issues Convention in the United States on foreign affairs, the changes uniformly exhibited a greater willingness to shoulder responsibility for global problems. It is a commonplace in public opinion research that if one asks the American public whether we ought to contribute to the solution of any worthwhile problem abroad or whether we ought to "deal with problems at home first," the latter option always overwhelms the former. Our initial surveys conformed to this pattern, with 53 percent choosing to "deal with problems at home first" rather than helping with world hunger and 50 percent choosing that option over dealing with AIDS in developing countries. But after deliberation, these percentages dropped to 29 percent and 20 percent, respectively. There were similar increases in willingness to assume more responsibility for global environmental issues—with a shift from 65 percent to 81 percent in support of more stringent fuel-economy requirements for cars even if this made them less powerful, and an increase from 70 percent to 87 percent in support of dealing with environmental problems through international agreements. And, as mentioned earlier, support for increased foreign aid went from 20 percent to 53 percent. More generally, participants entered the Deliberative Poll as citizens of the United States and left, to some measurable degree, as citizens of the world.[34]

These moves in the direction of greater public spiritedness recall a classical aspiration of democratic theory. John Stuart Mill famously urged the development of new institutions that would be "schools of public spirit." Heavily influenced by Alexis de Tocqueville's account of juries and town meetings in the United States, Mill also invoked ancient Athenian experience with the people's court (the *dicastery*), which used random samples of several hundred citizens to deliberate not just about legal cases but also about broader political issues. In all these institutions, the citizen "is called upon, while so engaged, to weigh interests not his own; to be guided, in case of conflicting claims, by another rule than his private partialities."[35]

Without such schools of public spirit fostering shared discussion, one "never thinks of any collective interest, of any objects to be pursued jointly with others, but only in competition with them, and in some measure at their expense."[36] The evidence from the Deliberative Polls held in Texas, in New Haven, and at the National Issues Convention suggest the significant promise of DPs — and by extension, DDay — in this regard. Both are potentially schools of public spirit, creating social contexts in which citizens can discuss public problems together.

A fifth area of change associated with DPs involves a classic problem of social choice theory. Since Condorcet's pathbreaking work in the eighteenth century, it has been well known that majority rule can fail to pick out a unique winner from the range of possible public policy solutions. For example, although a majority might vote for policy A over B, and for B over C, it might also prefer C over A in a pairwise comparison. And when this is true, the majority's choices can cycle endlessly through the three options without generating a determinate solution. In modern times Kenneth Arrow generalized this result, leading to a good deal of skepticism about the very coherence of the idea of the "will of the people." William Riker is perhaps the best known representative of this view. Building on Arrow's analysis, he charges that the notion of a popular will must be "meaningless" — since cycles show that the public's preferences have no collective consistency.[37] If we allow politicians to manipulate the agenda, they might be able to maintain the *appearance* of collective consistency, but that is only an illusion.[38] While option A might beat B on the surface of public life, A's dominance may endure only because politicians have somehow prevented option C from appearing on the agenda.

But voting cycles are only possible, not inevitable, features of democratic life. They can be prevented, for example, if all voters place the competing options on a single *dimension of value*.[39] For example, if all voters agree that options A, B, and C all fit along a single left-to-right or liberal-conservative spectrum, then no cycles are possible. While different voters might disagree about the relative merits of A, B, and C, majority rule will pick out a unique winner if all voters agree that A is to the left of B and B is to the left of C. We come, then, to a key question raised by the social choice literature: Are there methods a group can use to eliminate voting cycles by coming to an agreement that the competing options may be appropriately placed on a single dimension of value?

Here is where discussion and deliberation enter the argument. By talking over the issues, a group may not reach a clear policy choice. But they may well come to understand their disagreements well enough to place the choices along a common metric of evaluation. Riker himself recognizes this possibility,[40] and DPs provide an empirical way of testing this hypothesis. Thus far we have employed ranking questions (first choice, second choice, third choice, and so on) in ten Deliberative Polls. Analysis of those questions indicates that deliberation increases the level of preference structuration — their convergence upon a common metric — if not upon a single policy solution. There is an impressive relation between deliberation and increases in the percentage of the sample that places all the options on a single dimension for evaluation. And the larger the proportion of the sample that shares the same dimension, the more unlikely a cycle. For example, in the Texas electric utility DPs, respondents were asked to rank the order in which different energy sources should be exploited, choosing among coal, natural gas, conservation, and renewable energy (wind and solar power). These individual rankings exhibited a much greater convergence around a single dimension after deliberation. While participants continued to disagree about their individual rankings, they shared a more common understanding of what they were disagreeing about. Some DPers ended up valuing the least expensive options; some, the most environmentally friendly; and some took up a position in between. But many more came to understand the values involved, and so could locate each option on a single dimension that traded off economic cost against environmental value. This was enough to minimize the risk of the Condorcet cycles emphasized by social choice theory. In contrast, this risk was much greater on the basis of the preferences registered at the time of the initial questionnaire without much thought or information.[41]

A sixth finding of Deliberative Polls is that everyone can deliberate. When we started our research program, we worried that only the more educated were likely to change their opinions as a result of discussion. But the evidence from the DPs suggests that our fears were groundless. Opinion change does not seem to correlate with any of the standard sociodemographic factors, including education. The respondents, pretty much regardless of who they are, all have plenty to learn, from the process and from each other. Deliberation is not just for the more educated or more privileged; it is democratic in its potential for everybody.[42]

Last, but not least, the DPs demonstrated that deliberation is satisfying. When we asked the participants in the National Issues Convention to rate the experience on a one-to-nine scale, ranging from "generally a waste of time" to "an extremely valuable experience," 73 percent gave it a perfect nine rating, and more than 94 percent gave it a rating of seven or above. Perhaps this is not surprising since respondents had been on national television discussing high-profile issues. But we got the same results in the local electric utility polls — even when the participants were not on national television dealing with dramatic issues, they still found deliberative consultation extremely satisfying.

To sum up these first seven lessons: experience with Deliberative Polls suggests not only that participants change their political attitudes but that these changes are driven by better information. They suggest not only that these changed attitudes generate different voting intentions but that these preferences become more public spirited and collectively consistent. These changes occur throughout the population and aren't limited to the more educated. Finally, deliberation is intrinsically satisfying once people are given a serious chance to engage with one another in an appropriate setting.

On the Use and Abuse of Heuristics

These results contrast sharply with a growing literature in political science. On this view, well-informed citizens wouldn't vote very differently than they do today. To make their case, these analysts suggest that poorly informed voters already use various heuristics or simplifying devices to approximate the same conclusions they would reach if they were well informed. If citizens know, for example, who is for a proposal or who is against it, they can use this cue to guide their voting behavior without taking the trouble to study the issue themselves. Samuel Popkin argues that "low information rationality" of this kind can allow individual voters to approximate the same conclusions they would reach with high information rationality.[43] Arthur Lupia says that "shortcuts" can produce the same voting behavior as "encyclopedic" knowledge.[44] Another version of the argument is offered at the aggregate level. Benjamin Page and Robert Shapiro hold that despite individual ignorance and inattention, the errors of individual voters cancel each other out, and the aggregate voting patterns of the mass public are not different from what they would be if the population were well informed.[45]

Popkin introduces his thesis by presenting the example of President Ford choking on a tamale while campaigning against Ronald Reagan in the Texas Republican primary of 1976. The president didn't know that he was supposed to shuck the tamale before eating it and choked as a result. Popkin claims that Mexican-American voters could reasonably infer from Ford's ignorance about their food that he knew little about them or their culture As a consequence, Hispanic voters had good reason to prefer Reagan, without needing to know much about the detailed policy positions of the rival candidates. Unfortunately, Popkin's choice of an example serves as a caution about the potential abuses of informational shortcuts: the unshucked tamale did not, in fact, serve as a very good indicator of the comparative positions of Ford and Reagan.[46]

Apart from such anecdotes, the Popkin-Lupia thesis rests primarily on statistical models developed from survey data. These models compare the preferences of uninformed voters with those who are better informed but are otherwise similar. But as Larry Bartels has shown, it is perfectly possible to construct equally plausible models from survey data that lead to a very different conclusion—that the public's ignorance makes a real difference in how elections come out.[47] If people were more informed, they would vote differently, and these differences would be large enough to change election results. Given the limitations of the models and the evidence, we think that the evidence provided by Deliberative Polls is more decisive. As we have seen in the cases of Australia and Britain, relatively uninformed voters *do* change their voting preferences substantially once they deliberate on the basis of better information.

There is a partial truth in the "heuristics" literature. People do use informational shortcuts. For example, the participants in a DP or on DDay would likely be sensitive to which parties, political elites, or interest groups were for or against a given policy. The issue is whether heuristics of this sort reliably take low information respondents to the *same* conclusions and behaviors they would reach with high information. This claim seems dubious in the light of the DP results.

The Pathologies of Deliberation

But isn't there a darker side to deliberation? Some have argued that it can lead to pathological forms of groupthink and issue polarization. Our next task is to confront this common anxiety.

Cass Sunstein has recently emphasized the negative with regard to group deliberation. Working with a number of distinguished collaborators, he has propounded a "law of group polarization": discussion pushes a group to adopt a more extreme position than it held at the start of the conversation. He makes his point through experiments with mock juries dealing with issues in which there is a mathematically calculable midpoint — for example, in the award of damages, one can calculate the average amount different juries award mock plaintiffs making identical cases. He shows that if the jury starts at one side of the midpoint, it will move further in that direction after discussion. He calls this "polarization" and attributes it to two main factors. Since the group contains a disproportionate number of people favoring one side of the argument, there is an imbalance in the "argument pool." The group can also impose "conformity mechanisms" on its dissenters. These pressures to conform may come merely from the "information effect" generated when an individual learns that most others group members support a more extreme alternative. Or dissenters may suffer from a "reputational effect" if the group imposes sanctions upon deviant members — disparaging them publicly or threatening them with reprisals.[48] In emphasizing these pressures toward conformity, Sunstein leads us to recall an earlier literature elaborating on the dangers of groupthink.[49] The fear is that when groups deliberate, they come to think more alike. Note that groupthink can occur even without Sunsteinian polarization. While the group's opinions may be no more extreme at the end of the day, there may be a decrease in the variance of each individual's opinion around the group's mean.

We emphasize this point because groupthink raises very different issues from polarization. Imagine that you are in a mathematics class: at the beginning of the session, half of the class thinks that $2 + 2 = 3$, but at the end everybody believes that $2 + 2 = 4$. Rather than calling this a triumph of groupthink, we think of this as the product of education: deliberation has narrowed the variance because more members appreciate the force of the better argument. Of course, political discussion isn't mathematics, but this doesn't mean that some disagreements aren't based on demonstrable mistakes. To the contrary, given the low levels of information prevailing in the population, group members will often find that they had based their previous political opinions on mistaken "facts," and will therefore achieve previously unsuspected grounds for agreement. When this is so, we should interpret a reduction in variance of opinion not as the product of groupthink but as an entirely appropriate response to the force of better arguments. This example suggests that it isn't enough to look at quantitative data to establish the existence of pathologies; one must qualitatively explore the *reasons why* opinions seem to be converging.

Quantitative demonstrations of group polarization, however, raise more serious concerns. Beyond the obvious evil of coercive pressures, Sunstein's point about biased "argument pools" threatens the rationalistic ambitions of our project. What good is our effort to encourage citizens to use their reason if the exercise is subtly biased and will predictably generate unnecessary polarization?

These questions will recur in various forms throughout this book, and our answers will gain increasing political nuance as our argument proceeds.[50] But for starters, the results from Deliberative Polls suggest the need to treat Sunstein's law of group polarization with great caution. Quite simply, our analyses of the DP data provide no support for Sunstein's "law," nor do they suggest that deliberation leads to a reduction of variance in group opinion that might justify the (ambiguous) charge of groupthink.[51]

In his review of the literature, Sunstein recognizes that the DP data provide an exception to his "law."[52] But we would go further and deny the existence of any general law that causally links deliberation to polarization.[53] To account for the presence or absence of polarization and groupthink, we cannot rely on broad generalities but should focus on the impact of fine-grained differences in institutional contexts. Sunstein's mock juries differ significantly in their structure and motivation from the setups provided at DPs and DDays. By focusing on these differences, we gain a better sense of when and whether it makes sense to take seriously free-floating fears about the pathologies of deliberation.

Sunstein has come to basically the same conclusion. In his recent Holmes Lectures he explains: "Group polarization can be heightened, diminished and possibly even eliminated with seemingly small alterations in institutional arrangements. To the extent that limited argument pools and social influences are likely to have unfortunate effects, correctives can be introduced, perhaps above all by exposing group members, at one point or another, to arguments to which they are not antecedently inclined."[54]

Sunstein is right to emphasize two factors in his account of polarization: "conformity mechanisms" and "argument pool imbalances." We can show how the microdesign of DPs and DDays serves to undermine these forces, while the design of mock juries tends to exacerbate them. Begin with the conformity mechanisms generated by the typical jury procedures. Most obviously, jurors are obliged to reveal their bottom-line decisions to other jurors, but this is not true for either DP or DDay. In DPs participants' conclusions are solicited in confidential questionnaires; in the case of DDay, citizens express their final decisions in their secret ballots on Election Day.

In organizing their discussion, moreover, jurors engage in a more coercive format than the one contemplated in our initiatives. The point of a jury conversation is to come up with a single "right answer": guilty or innocent, and if legally responsible, a *particular* criminal sentence or payment of money damages. In contrast, DPers and DDayers focus on framing good questions, not final answers — questions that will open up further inquiries, not close them. Although participants may also state their bottom-line opinions, this is optional, not mandatory. Members holding minority opinions may avoid group sanctions simply by keeping to the announced task — proposing questions, not propounding answers.

Jury deliberations are particularly coercive when unanimous decisions are required in reaching a verdict.[55] In this context, continued dissent means that the group has failed to discharge its function. Little wonder that those in the majority may put pressure on dissenters in order to get the job done. In contrast, nobody expects elections to be resolved unanimously. A 60–40 vote represents a landslide in this context. Even when participants in a DP or DDay find themselves supporting a minority candidate, they know that tens of millions of others support the same choice.

DPs and DDays are also organized to undermine Sunstein's fears about unbalanced "argument pools." To be sure, the typical jury trial does seek to generate a balanced argument pool by inviting the competing sides to develop their strongest possible arguments for jury consideration. But once the judge gives the case to the jury, the panel cannot consult with others — they are locked into a single conversation until they reach their verdict. As a consequence, a majority's forceful selection of certain arguments may well have a significant impact on the deliberations of the minority. In contrast, DPers and DDayers are never locked into their small groups to make a final decision. Instead, small group members are constantly moving out into larger assemblies where competing opinion-leaders try to provide greater balance to the argument pool. This back-and-forth motion generates a very different dynamic from the closed conversation of the jury room.

It should be no surprise, then, that the DP data don't support Sunstein's law of group polarization. The microinstitutional structures that generated Sunstein's findings have a very different spin in the formats we are elaborating. At the least, this means that our critics must travel a much longer road if they wish to defeat our claims for Deliberation Day. They can't hope to invoke some globally applicable "law" to dismiss our project from the field of contention. Since DPs establish that ordinary citizens *can* constructively deliberate on pressing political issues placed before them, critics must frame their objections to DDay at retail rather than wholesale. To make their case against our proposal, they can't disparage citizen deliberation as a hopelessly utopian notion. Instead, they must point to *particular* features of our DDay proposal that diverge from the institutional format developed for DPs, and explain why these fine-grained institutional differences will prevent ordinary citizens at DDay from replicating their achievements at the DPs.

This is a more complicated form of critique. But in the end, it will prove more worthwhile. We believe that a fine-grained exploration of the similarities and differences between the formats of DP and DDay suggests cautious optimism as to the likely consequences of collective deliberation at our new holiday. But even if you disagree in the end, the effort will help refine an appreciation of the complex ways in which the art of institutional design can shape the future of deliberative democracy.

The Art of Institutional Design

In introducing the basic framework for Deliberative Polling, we have already noted many resemblances to the format we have proposed for Deliberation Day. But there are significant differences as well. Our present task is to consider those differences more systematically. Are they so significant as to put in doubt the applicability of the success stories from the DPs? Although ordinary citizens can engage in constructive forms of deliberation at DPs, will they be blocked from similar achievements by the differentiating features of DDay?

Since DDay doesn't exist, we don't have any hard data to answer this question. But we can consider how other real-world institutions handle comparable problems — if similar ones operate with moderate success, this should ameliorate concerns about DDay.

This search for analogues is especially rewarding when it comes to one key difference between DPs and DDays. In our social science experiments, each small group's deliberation is guided by a trained moderator; but at the new holiday, citizen-foremen will be charged with this task. The costs of training millions of moderators would be high, but this isn't the main reason why we have made this shift. Even if we were willing to pay the economic price, the creation of a "moderator corps" strikes us as a terrible idea. Even if the initial corps were largely composed of paragons of fairness—itself a doubtful proposition—it would be far too tempting a target for takeover by one or another ideological movement. This possibility suffices to dismiss the proposal out of hand. Above all else, we have imposed an "anti-tyranny" constraint on every aspect of our design proposal: *Any* proposed feature that generates even a remote risk of centralized political control over the course of deliberation is beyond the pale.[56]

While a moderator corps is a normative nonstarter, the absence of moderators is potentially important as an empirical matter. In reflecting on our DP experience, we have found that the social skills of the moderator have been useful in keeping the flow of conversation going and encouraging an atmosphere of mutual respect. Although romantic democrats may find it easy to suppose that ordinary citizens can discharge this task without guidance from so-called professionals, is there any evidence to back this up?

Happily, the answer is yes. Jury deliberation in the English-speaking world has been superintended by citizen-foremen for centuries, and it has survived centuries of contestation. This fact alone should assuage anxieties. There are only a handful of social institutions that have withstood the test of time as successfully as the citizen-jury led by a citizen-foreman. In extending the role of citizen-foreman to DDay, we are building on a time-tested practice, not invoking a utopian ideal.

But the idea of the citizen-foreman has more than history going for it. Over the past half-century, social scientists have contributed a lot of insights into jury deliberation. As Sunstein's recent work suggests, not all of it has been laudatory. We have already explained why his findings about polarization don't apply to the DDay format. In any event, our present purposes lead us to concentrate on different social science studies. The key questions here involve process more than outcome: Do citizen-juries led by citizen-foremen do a relatively good job focusing deliberation on the central issues before them? Or do they waste their time on peripheral matters of no importance to the issues they are supposed to decide?

Our review of the literature suggests the need to distinguish between questions of fact and questions of law. As to the former, there is unanimous agreement that juries successfully winnow away irrelevant facts and focus their attention on the key issues in dispute. But it is less clear whether juries understand the precise legal issues presented by the judge before they enter the deliberation room. In her impressive work with mock juries, Phoebe Ellsworth rejects the notion that this disparity is "a function of [the jurors'] mental capacities."[57] Instead,

> it seems more plausible that the system is set up to promote misunderstanding: The convoluted, technical language, the dry and abstract presentation of the law following the vivid, concrete and often lengthy presentation of evidence; the requirement that jurors interpret the evidence before they know what their decision choices are; the fact that juries usually do not get copies of the instructions to take with them into the jury room; the lack of training in the law for jurors as part of their jury duty; the general failure to discover and correct jurors' preconceptions about the law; the failure to inform jurors that they are allowed to ask for help with the instructions; and the fact that those who do ask for help are often disappointed by a simple repetition of the incomprehensible paragraph.[58]

These barriers to comprehension won't generally carry over to Deliberation Day. Rather than restricting themselves to legal arcana, the party representatives at the citizen-assemblies will have every incentive to answer questions in terms that the general public will find intelligible. The evidence that juries do in fact succeed in mastering the facts is more relevant to our concerns. Consider Ellsworth's picture of jury deliberation on a homicide case: "In summary the process of deliberation seems to work quite well in bringing out the facts and arriving at a consensus about their sequence. Errors are corrected, and irrelevant facts and implausible scenarios are generally weeded out, at least in deliberations over this relatively simple homicide. The juries do a good job of gradually narrowing down discussion to important issues."[59]

This demonstrated capacity of ordinary citizens to deal with facts gains special importance in the light of our findings about Deliberative Polls. All the Deliberative Polls thus far, whether in a campaign or a policy context, show impressive information gains as measured by knowledge questions. And our best model for explaining change in the Deliberative Polls focuses on true information gain as the key explanatory variable.[60]

Those who learn the most are also those whose opinions change the most—suggesting that change is occurring on the basis of factual learning and reasoned argument. Ellsworth's work suggests that these conclusions are not dependent upon the presence of professional moderators, and that fact-based learning is well within the capacities of citizen juries led by citizen-moderators.

These conclusions are reinforced by the classic study on the American jury by Harry Kalven and Hans Zeisel.[61] In contrast to later work, this study did not analyze the behavior of mock juries but followed real juries into the deliberation room. The resulting furor generated changes in the law that made it impossible for subsequent researchers to replicate Kalven-Zeisel methods. It therefore provides a unique insight into the way real jurors actually discharge their deliberative responsibilities—findings which lead to an even more optimistic assessment than do Ellsworth's.

For our purposes, two of their conclusions about jury comprehension are crucial: first, "that the jury does by and large understand the facts and get the case straight," and second, that the "jury's decision by and large moves with the weight and direction of the evidence."[62] Kalven and Zeisel compared the decisions of judges and juries in "hard" and "easy" cases and "clear" and "close" cases (as classified by judges). They hypothesized that "if the jury has any propensity to misunderstand the case it will be more likely to disagree with the judge in those cases it perceives as difficult." However, this was not the case. The rate of disagreement between judge and jury was virtually identical for each of the four possible categories: clear and easy, clear and difficult, close and easy, and close and difficult. Kalven and Zeisel offered these results as a "stunning refutation of the hypothesis that the jury does not understand."[63] And as a later study noted, "the judges in Kalven and Zeisel's study almost never attributed their disagreements with the jury to the jury's inability to grasp the case facts; in fact this attribution was made only once in the 3,576 cases sampled."[64]

These findings provide additional support to more recent work and permit reasonable confidence about the capacity of DDay groups to perform their core function without the assistance of trained moderators. As in the case of traditional juries, they should generally be capable of honing in on important questions of fact and value left unresolved by the debates between presidential candidates and local party representatives.

But in our experience with DPs, moderators are useful not only for discharging this core function. They also serve two other roles. First, they encourage conversationalists to proceed in ways that express mutual respect. Second, they help the group reach consensus on the questions they wish to pose in the plenary sessions. In the place of moderators we propose to discharge these functions with a few simple rules. The discretion of citizen-foremen is strictly limited by our time-clock system that grants each participant the right to gain recognition for ninety-second segments. Similarly, citizen-foremen are not free to decide which of the group's questions should be forwarded to the citizen-assemblies. This is a decision made by all group members using a system of approval voting that gives priority to issues that gain the broadest support from participants. Is there any evidence from jury deliberations that bears on the viability of these rule-bound strategies?

For starters, jury foremen are not notorious for abusing their position. Remarkably few incidents have surfaced over the centuries. This augurs well for the behavior of citizen-foremen on DDay. Nonetheless, problems remain. Although the ninety-second rule grants equal rights of participation to each member of the group, individuals are free to waive their rights and remain silent. And in similar circumstances, social science studies of jurors have regularly unearthed a troubling pattern. Even though the rules grant jurors equal rights, everybody doesn't participate equally. Instead, the big talkers tend to be white and male, richer and better educated.[65] In recognition of these realities, the trained moderators at DPs make special efforts to draw others into the conversation. But in their absence, there is good reason to believe that the jury results will be replicated, at least to some degree, on DDay. We say, "to some degree" because the severe time constraints we impose are designed to limit the opportunities for anyone to dominate the discussion. We shall also be noting some other mitigating factors as our discussion proceeds.

Some significant inequalities will undoubtedly remain. This is regrettable, but we don't think the shortfall is nearly enough to render inapplicable the broad empirical findings that emerge from the DP experience. Even when small-group members don't talk, they can learn a lot from the ongoing exchange both within the group and at the larger citizen-assemblies. And as we have seen, learning drives changes in political preferences.

The tendency toward differential participation may also be ameliorated by a second factor. When assembling a group of participants for a DP, we take care to bring together a cross-section of the relevant constituency—which typically includes the entire nation or some large region (like Texas or the New Haven metropolitan area). Thus each DP is certain to contain a substantial number of relatively wealthy white males who might dominate the conversation by invoking the ninety-second rule more frequently than others. In contrast, each assembly at DDay will be drawing its five hundred citizens from a much narrower geographic area—with DDay participants at each neighborhood school or community center drawn from within a three- to five-mile area.

This "neighborhood model" of deliberation contrasts sharply with the procedures we have used in organizing a DP. After all, the DP's aim is to simulate the thought processes of an entire nation or region, and this couldn't be accomplished if all DP participants were drawn from a single small neighborhood. But such a model makes sense during DDay, when the entire nation will actually have the chance to deliberate. Given this fundamental shift in ambition, it is no longer necessary to make each citizen-assembly into a statistical microcosm of the larger nation. Instead, our overriding aim should be to maximize turnout, by inviting each citizen to participate at a place near his home.[66] Given existing patterns of residential segregation, this means that upper-class citizens will concentrate in their own neighborhood centers, providing space for other classes, races, and ethnic groups to participate more actively at their own neighborhood DDays.

Of course, prevailing patterns of racial, ethnic, and class concentration will have other important consequences—but we defer a treatment of most of them to Chapter 4, where we try to assess DDay's impact on the larger process of national politics. For the present, we bracket these larger inquiries to focus on a single issue: Does the neighborhood model of deliberation make it harder to extrapolate the basic empirical findings generated by DPs to the likely deliberative performance at DDay?

While geographic concentration helps ameliorate the problem of unequal participation, it may have a negative effect along another dimension. Since DPs contain a random cross-section of the entire community, they maximize the chances of cross-class encounters that often enrich the normative discussion. Our society offers few opportunities for rich suburban-ites and poor immigrants to deliberate on matters of common concern. And we have already offered anecdotal evidence suggesting that such encounters sometimes lead to breakthroughs in mutual understanding — breakthroughs that will occur less often in more homogeneous groups.

Nevertheless, one should not overestimate this point in the overall scheme of things. At present, the overwhelming majority of political conversations take place amongst family and friends. One study of British and American political conversation found that at least two-thirds in each country "never or only rarely discuss political topics" in social interactions with those they do not know very well.[67] For most Americans, the neighborhood assembly will represent a vast increase in the range of views and interests encountered in face-to-face conversation. This range may fall short of the full diversity of opinion in the nation as a whole, but it will be more than enough to prompt a great deal of reflection by each group member as he or she tries to understand why others approach the issues so differently. In short, the data from the DPs can serve as a rough and ready approximation for the likely consequences of neighborhood deliberations — though it will be valuable to refine these estimates with more focused research in the future.

Research on National Issues Forums (NIF), deliberative discussions held in communities around the country, show very similar effects to those of the DPs in terms of learning and increases in civic engagement. In addition, "NIF participation increased the diversity of participants' conversational networks" after the forums.[68] Such studies are instructive, as they concern deliberative forums that are community based and in that sense offer a closer parallel than national DPs to DDay.

Citizen-foremen, neighborhood deliberation. These differences between DP and DDay are significant, but they don't prevent a cautious extrapolation of the DP findings to DDay — though the DP data should be treated only as suggestive of the orders of magnitude of learning and opinion change that is likely. Fortunately, we can be more confident about a third significant difference — and that is the sheer amount of time provided for deliberation. Participants at DPs typically devote nine hours to deliberation in their small and large groups, while DDayers will spend only six hours in a similar enterprise. Yet we have reason to believe that this is more than enough for significant effects. In the New Haven Regional Deliberative Poll, we launched a second wave of our questionnaire at midday on Saturday, after only a morning of deliberation, and we found large shifts of opinion.[69] Moreover, DDay will be preceded by a period of buildup and anticipation. Knowing that they will participate in a discussion, citizens will respond in the same manner as they do in preparation for Deliberative Polls — paying more attention to the media and talking with friends and family about the issues. There is good reason, then, to expect that the six-hour engagement at DDay will suffice to generate substantial learning, and learning-induced changes in opinion.

There is a final difference. DPers are celebrities of a sort. They are treated to a weekend away from home; they may encounter leading politicians or prominent experts; their experiences are chronicled in the newspapers, and the folks back home may even catch a glimpse of them on television. This is a once-in-a-lifetime event for almost all concerned — it is no surprise that they prepare seriously and try to make the most of it. Will the same be true on DDay?

Like the DPs, the new national holiday will lift participants out of the routines of everyday life. There will be an air of anticipation as tens of millions prepare for the day's discussions. While there won't be many TV stars, participants won't want to make fools of themselves before their neighbors. Millions will start paying more attention to the news, and their dinner table conversations will begin to focus on DDay as it approaches. There will also be lots of hubbub during and after the holiday — exit polls, countless conversations, and media commentary. The overall level of popular engagement will far exceed that of any DP in the past or future. And at the core of the event, DDay will display the same features that have made DPs such a powerful tool for reflective decision making: in both events, each deliberator will be one voice in fifteen in a small group and one voice in a few hundred at the plenary sessions. We may be old-fashioned, but we continue to believe that substance counts for more than media hype. DDay will provide tens of millions with the opportunity to take the great phantom of "public opinion" away from pollsters and political advertisers, and make it a creation of popular deliberation. Never underestimate the power of simple ideas to inspire genuine commitment.

Of course, DDay may turn out to be a flop, with fewer and fewer folks turning out with every passing year — in which case, we will sadly support a proposal to rededicate the holiday to Presidents Day Sales and the Greatest Ski Weekend of the Year.

But in the beginning, we anticipate a good deal of popular excitement at the prospect of genuine national dialogue. And if the first few DDays succeed, tens of millions of Americans will begin to cultivate civic habits of attendance and preparation. This developing civic culture will serve as a far more enduring motivation for active engagement on Deliberation Day than the prospect of weekend celebrity offered by the Deliberative Poll.

We have reached an important resting place in our journey. We began with forty million Americans watching the televised debates between Bush and Gore. This eloquent fact testifies to the broad popular desire to penetrate the haze of media sound bites. We continued with the accumulating experience with Deliberative Polls. Our analysis of this data suggests that we aren't making the best civic use of these ritualized television encounters between the candidates. Instead, one of these debates should serve as the prologue to a day of deliberation modeled on the Deliberative Poll. DP data suggest that Deliberation Day may well provide a suitable context for ordinary Americans to deliberate in a mutually constructive fashion. If our DP results generalize, Americans emerging from the experience will not only become better informed and more public spirited. They will change their bottom-line choices, and in ways that display greater collective consistency. They will, in short, express a public opinion that is worth listening to.

Welcome to the Enlightenment.

But perhaps our greeting is premature. As we have been emphasizing, Deliberation Day departs significantly from the real-world formats used in Deliberative Polling. We have already begun investigating whether these differences — individually or cumulatively — should caution against an extrapolation of the DP findings to the DDay proposal. Our initial exploration of four key differences — citizen-moderators, neighborhood assemblies, single-day deliberation, and absence of celebrity — hasn't discouraged us from cautious optimism.

Nevertheless, we still have a long way to go before coming to a final conclusion. In comparing DP with DDay, we have thus far stayed clear of one big difference between the two enterprises: since DPs are social science experiments, the format seeks to make it impossible for external political forces to manipulate the proceedings for partisan ends. Great care is taken to prevent Democrats or Republicans, or any political interest group, from stacking the deck. In contrast, DDay is designed for the hurly-burly of real political life, and we have yet to consider how partisans might seek to exploit the new holiday for their own narrow purposes. To consider one obvious and important example, won't ideological extremists try to capture DDay by flooding the assemblies with their own activists, who then seek to focus the entire conversation on their own fringe agenda?

Such a maneuver is impossible in a DP, whose membership is generated by random-sampling techniques. Given this statistical approach, ideological positions held by members of a plenary assembly at the DP will be roughly proportional to those held in the general population: if 1 percent of Americans hold a particularly Extreme Position, about 1 percent will voice similar sentiments at the DP. But there is no similar guarantee of proportionality at DDay assemblies, especially if turnouts are low. If large numbers of centrists refuse to show up, what is to stop highly motivated extremists from dominating proceedings in one or another neighborhood assembly?

Problems like "extremist capture" emphasize the crucial importance of inserting our new institution into realistic models of modern politics. We shall take up this complex task shortly by considering how our new holiday will create new incentives both for governing the country and campaigning for office. Only then will we be in a position to come to an overall assessment of DDay.

Nevertheless, the present chapter's focus on the micro-organizational relations between DDay and DP has been important. We think it establishes that DDay isn't merely a utopian pipe dream, but a serious real-world option for enriching the democratic quality of our public life.

Perhaps you may think it is a bad idea once we place it in larger political context; perhaps not. But the real-world experiments with Deliberative Polling do suggest that the proposal deserves to be taken seriously.

And that is no small matter.

4

CYCLES OF VIRTUE

So ordinary citizens *can* reason with one another constructively, and this effort at public reasoning *can* make a difference in how people think about politics and how they vote. A democracy that reasons together is likely to have different views and reach different outcomes. Deliberation makes a difference.

Our next task is to locate the new holiday within the larger setting of American democracy — a notoriously complex system, full of Madisonian checks and balances. We cannot come to a mature assessment of Deliberation Day until we consider its dynamic interaction with the other moving parts of an intricate Enlightenment machine. This exercise may suggest that DDay will create unsuspected frictions, eroding the equilibrium of the existing system, or it will generate remarkable synergies strengthening core constitutional values — or both.

We hope to convince you that, on balance, systemic effects are strongly positive. DDay's impact on other institutions may well prove more important than anything that occurs in the citizen assemblies themselves. To see why, we must return to consider the basic aspirations of the Madisonian system, and how DDay may sustain their realization under the likely conditions of twenty-first-century political life.

Begin with a tension at the heart of modern democratic practice. On the one hand, our elected governors are supposed to take the basic interests of *all* citizens into account, and not only the narrow interests of the majority that voted them into office. On the other hand, we don't expect voters to take the obligations of citizenship very seriously. They can be as uninformed and self-interested as they like, and nobody will blame them as they enter the polling booth. To the contrary, political participation has so declined (and not only in America) that voters bask in the faint glow of community approval if they merely take the trouble to go to the polls — regardless of how ignorantly or selfishly they cast their ballots in the privacy of the ballot box. The problem this raises is obvious: Why should politicians consider the interests of all citizens if voters are uninformed and selfish?

This is not a new question. Since the days of Madison, constitutional thought has struggled with the problem — and there is no reason to think it will ever be solved definitively. Nevertheless, the political world constantly is changing, and these changes alter the terms in which the problem is expressed, and the institutional modes through which it may be ameliorated, if not resolved.

Madison famously focused on the capacities of political elites to filter out the most irrational and self-interested aspects of public opinion. One of the great aims of the Federalist Papers was to defend the design of a constitutional framework that subtly rewarded elites for filtering, rather than mirroring, these selfish impulses, thereby encouraging leaders to steer the Republic in more enlightened directions. Our first task is to consider how the introduction of DDay might contribute to this filtering process.

Our argument proceeds by appealing to the "law of anticipated reaction": Politicians try to look ahead and adapt their behavior to new risks as they emerge on the horizon. Suppose that a groundswell of popular support finally pushes our proposal through Congress in the form of the Deliberation Day Act of 2012. To fix ideas, put yourself in the place of the man or woman who has been elected president of the United States in that same year. The new statute means that you are the first sitting president who will be obliged to suffer the hazards of Deliberation Day upon seeking reelection. Like any good politician, you want to be prepared. Rather than allowing your opponent to exploit the new holiday to his electoral advantage, you will factor Deliberation Day into your political equation throughout your first term in office. As you design and execute policy during your first four years, you will consider which options will enable you to present the most persuasive case to the American people on Deliberation Day.

Obviously, you will be worrying about lots of other things as well — sometimes the prospect of Deliberation Day will be swamped by more pressing concerns, but sometimes it will seem quite important and as the years roll on, and reelection comes closer, your mind will recur to Deliberation Day more frequently. For analytic purposes, we won't try to model these complexities. We will be simplifying our problem by indulging in a familiar form of social science analysis. We shall focus on the marginal impact of our proposed innovation: *Other things being equal,* how will the introduction of Deliberation Day modify your political calculus as president?[1]

Consider a central aspect of modern politics: government by public opinion poll. No sitting politician would think of taking an important step without hiring a pollster or two to test the waters, and the modern White House is famous for its elaborate polling operations. Deliberation Day will require the president to rethink his relation to this steady stream of polling data, and in ways that promise a more reflective relation to the public good.

Every politician must engage in a predictive exercise before making sense of polling results. The key question is not what constituents think about the issues today but what they will think on Election Day: After all, the politician's fate will be determined only when the next set of votes is counted. Predictions of this kind are always hazardous — six months is an eternity in politics, and a sitting politician's day of electoral reckoning may be several years away. Nonetheless, the existing set-up allows for one important stabilizing element.

Polls can only attempt to measure what exists — and we have seen that citizens generally have poorly formed preferences based on very weak information. Call these *raw preferences,* and consider how Deliberation Day will transform their status in a politician's calculation. At present, she has no reason to believe that her constituents' preferences will be much less raw on the distant day they go to the polls — the campaign mobilization may make some difference, but not a huge one. As a consequence, the politician can extrapolate existing polling data to the future with a certain degree of confidence.

But not when Deliberation Day comes into the picture. To make our point, we need not predict that our new holiday will be a great success, attracting a huge turnout to the nation's schools and community centers. The key question is not how many Americans use the holiday as a convenient excuse to catch up on their sleep, but whether the folks who do show up can swing the election. Call this a critical mass. We will have more to say about its size and composition later.

The important point is this: if a critical mass does show up, modern polling will suddenly seem old-fashioned, and present-day techniques will dramatically depreciate in political value. Sophisticated politicians will no longer be so interested in monitoring the existing patterns of raw preferences. They will want to know about their constituents' *refined preferences:* what the voters will think after they have engaged in the course of discussion and reflection precipitated by Deliberation Day.

There are two ways to make a guess, and both represent a Madisonian improvement on the status quo. Most obviously, politicians will have a powerful new incentive to engage in some deliberation for themselves: Since a critical mass of their constituents will be discussing their performance at length, it is now in their self-interest to ask themselves what policies are in the public interest and whether they might use Deliberation Day to defend their conduct in front of their constituents at the citizen assemblies.

The second tactic might be to cough up the money required to conduct a suitably structured Deliberative Poll. By simulating the conditions prevailing on DDay with a representative sample,[2] our politician might get a better handle on the way the public will ultimately come to view the alternative actions she is considering. But conducting such polls will be expensive, and the findings of the deliberative pollster can serve only as a supplement to her own deliberations. After all, she will still have to extrapolate today's results to future elections, and this can be a tricky business.

One thing is clear: whatever technique politicians use to anticipate the judgment of their constituents on Deliberation Day, they will no longer be slaves to the high-tech methods of conventional polling that seem so sophisticated today. In making this point, we do not suppose that our holiday will generate a miraculous increase in the statesmanship of the average politician. We are appealing instead to his enlightened self-interest: raw preferences simply won't be as good a guide to electoral success, and so there won't be the same incentive to use the polls as if they were the alpha and omega of political survival. Rather than slavishly following the numbers, incumbents will be driven by electoral self-interest to exercise their own political judgment in ways that seem persuasive to their more informed constituents on DDay.

Our argument seeks to sustain the tradition of political reasoning exemplified by the Federalist Papers. The constitutional thought of James Madison and Alexander Hamilton seeks to define a middle way in its assessment of politicians — neither demonizing them nor idealizing their devotion to the public good. Instead, it views politicians as mixing selfish and public motivations in complex tangles that elude careful deconstruction. The challenge is to design institutions to encourage them to make good use of whatever political virtue they might possess — creating institutional incentives that make it in their self-interest to restrain, not exacerbate, the pathologies of popular government.[3]

The particular pathologies of concern involve citizen ignorance and the political temptation to exploit it for short-term purposes. While we called it "government by opinion poll," the Founders had a less polite term: demagogy. Our simple, but basic, point: a good way to reduce the risk of demagogy is to force politicians to reckon with the realistic prospect of a deliberative citizenry.

Our second argument also follows in the footsteps of the early American Founders. It targets a different abuse: the Founders called it faction, but moderns call it special-interest politics. The problem is that well-organized interests exploit the ignorance of the general public by rewarding politicians for actions that they would not endorse if the folks back home were paying attention.

In assessing this factor, we distinguish between high- and low-visibility issues.[4] When a politician believes that her conduct will gain broad attention back home, interest group pressures will be attenuated. While well-organized groups can provide valuable campaign contributions, this will be small consolation if opponents can effectively portray the incumbent as betraying the constituents' political values. It is to ward off this prospect that modern politicians pay such heed to public opinion polls.

But high-visibility issues represent a small proportion of the decision agenda in Washington, D.C. Interest groups are far more powerful when the general public is asleep. This is, of course, almost all the time, and so, on the vast majority of issues, interest groups operate as attentive subpublics, rewarding compliant politicians without much risk of penalty from broader constituencies. And it is here where the prospect of Deliberation Day promises to destabilize the existing terms of political trade.

The advent of the new holiday makes it far more difficult for politicians to predict which of their actions and votes will remain safely on the low-visibility end of the agenda. Given the abysmally low levels of information now prevailing among the general public, seasoned politicos can safely assume that low-visibility deals will remain low-visibility on Election Day. But DDay introduces new uncertainties. A month before the new holiday, each candidate will place two "major issues" on the agenda for discussion by the citizen assemblies, and these issues will attract far more attention than they would otherwise.

This will cast a large shadow on prospective dealings with special interests. Politicians will now be obliged to peer into the future and consider the potential evolution of public concerns over many years — when DDay is extended to Congress as well as the presidency, members of the Senate must sometimes adopt a six-year time horizon. Nobody in politics possesses a crystal ball, and even special-interest deals that seem far removed from center stage suddenly carry a new risk. Will they get caught up in the glare of Deliberation Day at the crucial moment of reelection?

Incumbents will become anxiously aware that the sleeping public may become a roused giant. And as a consequence, they will take a different attitude to the proffer of campaign funds and similar political services from attentive interest groups. They will continue to value these resources, of course, but they will subject them to a new and substantial discount: call it the "high-visibility discount."

We do not claim that all low-visibility decisions will be subject to this discount. While Deliberation Day will vastly expand the existing informational base for electoral decisions, it does not promise anything like an exhaustive review of each incumbent's performance. Perhaps a senator can remain quite confident that his decisive action in a legislative committee on behalf of Section $4379(A)(iii)(k)(2)$ will be appreciated only by the attentive subpublics who stand to benefit by a billion dollars a year. But even this is not so clear if his or her opponent tells a story on Deliberation Day that portrays this action as part of a pattern of special-interest dealing opposed by the majority of constituents.

To put the point technocratically, the high-visibility discount will be a variable, not a constant, leading to a broad devaluation of many political resources proffered by special-interest groups. To use a more classical idiom, politicians will have a new incentive to rise above faction because their special-interest deals will be a likely target for criticism in the citizen assemblies.

We have been approaching our problem cautiously — identifying pathological features in our present situation, and exploring how our institutional innovation might help ameliorate them. Having come this far, we can ask a more affirmative question: Once the constraints of public opinion polling and special-interest dealing are loosened, how will incumbents use their newfound freedom? Will the prospect of Deliberation Day subtly influence the sorts of issues they will introduce into the public debate?

Begin by reflecting on the televised event that opens Deliberation Day during presidential contests: the seventy-five-minute debate between the leading candidates on major issues. This format builds on the nationally televised debates that have become familiar since the Kennedy-Nixon election. While the candidates are free, of course, to continue organizing debates on their own, the one on Deliberation Day will be a much more significant event. First, there is the matter of timing. There is currently no guarantee that presidential debates will occur at all, let alone at a time when public interest in the election is reaching its peak. Even more important is the larger context. While tens of millions of Americans presently flock to their televisions to see the candidates debate, the new setting will allow them to expose their claims and counterclaims to serious scrutiny. Both contenders will know that their initial assertions will only serve to set the agenda for further give-and-take, with local party representatives obliged to defend their candidates against charges of misrepresentation and exaggeration.

The prospect of daylong examination plainly tells the sitting president that a few rhetorical gestures will not suffice to deflect serious examination of his record. It also puts him on notice that, in seeking reelection, he will be required to say the same thing to all the citizens of America. This basic point will shape the flow of administration activity throughout the president's term in office.

Speaking broadly, presidents use two strategies to sustain their grip on office. One exploits the distinctive logic of the Electoral College and seeks to deliver government benefits selectively to those states that are crucial in providing him with an Electoral College majority—if he is counting on the farm states, then he will pump up agricultural subsidies; if he plans to win without California, he will be relatively stingy on high-tech development; and so forth. In contrast to this strategy of selective reward, the second approach seeks to gain electoral credit by presenting the presidency as a steward for the nation as a whole. The emphasis here is on the identification of nationwide solutions to nationwide problems.

The format of Deliberation Day militates against the strategy of selective reward. A candidate for reelection will, of course, continue to emphasize his support for agricultural subsidies in campaign ads selectively beamed to the farm states, out of the earshot of the big-city consumers who are paying the bill. Given the increasing technological capacity for "niche advertising," the strategy of selective reward has a vibrant future in presidential politics. This gives us all the more reason to applaud the contrary tendency of Deliberation Day. Despite the technological temptations to pinpoint narrow audiences, our new civic holiday will serve as a bulwark for national stewardship. When defending his administration on Deliberation Day, the president cannot say one thing to the farm states and another to the high-tech areas. The format virtually compels him to demonstrate accomplishment on issues of importance to the nation as a whole.

And a good thing, too. While the strategy of selective benefits may sometimes serve a larger interest, it is generally a recipe for the politics of faction—enabling electorally strategic regions to raid the federal treasury.[5] A strategy of national stewardship is, in contrast, precisely the Madisonian tendency our institutions are supposed to encourage.

A second feature of the televised debate also strikes us as desirable. One month before DDay, each side will specify two major issues for the televised debate. The need to come up with compelling themes will have an impact on the sitting president years before he makes his Deliberation Day appeal for reelection—putting pressure on him to organize his national problem-solving activities around a few leading ideas or concerns. This drive to articulate a few big themes is already a characteristic of the modern presidency—but all too often, it amounts to little more than empty sloganeering that bears little relation to actual decisions made by the administration. The prospect of Deliberation Day will exact a salutary penalty on empty rhetoric—since the opposing candidate will predictably encourage citizen-deliberators to spend their day examining the failure of the president to carry through on his main promises.

Moving beyond the television debate, another feature of the DDay format will have a significant impact. Recall that the competing candidates can't monopolize the agenda for discussion on the holiday. While the major issues debated on television will influence the subsequent discussions in the small groups, ordinary citizens have the right to raise their own concerns to their fellow members, and if these issues gain sufficient support at the end of the discussion period, party representatives may have to confront them at the citizen assemblies.

This procedure will give new leverage to ideological groups with mass memberships—ranging from the Sierra Club to the National Rifle Association, from the Christian Coalition to the NAACP, and beyond. Throughout his term in office, the president will know that such groups can make trouble for him on DDay. And each of them can be expected to make use of this prospect as it puts pressure on the administration: "If you don't support our right-to-life proposal, hundreds of thousands of our followers will be denouncing you on Deliberation Day!" Given the number and ideological diversity of grassroots groups, this new weapon will be wielded on all sides of an issue, often leading to its neutralization. Just as right-to-lifers may warn the administration of a massive DDay campaign, so too may the freedom-of-choicers—and both, or neither, may be bluffing.

One thing is clear: the new holiday will, on the margin, strengthen the bargaining hand of grassroots groups in day-to-day politics. But to have impact, it will not be enough to provide a show of numbers; grassroots movements must articulate their arguments and concerns in deliberative forums in which many other citizens, not part of any particular interest group, will constitute the relevant audience. At the moment, interest groups mobilize to present a picture of mass support. On DDay, they will have to mobilize to express their views in public dialogues across the country. Broadly speaking, this is a good thing—the whole point of our initiative is to permit the concerns of ordinary Americans to express themselves more effectively in American government. But as always, it is well to consider the possibility of pathology.

Suppose, then, that some grassroots groups carry out their DDay threat and organize their followers to raise a series of pointed questions for adoption by their small groups. Won't these campaigns generate heightened tension in small-group discussions, leading to more breaches in civility?

We doubt it. Groups capable of organizing a large-scale effort will recognize that strident and self-righteous demands only serve to alienate uncommitted citizens. Stridency will be particularly counter-productive on DDay, when small groups will submit to the larger assembly only those questions that gain the broadest support among their fifteen members. And given random assignment to small groups, it will be difficult to pack an individual group with a majority representing a given viewpoint. Within this setting, organized campaigns will emphasize that activists should present their concerns in a civil fashion calculated to appeal to the open-minded.[6] Loud and assertive opinions are more likely to be voiced by individuals speaking for themselves than by people who have been prepped by grassroots organizers.[7]

Another scenario strikes us as more serious. If many large groups organize massive campaigns, their partisans might outnumber ordinary citizens without a particular axe to grind. Since the activists have made up their minds (on different things!), the tone of the meetings would be less congenial to open-ended exploration, and less productive of considered changes in opinion. They also might be less fun for ordinary citizens, who might respond by using the next DDay to catch up on their sleep. A debilitating cycle threatens: a massive turnout of activists drowns out ordinary citizens, who respond by reducing their attendance at the next election, making it possible for a smaller number of activists to drown out ordinary citizens, and on and on.

It is important, then, to assure a large turnout from ordinary citizens. This is one of the important reasons for offering a generous daily stipend of $150 for participating in Deliberation Day.[8] Especially during the early period, when habits haven't yet formed, a generous citizen stipend will signal the social importance of the new holiday and serve as a magnet attracting millions of Americans who are uncertain about participating. By starting out with large numbers of open-minded citizens, we prevent the "drown-out" cycle from starting in the first place.

We will return to this problem later, but assuming it is under control, our new civic holiday promises to have a series of positive effects on the conduct of day-to-day government: it will reduce the influence of conventional public opinion polling, reduce the power of special interests, increase the incentive to launch a sustained program aimed at solving some crucial national problems, and increase governmental responsiveness to ideological groups with genuine grassroots support. More generally, it will encourage a more deliberative attitude from the administration — emphasizing the imperative of transcending the passions of the moment in order to prepare the president's case for reelection on Deliberation Day. Not bad for a day's work.

There is no need to overstate our case. The new civic holiday will not transform presidents into paragons. There are many other factors influencing a president's reelection chances, and these may push him in very different directions. Our basic argument also depends on the law of anticipated reaction, and this will be modulated by each president's psychology. Some may be extravagantly confident of their rhetorical ability to mold public opinion and may dismiss the prospect of Deliberation Day with a wave of the hand — in which case our argument won't apply.

But this cavalier reaction doesn't seem likely in the present era of media-managed presidencies. To the contrary, Deliberation Day is more likely to provide presidents with a useful rhetorical technique for putting media-driven advisers in their place: "That sounds good today, but how will it sound two years from now on Deliberation Day?"

Our new civic holiday won't work miracles, but it will provide a new framework encouraging presidents to look beyond the moment and reflect seriously on the nature of the public good.

Up to now, we have been focusing on a single question: How will DDay invite a sitting president to redefine his administration's agenda for action during his first four years in office? But consider a second and closely related question, that of campaign strategy. Whatever the president has or hasn't done, he will still want to get reelected, and this will require vast sums of money for campaign advertising. How will the prospect of DDay change the calculus involved in selling the president?

And we do mean selling. It is hard to be too cynical about the merchandising of politicians. There are more constraints involved in selling toothpaste or automobiles than in selling a presidential candidate. It's easy to get in trouble with the law if you misrepresent the basic facts about a commercial product. But the First Amendment provides sweeping protection when it comes to selling the president. The most important consideration is coming up with sound bites of ten seconds (or less) that generate hot-button responses from focus groups.

One might imagine a presidential candidate taking moral responsibility for this dreadful situation, and deciding to rein in his Madison Avenue merchants — for example, by forbidding them from buying time slots less than five minutes in length, and requiring them to fill these slots with real political argument. But in the real world of American politics, such a suggestion would be viewed as conclusive evidence of ivory-tower naïveté, rather than as a bit of Madisonian common sense. To be sure, there have been rare politicians who have demonstrated moral leadership. Senator Russell Feingold, for example, refused all large contributions of "soft money" to his campaign for reelection in 2000 and managed to win despite this act of unilateral disarmament. But few will follow Feingold in risking political suicide in the noble struggle for a higher campaign ethic.

The only serious solution is to change the normal politician's electoral calculus — and this, of course, is the object of DDay. As the holiday becomes part of the election schedule, it will no longer seem rational for media managers to buy an unending series of ten-second spots for hot-button advertisements. These staccato messages will now get fewer dollars in competition with five- or ten-minute infomercials. After all, these longer messages have a better chance of attracting the attention of voters who are planning to show up at DDay. As the civic holiday comes closer, the commercials will grow longer, and more discursive — not out of a sudden burst of civic virtue, but from a sober calculation of political self-interest. A media strategy that would seem quixotic under today's conditions will suddenly seem like political common sense during the run-up to DDay, as we expect DDay will, in effect, create a market for more informative broadcasts.

Medium will affect message. Many ideas can't be conveyed in ten seconds — or even in a minute! Once the time frame opens up to five or ten minutes, a lot more things become sayable. There is no guarantee that the folks on Madison Avenue will make good use of their expanded time slots — longer bits of fluff are also possible. But we hope that an organizational detail will push the media managers in the right direction. One month before DDay, each of the major candidates will be asked to define the major issues — no more than two — which he wants discussed at the televised debate that will open up DDay. We expect these announcements to trigger a media campaign that is both focused and substantive. If one side contents itself with fluff, the other can use the two-week run-up to frame the major issues in a way that redounds to its decisive advantage at citizen assemblies throughout the land.

Our institutional innovation, in short, promises to reverse the incentives now prevailing under the malign guidance of the invisible hand. Nowadays, it is almost crazy to follow Ross Perot and spend millions of advertising dollars on serious and sustained communication to ordinary Americans; under the new regime, it would be almost crazy not to.

This prospect provides the basis of a leveraging strategy: By placing DDay near the end of the campaign, we hope to reshape everything that goes before. Indeed, if we are successful in enhancing the quality of the *ex ante* debate, our intervention might have the paradoxical effect of diminishing the impact of the conversations that take place on Deliberation Day itself. Since more voters will have better information coming into the Day, fewer may find themselves changing their minds on the basis of face-to-face discussions.

Such an outcome would be a marker of Deliberation Day's success, not of its failure. It would suggest that, by inserting a formal moment for collective deliberation into the larger process, the community had managed to leverage its entire political conversation onto a higher plane.

By pursuing the law of anticipated reaction, we have developed two important conclusions. The prospect of Deliberation Day will both improve the character of decisions by sitting politicians and create a higher level of political debate during their campaigns for reelection.

We now propose to shift focus, and turn away from the *ex ante* perspective of the forward-looking politician to the holiday's *ex post* consequences: How will DDay shape the race during the last days of the run-up to Election Day?

Begin at 5:01 P.M. on DDay: As millions of deliberators stream out of the nation's schoolrooms and community centers, their way will be blocked by smiling exit pollsters seeking a word or two. Participation will be strictly voluntary, but candidates and media will be desperately seeking a reliable sense of whether and how deliberation has changed the likely result on Election Day.

The candidates' needs will be especially urgent if we persuade you to adopt a final feature of our proposed format. DDay is a two-day affair: while the basic plan shouldn't change from one day to the next, a question of institutional design arises when it comes to the televised debate for the second day. Should the debate on day two simply be a recorded rerun of the one presented on day one, or should the presidential hopefuls engage in a second live encounter?

By all means, another live debate. One of our great aims is to organize a genuine dialogue between ordinary citizens and political leaders. As day one progresses, the political conversation has moved from the national level to small groups to local leaders, and then back to small groups, to local leaders, and then to small groups once again. The second televised debate will return the give-and-take to the national level, providing the candidates with an opportunity to respond to the controversies bubbling below: "There have been lots of questions raised about my position on a war with China. Let me make myself clear . . . "

This performance will contrast sharply with the one-way communication pattern of modern campaigns. When voters find themselves on the receiving end of an endless barrage of ten-second sound bites, their reaction is to tune out rather than to talk back. Even when candidates cautiously emerge into more conversational settings, their handlers make heroic efforts to protect them against follow-up questions that might force them into complexities. Little wonder, then, that the televised presidential debates now serve as the high point of the campaign—they represent one of the rare occasions when the candidates can't count on weaseling out of embarrassing questions. But the debate on day two promises something much more worthwhile than any other encounter—since the candidates will be responding to the leading concerns voiced throughout the nation's citizen assemblies.

The exit polling and extensive coverage will create a media environment in which the voters and the candidates will be well aware of the key concerns expressed on the first DDay. At the second candidate debate, the citizens deliberating at the national "town meeting" will build on the dialogue in the first round. The informed microcosm will carry the dialogue further, building on its understanding of what the candidates said last time—on what they answered and failed to answer.

The candidates' answers won't only serve to kick off the second round of DDay conversation. Many day one participants will also tune in to the day two debate (rebroadcast later in the day for late sleepers). After all, they will have spent lots of time discussing the key issues on the preceding day, and many will be genuinely curious to see whether the candidates have responded to their concerns. Even if both presidential hopefuls evade or ignore their major concerns, viewers will get a chance to reflect further on their prior conversations, and that is a gain in itself.

Day two's debate will be a highpoint for the citizenry, but it will be hell for the candidates. If one or another contender responds clearly and forcefully, he is bound to alienate large chunks of his audience. Given this fact, he would normally be tempted to waffle. But as a consequence of their previous experience, day one viewers are expecting serious answers and will react with disgust if they hear the usual blather. The contenders, in short, will squirm mightily as they find themselves between a rock and a hard place. How to respond?

The question will be the subject of much heated debate as exit polls flow into each candidate's headquarters throughout the evening of day one. We can already hear the paid consultants yammering to "their" presidential hopeful as they brandish reams of "expert" data analysis. If the candidate is wise, he will recognize that these instant analyses couldn't be worth very much. Rather than engage in shadowboxing, perhaps he will cut through the chatter and resolve to answer questions in a straight-forward fashion — or at least something pretty close. But if he chooses to indulge in evasive obfuscation, at least he is likely to pay a price.

Apart from shaping the day two debate, the exit polls will have a second immediate impact. By next morning at the latest, newspapers and television will be full of the latest predictions about the electoral horserace: "Coming into Deliberation Day, the president was leading by 6 points in the polls. But after the first day of citizen assemblies, his lead has shrunk to 2 points. Voters seem to be having trouble accepting his position on taxes. Will he launch an effective come-back?" These excited summaries will escalate after the close of the second day's deliberations. The world will be full of ten-second sound bites — but this time they will be reporting the results of Deliberation Day!

Given our scornful dismissal of sound-bite campaigning, we hope you will forgive us for making an exception in our own case. But we do have our reasons, which require a return to our discussion of the heuristic devices that citizens use as shortcuts in deciding how to vote.[9] As we made clear, we do not deny that voters use shortcuts in figuring out which candidate is on their side. We deny only that the cues they ordinarily employ are reliable: Despite the opinions of leading political scientists, President Ford's failure to shuck his tamale is not a good indication of his positions on issues of importance to Hispanics. Given the prevalence of such poor cues, it may well make sense for some voters to use the DDay headlines as one of their principal guides to making their decision.

To see our point, put yourself in the position of a registered voter who fails to show up at DDay, using the holiday for some private purpose. Despite your absence, you still intend to cast a ballot on Election Day. Pondering your choices, you turn on the television news and hear that "Candidate A's lead in the polls has completely disappeared as a result of his poor performances at Deliberation Day, and his rival is now narrowly ahead." If you are otherwise poorly informed, isn't this sound bite particularly worth thinking about?

It tells you that millions of Americans who have spent lots more time than you have on the presidential race have found Candidate A surprisingly weak as a serious prospect. This is a lot more informative than observing the candidate's gracelessness in eating a hot tamale!

If a voter is going to content himself with "low-information" rationality, he could do a lot worse than follow the sound bites in the aftermath of DDay. Indeed, we have detected some cueing of this sort in our experience with Deliberative Polling.[10] We expect that a much more powerful "cueing effect" will emerge from DDay. First, reportage will be much more pervasive. DPs are news on the day their results are announced, but they compete with many other late-breaking stories for public attention. In contrast, the exit polls coming out of DDay promise to become *the* story that dominates much of the news and punditry during the final days of the campaign. As soon as the headlines scream that one or another candidate has gained an advantage on DDay, news commentators will begin speculating about why, and the rival campaigns will begin desperately spinning the reported outcomes.

The subsequent stream of talk will defy a favorite distinction made by specialists on public opinion. Political scientists have long distinguished between media commentaries that discuss substantive issues and those that focus on the "horserace" aspect of the struggle — who's ahead, who's behind, and what are the chances of change. Over the past thirty years, the percentage of commentary devoted to the horserace has increased dramatically at the expense of more substantive discussions.[11]

But DDay will predictably disrupt this disturbing trend by making the candidates' substantive positions decisive in commentary about the horserace:

> PUNDIT 1: Candidate A lost ground because deliberators believed that his position on taxes had lots of holes in it. His campaign has just issued a statement saying that A has learned a lot from the dialogue and is thinking about changing his stance. What do you think about this exercise in damage control?
>
> PUNDIT 2: It's better than nothing, I guess, but I think it's a case of too little and too late. Candidate A had his chance on day two. I think he's blown it.
>
> PUNDIT 1: Well, there's only one way to find out. As soon as A makes his clarifications, we'll be telling our audience whether they are important enough to warrant giving the matter another thought. And we'll be polling, of course, to see whether this last-minute swerve is having an impact.

By setting the agenda for media discussion, DDay will have a much more lasting impact than the coverage provided by even the most successful DPs. The reportage will also seem much more relevant to ordinary people. So far as they are concerned, news about a DP tells about a far-off event distant from ordinary life: Most Australians will never actually meet any of the four hundred deliberators who traveled to Canberra to discuss the merits of a republic. But every voter who fails to show up on DDay is virtually guaranteed to meet lots of real-life deliberators as soon as the holiday comes to an end. It may be at the workplace, or the neighborhood bar, or the family dinner table, but it will be hard to avoid vivid accounts of personal DDay experiences: "I was sitting next to a real jerk in the morning—but you know, I got a lot out of it in the end . . . "

This means that nonparticipants will be gaining a good deal from DDay—by cueing on news reports, learning from personal conversations, and viewing improved issue analysis in the media. This is especially significant, given the likely class distribution of attendance on the day itself. DDay will seem an especially scary prospect for citizens with poor educations, and especially those whose native language isn't English. Since these people are disproportionately poor, the $150 stipend will operate as a counterbalance—the money will seem more important to a person making the minimum wage than to a professional earning $5,000 a month. Nevertheless, the fear of "making a fool of myself" is a very potent force, and it is hard to predict how many will find it an insuperable obstacle to attendance.

The prospect of class and ethnic bias in the turnout is troubling. But these concerns are ameliorated—if not eliminated—by the countless second-order conversations that DDay will precipitate during the run-up to the election. While the ongoing discussions among DDay participants will encourage them to reflect further on their choices, conversations with nonparticipants will be especially important. Even if DDay seemed too intimidating or boring (or both!), the no-shows may be drawn into the second-order conversation with some especially trusted friends or family members—and thereby increase their interest in, and knowledge about, the election.

This may, in turn, have a positive impact on Election Day. At present, turnout is not only low but badly skewed along class and ethnic lines.[12]

If second-order conversations draw more of the underrepresented into the network of civic concern, they will be more likely to cast a ballot in the end. So a disproportionately low turnout on DDay may be counterbalanced by a countervailing improvement on Election Day.

This dense network of ongoing talk will also provide a new framework for the advertising blitz that saturates the country during the final run-up to Election Day. Given the increasing clarity of the candidates' stand on the leading issues, it will no longer pay to buy ten-second sound bites that distort a rival's position. It will make more sense to use the airtime to respond to shifts in public opinion detected by the ongoing polling operation—buying longer spots when needed to broadcast key clarifications in a way that will be persuasive to voters who remain undecided. This will substantially increase the number of people going to the polls with a better understanding of the stakes involved.

It may, once again, help improve the overall turnout. Although social science analysis doesn't unequivocally support the claim, there is a widespread suspicion that the increasing use of "negative advertising" has alienated the electorate, diminishing voter turnout.[13] If this is so, the shift away from brief and personal attacks toward longer and more issue-oriented advertising should make a perceptible difference on Election Day.

We are more confident in making a final prediction. Turnout is lowest amongst younger voters—and it has been declining at alarming speed over the past generation. Deliberation Day promises to make a real difference here.[14] Younger voters are the best educated in the population, and will, ceteris paribus, find DDay less daunting. They are also the most poorly paid, and so will find the citizen stipend relatively attractive. (We will talk about babysitting arrangements later.) Making DDay into a civic holiday also strikes at the roots of youthful nonengagement—since voting is an unfamiliar ritual, it takes time to accumulate the civic ties that make it seem an important civic duty. Rather than wait for time to take its course, the holiday positively invites involvement—and the hubbub of activity will make it seem attractive for youthful engagement.[15]

There is no need to exaggerate. About a quarter of Americans never talk about politics, and many of them will successfully avoid the secondary conversations generated by DDay.[16] But there is reason to expect that the new holiday won't merely make more people better informed. It will also encourage more of them to take the time to vote on Election Day.

We have been tracing the influence of Deliberation Day over a single electoral cycle. The first stage of our argument considered how a sitting president will adapt his actions to the prospect of a new deliberative test—other things being equal, he will deemphasize normal opinion polls, deflect the pressures of special interests, give new attention to grassroots groups, and focus on substantive problem solving as his best hope for reelection. The second stage used the law of anticipated reaction to show how the holiday will create new incentives as the president and his rivals chart their campaign strategies—pushing their advertising campaigns away from the spirit of Madison Avenue toward the spirit of Madison. Our final stage considered the way the Day's activities will change the secondary conversations and mass media presentations during the run-up to Election Day. This allowed us, once again, to see how Deliberation Day's impact will ripple far beyond those who actually attend—allowing nonparticipants to take advantage of better cues in making their final voting decision and encouraging them to turn out in greater numbers.

Now is the time to step back and view these arguments from a long-run perspective. All these effects will accrue gradually over time, generating the cycle of virtue promised by our chapter title. If Deliberation Day comes off reasonably well the first time around, tens of millions of Americans will have had a pretty good time and they will resolve to turn out again the next time around. They will also recommend the experience to others, who will be tempted to try it out.

This will increase the importance of Deliberation Day in the political calculus of the sitting president: The holiday was merely a prospect the first time around, but it is now an established reality that has induced a palpable shift in campaign strategies. This increase in political saliency will occur even if the first Deliberation Day didn't generate much of a shift in citizen preferences; but its effect will be greatly enhanced if a significant shift did occur, and if the sitting president attributes his electoral success to his DDay performance. Under this scenario, he will naturally bask in the glory of his achievement as the first president in American history to survive a process expressly designed to solicit the *considered* judgments of the people. By promoting himself, he will be promoting Deliberation Day; and the more he emphasizes this aspect of his achievement, the more he will look forward to the next Deliberation Day as a final vindication of his next four years in office. If the sitting president is eligible for reelection, this is only a matter of enlightened self-interest; but even if he can't run again, he will tend to view the judgments reached on Deliberation Day as a significant marker in his quest for fame and historical recognition. Whatever his motive, the increasing salience of the holiday in his political calculus will tilt presidential policies in generally desirable directions.

Campaign advertising will also be better. Media merchants will spend only some of their time searching for hot-button issues presentable in ten seconds. They will also be thinking about the mistakes they made in presenting their candidates' stands on the major issues during the run-up to Deliberation Day — devising new strategies and formats that promise to present the crucial facts and values in especially vivid ways. And they will be devising new schemes when their candidates lose ground on Deliberation Day and must desperately try for a comeback in the final weeks.

We're not promising miracles. Mudslinging and media hype will still abound, but there will also be new pressures to respond effectively to the issues that Deliberation Day will make more prominent. And this concern will encourage Madison Avenue to figure out clever ways of arresting the attention of normal Americans and speaking about the issues in a language that they can understand. As always, our relevant reference point is not some hypothetical philosophy seminar, but the egregiously commercialized status quo. And by that measure, the new incentives should significantly improve the public's understanding of the major issues as the media merchants master their new trade over time.

Or maybe the first DDay will be a flop — an organizational nightmare marred by millions of fistfights. Maybe we will find that ordinary Americans don't have what it takes to conduct a civil civic conversation. Or suppose that the victorious president hates DDay and tries to destroy it. Or suppose . . .

If things turn out badly enough, maybe we should call it quits. But we still wouldn't consider DDay a total failure. Democracy *is* an experiment in self-government, and some experiments will fail. The question is whether the upside potential is large enough to justify the gamble.

To explore this question further, follow us on a further exploration of the upside. Suppose that the first two rounds of Deliberation Day initiate a cycle of virtue — tens of millions of Americans form a new habit of citizenship, presidents increasingly use Deliberation Day as a reference point in their governmental decisions, election campaigns become less like merchandising extravaganzas.

Now is the time to take the next step and extend our innovation from the quadrennial election for president to the midterm congressional elections. To what extent does Congress Day require a different format? Will it create different political incentives from those generated by Presidents Day?

5

EXTENDING THE PARADIGM

We have been focusing on the contest for the presidency. But does our initiative make sense when extended to other contexts? We begin with Congress Day and then move further afield. Other countries may be interested in some version of Deliberation Day, and we consider how our proposal may be adapted to parliamentary systems common in the rest of the world.

We then consider DDay applications that may work on an ad hoc basis. This would permit real-world experience without committing a political system to a permanent reform. The most promising area here is the occasional referendum that nations increasingly use to resolve a matter of high importance: Isn't DDay an ideal tool for a country considering a fateful choice, like joining the European Union or NATO?

We conclude by extending the paradigm to embrace changing technologies of communication: Does the rise of the Internet provide a better alternative to old-fashioned face-to-face neighborhood meetings?

Congress Day

The American system is based on the separation of powers, and the selective introduction of Deliberation Day may subtly shift this balance in a presidentialist direction. During the first two cycles, more citizens will be paying more attention to the contest for the White House. This increasing political engagement may or may not carry over to the races for Congress. Some may get curious about the campaigns for the House and Senate; but others may cut back the time and energy they otherwise spend on politics, and reduce their attention to congressional races. It is hard to guess the net effect of these competing factors — though data from Deliberative Polls suggest that experiences with collective deliberation tend to increase civic engagement and interest in politics and public policy more generally.[1] If this turns out to be true, DDay will probably improve the informational link between voters and Congress — a good thing, given the weakness of the link at present.

Even if they are learning more about congressional races, citizens may come to think about their choices differently, and in a way that will subtly enhance presidential power. As they get more interested in the issues raised by the presidential hopefuls, they may become more impressed with the importance of assuring the president a solid majority in Congress. The result would be an increase in the president's "coattails" — his effective capacity to swing marginal congressional seats into his own party's column. How should we judge this likely outcome? Is it an additional plus for Presidents Day, or is it a significant minus?

We incline toward the positive view, especially during an era when presidential coattails are very short indeed. Members of Congress have proved remarkably successful in immunizing themselves from the vagaries of presidential politics — achieving reelection rates in the 1990s that usually soared above 90 percent and never dropped below 80 percent.[2] Indeed, the existence of so many "safe seats" has permitted Congress sometimes to escalate its institutional struggle with the presidency to pathological heights — or so many scholars believe.[3]

Reasonable people can disagree: Within the American tradition of separation of powers, it is always tough to say how much congressional independence is too much. But fortunately, it isn't necessary for us to resolve this — probably interminable — debate. Given its essentially contestable character, it seems particularly appropriate for citizens to resolve the question on an election-by-election basis. If their deliberations on Presidents Day lead more constituents to reward congressional candidates for supporting their party's choice for president, who are we to say they are wrong? To the contrary, this decision exemplifies the way that deliberation can lead to the more thoughtful exercise of citizen sovereignty.

Whatever the impact of Presidents Day, it would be a mistake to deny Congress its own place in the sun during the off-year elections when the White House is not at stake. Casting a quadrennial spotlight on Congress is important as a constitutional matter—to emphasize its standing as a coequal branch of government in the American system. And it is important as a practical matter—since off-year contests have often swept a different party into power, leading to dramatic changes in public policy (as in 1994 and 2002). Despite their constitutional and practical importance, these elections have been attracting fewer and fewer voters. If presidential turnouts are disappointing, off-year participation is utterly embarrassing—about half of the voting-age population goes to the polls during presidential elections, but less than 40 percent manage to cast a ballot during off-years.[4]

Congress Day will help stop this slide, inviting citizens to take seriously the great importance of Congress in the American scheme of government. To be sure, the decline in participation has its source in deeper causes. The Constitution requires redistricting in the House every decade, and computer technology now permits partisan gerrymandering with ever-greater precision. As a consequence, incumbents can reliably design safe seats for themselves, to the point where a shocking number win re-election unopposed by a major-party candidate—ninety-eight in 1998, seventy-six in 2002—and many others encounter only nominal opposition.[5]

With so many incumbents cementing themselves into seemingly impregnable districts, there is little wonder that voter participation is in sharp decline—why bother voting when the outcome is foreordained?

Worse yet, incumbents have powerful tools to maintain themselves in office—most important, sedulous service to powerful local interests generates enormous advantages in fund raising.

Nevertheless, it is a mistake to underestimate the role played by a final factor in this dismal story. Constituents simply fail to pay attention to the most basic issues raised in the elections. Given this failure, the name recognition achieved by incumbents serves as a formidable obstacle to serious electoral contestation.[6] It takes too much money for a challenger to penetrate the attention barrier during the short space of a campaign. It is little surprise, then, that both parties focus an enormous amount of their time and money on open seats created by retirement, death, or decennial reapportionment. Generally speaking, this is the only moment when the two sides compete on relatively equal terms.[7]

Sadly, this means that the greatest opponents of Congress Day will be the members of Congress themselves. The present fog suits them just fine. The only thing they have to fear is a whole day devoted to monitoring their activities. To be sure, a representative or senator might use the time to demonstrate how good a job he or she is doing in Washington. But why give a challenger the chance to make the contrary case?

It is far safer to keep the hurdles high, and oppose extending Presidents Day to Congress Day. A similar logic is already at work when it comes to campaign finance reform. During the Watergate crisis, Congress was happy to pass a campaign finance law that offered fairly generous public subsidies in presidential races. But it refused to grant similar subsidies for congressional races. Since this would involve giving challengers equal access to funds, it was much safer for incumbents to rely on their existing advantages in the private fund-raising market. By the same reasoning, incumbents will pause for a very long time before granting their opponents equal access to constituents on Deliberation Day.

But this only suggests how important it is to extend the deliberative paradigm to embrace Congress. The point of this book is not to pander to incumbents but to explain to Americans how they might recapture a portion of their democratic sovereignty. So the obvious fact that it will take a big political struggle to wrest Congress Day from Congress shouldn't block further analysis. The question is whether it would be worth the effort to launch a serious campaign for Congress Day. Answering this question requires us, first, to identify any new practical or theoretical problems raised in extending the deliberative paradigm beyond the presidency, and second, to consider whether these problems are serious enough to eliminate Congress Day from the next generation's reform agenda.

The practical problem is clear enough: Presidents Day concerns a single national office, but Congress Day deals with 33 or 34 senators and 435 representatives. When citizens go to their gathering places, they will always be considering the race for their local House district, and two-thirds of the time both House and Senate seats will be up for election. Moreover, two aspects of each race will be relevant. The voters are choosing local representatives, but their choices also add up to a national decision giving the Democrats or Republicans control over one or another congressional chamber. Two perspectives on two races generates four informational dimensions — Presidents Day involves only one. This simple point raises the problem of information overload. A multiplicity of candidates, issues, and perspectives may lead to the cannibalizing of Deliberation Day into too many tidbits. Rather than engaging ordinary citizens in a sustained conversation, a morselized Congress Day might simply generate confusion or boredom or both.

Two additional design imperatives increase the problem's complexity. First is fairness: Each serious candidate must be given a chance to state his case. The second is openness: The format can't be seen as arbitrarily cutting off important dimensions for discussion. How to achieve these two goals without generating a disjointed cacophony of voices?

Begin with the two faces of congressional elections — each seat is part of a national party struggle for congressional control, but it is also a local contest between particular candidates, who may disagree with the national leadership on major issues. Different voters will rank these two dimensions differently — many believing that it is the character of their representative, and his particular positions, that count; others giving substantial importance to the question of national party control. To make matters more complicated, the relative salience of these dimensions will differ from district to district and shift from one election to the next. How to manage this complexity?

We propose leaving the matter principally to the local candidates. Let the rivals decide how much importance to give to the national dimensions of their contest. They have the greatest incentive to frame the matter in a way that the voters will find important. If a national party's positions are unpopular in a particular constituency, the opposing candidate can be expected to emphasize this point in his or her own presentation. And the same is true when a particular race is crucial to determining party control over the House or Senate.

As a consequence, our format gives pride of place to the local candidates. In place of the National Issues Debate on Presidents Day, Congress Day begins with a televised debate on major issues between the leading candidates for local office—giving forty minutes to the Senate race (if there is one), followed, after a ten-minute break, by forty minutes for the rivals for the House. The first half-hour of each debate will be in question-and-answer format, with the concluding ten minutes for closing statements. Questions will be generated by a Deliberative Poll composed of five hundred residents from the appropriate constituency (statewide for Senate races, districtwide for each House race). Different deliberative panels can pose questions for each of the two days. The second day's questions will benefit from the first day's discussions and reactions to them as they are filtered through the concerns of these representative samples of local residents.

As with Presidents Day, the candidates specify major issues for the debate one month in advance. But this time each names a single issue—creating four fifteen-minute segments for Q and A. This set-up encourages Senate and House candidates of the same party to consult before exercising their agenda-setting options, but there is no requirement of an agreement: each House candidate determines the issue for fifteen minutes of debate regardless of the desires of his or her Senate counterpart, and vice versa. As a consequence, the themes in the House debates may well vary from district to district across the state—though there may also be coordination, with Republican candidates from northern California focusing on a particular issue, and those from the Central Valley on another. By using a clear rule to allocate agenda control to particular candidates, we do not preclude coordination; but we place the burden for coordination where it belongs: on individual candidates, who have the most to gain or lose from making common cause.

These decisions, in turn, will prompt a complex set of coordinated advertising campaigns during the run-up to Congress Day, providing a focused stream of communication to the voters—particularly valuable for penetrating the low levels of citizen attention that have come to prevail during these elections.[8]

As Congress Day approaches, we supplement the flow of discussion in another way. On the evening before each day's discussion, the major networks will be required to give prime time to a preliminary debate from the congressional leaders of the two parties—the speaker and minority leader of the House and the majority and minority leaders of the Senate—

similar to the one that has already been organized by PBS during several recent elections. The PBS national congressional debates have been coordinated with local debates for congressional candidates around the country that are broadcast in their respective districts.[9] With Congress Day, we propose to build on a similar national-local dynamic.

The televised national debate will provide citizens with a clearer sense of the larger issues at stake in the national struggle for control over Congress, and invite the local candidates to explore their differences from the national party line in a more nuanced fashion.

The PBS debates have attracted small national audiences,[10] but these will expand when all major networks carry them as an integral part of a national holiday. And even though many people won't watch before they show up at their neighborhood centers the next morning, the debate will have an indirect impact. Local candidates will use the remarks of the national leadership as a springboard for their own televised debates on Congress Day. Citizens will refer to the national leadership's arguments in their small and large groups. This may lead many people to view a rerun of the telecast when they return home, and to discuss its significance in later conversations.

Or it may not. Much depends on how national party leaders make use of their conversational opportunity. The key point is that, by assigning these leaders a background role, the formatting problem becomes manageable. When both House and Senate seats are up for grabs, the Candidates' Debate will last ninety minutes (including the ten-minute break between the two segments) — fifteen minutes more than the National Issues Debate on Presidents Day (but this seventy-five-minute debate occurs without any break). It will be easy to make up the extra time by shaving a few minutes from other activities during the rest of the day.[11]

Some might protest that these debate times are too short. Twenty minutes on a side is a lot longer than a sound bite, but is it really enough to present a serious argument?

But recall that the Candidates' Debate only serves to kick off a daylong conversation. And it would be a mistake to allow the television show to cut too deeply into the heart of the process — the give-and-take among ordinary citizens and local opinion leaders. This dynamic will lead to something that no amount of television-watching can yield — an engaged understanding of the leading issues, not the passive acquaintance that comes from exposure to talking heads. If the candidates want to supplement their presentations, they are perfectly free to broadcast lengthy infomercials before or after Congress Day.

A relatively short television debate responds to another potential problem: boredom. One of the races may be so one-sided that it generates little real interest: Everybody knows that the underdog has no chance, so what's the use of talking?

Fairness requires that the sure loser be given equal time debating with the sure winner. The best we can do is to keep the total time relatively short. During the rest of the day, deliberators are free to focus their attention on the race that generates greater interest, allowing the concerns expressed by the sure loser to remain on the conversational periphery.

What if there isn't such a race? Most Senate races are energetically contested, but even here there is a problem—in 2002, six states saw incumbents win reelection against opponents who failed to gain 20 percent of the vote![12] But the boredom problem will be most acute when there is no Senate race at all and the House incumbent is a shoo-in—as we have seen, there were no fewer than seventy-six races in 2002 without a major-party opponent. With the outcome preordained, won't DDay be a total failure in many congressional districts throughout the land—with minuscule turnouts and desultory conversations among those who take the trouble to show up?

There is definitely a problem here, though Congress Day will help ameliorate it. Incumbents have such an easy time partly because constituents are paying so little attention. Since Congress Day will lower the ignorance barrier to effective campaigning, it will encourage more formidable challengers to enter the contest. This, in turn, will make for more competitive races—another cycle of virtue?

The passage of time will diminish the difficulty in a second way. Congress Day will be held every four years, but Senate terms last for six. This means that districts will rarely encounter the boredom effect twice in a row. If they lacked a Senate race on one Congress Day, they are sure to have Senate contests the next two times the holiday rolls around, and as we have seen, these races tend to be vigorously contested (though even here there are exceptions).

Yet when all is said and done, there *is* a serious problem, reflecting deep pathologies. The obvious solution is to attack these pathologies as well—for example, states like Iowa currently fight partisan gerrymandering by relying on a nonpartisan commission to draw district lines;[13] and the fund-raising advantages enjoyed by incumbents can be controlled by effective campaign finance reform.[14] But in the meantime, it might be appropriate to cancel Congress Day in districts suffering from an acute case of democratic default. So long as a major party is contesting the relevant House and Senate seats, DDay should go on. But if no major-party challenger takes the field, the celebration should be canceled if polls show that third-party candidates have failed to gain the support of 20 percent of likely voters.[15] Even when there is a local cancellation, it would be too quick to conclude that Congress Day has been a total failure. A great deal of the holiday's salutary impact operates via the law of anticipatory reaction. Put yourself in the place of a representative in a "safe seat" looking forward to the next election. By making it easier to penetrate the ignorance barrier, the holiday increases the probability of a serious challenge by the out-party. As a consequence, the incumbent must be on his guard. If and when a serious challenger appears on the scene, he can take the incumbent to task for his or her past low-visibility deals with special interests. This prospective critique makes these deals look less attractive even when no challenger has yet appeared on the horizon.

The result will be less pork-barreling—or at least, less pork-barreling of a certain kind. Congress Day will be especially good at deterring deals through which concentrated producer groups use state power to exploit masses of unorganized consumers. Partisans of sugar tariffs will be less powerful in their war for high sugar prices; organized groups of polluters will be less successful in externalizing their costs onto the consumers of clean air. As a matter of narrow cost-benefit analysis, the dollar savings on porkish legislation could easily dwarf the costs of running Congress Day.

Although the holiday will reduce the supply of industrial pork, it won't have the same effect on another familiar variety. So long as congressmen are elected from particular geographic areas, they will have an enduring incentive to bring home the bacon. Call it the logic of localist pork, which proceeds from a deep asymmetry between the distribution of benefits and burdens created by our system. Quite simply, almost all local projects are financed by national taxes. This means that local constituents must pay only a small fraction of the national taxes necessary to finance each local project. Since the locals get the lion's share of the benefit, they will predictably applaud whenever their senator or representative announces the construction of a new highway or dam—even if the total costs of the project are much larger than the benefits.[16]

DDay won't change this basic fact. But even here, it will change the kind of pork of maximal interest. Rather than pushing projects that reward a few big private givers, congressmen will look for those that could generate lots of votes from ordinary constituents. This means more neighborhood centers for the masses, fewer irrigation projects for desert agriculture.

At the same time, Congress Day will make even the most entrenched incumbent more responsive to public-interest groups with real grassroots support in his district. Sometimes this will favor the Right, sometimes the Left—depending on whether the National Rifle Association or the Sierra Club is more likely to mobilize lots of deliberators on Congress Day. Regardless of the ideological spin, the holiday will make incumbents more responsive to the evolution of public sentiment.

As a consequence, incumbents may also place greater emphasis on developing positions on national, rather than local, issues. They will be moved in the same direction by the pre-Congress Day debate of national party leaders. Generally speaking, incumbents can count on citizen ignorance to insulate themselves from some of the backlash when leaders of the national party take positions that are unpopular with local constituents. But the prospect of the national debate by congressional leaders puts them on notice that some of this insulation may be stripped away— and that they should, in their own self-interest, engage in more serious efforts to push the national party in the direction that they, and their constituents, favor.

This effect will be enhanced by a final formatting decision. When Congress Day convenes in a House district without a Senate race, we suddenly have time to burn during the period slotted for the Candidates' Debate. We propose to supplement the forty-minute period between the candidates with another forty-minute debate by the two national leaders of the House—the speaker and the minority leader.[17] Given the absence of informational overload in these districts, we think that the overwhelming majority of citizens will find their subsequent deliberations enriched by these party leaders' efforts to explain the national stakes hinging on their local decision.

To sum up: Congress Day will have an impact on the reelection calculus of incumbents that is roughly similar to the one that Presidents Day had on the sitting president—pushing incumbents away from low-visibility deals with organized interests and toward public-interest groups with strong constituency support, and inviting them to take a national perspective.[18] As always, we are speaking in terms of the marginal incentives on each incumbent's reelection calculus. Representatives and senators will still be pushing for special projects for their district or state (though their porkish projects will have greater mass appeal). But their localist ardor will be tempered on the margin, and they will take more seriously the larger national interests involved.

This realignment of political incentives strikes us as all to the good—indeed, very much in the spirit of the Founding enterprise. Pork-barreling is simply an aspect of the "politics of faction" that was of such great concern at the Constitutional Convention. As Federalist 10 emphasizes, politicians bent on reelection will forever be tempted to use the power of the state to gain the support of well-organized groups at the expense of the general public. There is no magical cure for this disease. The best we can do is to follow in the Founders' footsteps and try to design institutions that will encourage politicians to restrain their worst factional tendencies. From this perspective, Congress Day might well have merited Madison's respectful attention, and perhaps his considered approval.

But on a technical level, there is some tension between the Founders' eighteenth-century design and our twenty-first-century innovation. Our schedule for Congress Day doesn't mesh with the electoral calendar set out by the Framers: while Congress Day comes only once every four years, House members are elected every two, and senators every six. This will be especially significant for senators. Members first elected in presidential years will face the rigors of Congress Day upon their first reelection; but senators who initially gain office during the midterm election will find that their reelection campaign coincides with Presidents Day, and that they can wait twelve years before they must confront their constituents on Congress Day.

There is only one way to cure this deficiency — schedule Congress Day every two years, creating a double holiday when Presidents Day comes around on a quadrennial basis. But such a step strikes us as distinctly premature — even if Congress Day turns out to be a success, it might make more sense to extend DDay next to state and local races.

Within the foreseeable future, we must choose between Presidents Day and Congress Day when both branches are up for grabs. And given this necessity, we plunk for Presidents Day, given its great importance. This choice is made easier by the fact that senators will still be required to confront DDay at a relatively vulnerable moment in their careers — if they manage to avoid it on their first run for office, they will be obliged to confront Congress Day six years later, when running for reelection. Only long-term senators will gain the advantage of a full twelve years between deliberative tests. This is too bad, but it is a price worth paying to retain Presidents Day as the core element of our proposal. If Deliberation Day makes any sense at all, it should be used to restore a sense of citizen sovereignty to a contest where the stakes are highest and the interest is greatest. Only if Presidents Day proves to be a success does it make sense to follow up with Congress Day.

Assuming that things go well during the first two DDays for the presidency, this is the time to introduce CDay into the holiday calendar. By this point, the relatively low turnouts prevailing in midterm elections won't be as much of a barrier to success. Once Americans get into the habit of deliberating on their presidential choices, it will seem more natural to turn out for a similar exercise for the midterm elections. To be sure, CDay won't be as big a success as PDay until other steps are taken to increase the competitiveness of congressional races. Nevertheless, it should be successful enough to halt the troubling slide of voter participation and greatly increase the sense in which off-year election results represent the considered expression of public opinion.

Parliament Day

We have been struggling with the implications of one large fact about the American system: its separation of power between an elected president and an independently elected Congress. Separationism is embraced in many other places as well — including Brazil, France, and Mexico. While some version of Congress Day may make sense in these countries, our particular format may not travel very well. In designing Congress Day, we have not been searching for some universal model. We have formulated our basic proposal with the peculiarities of the American system in mind. Reformers in other countries should do likewise, using our proposal as a provocation more than as a guide.

Our general project is greatly simplified, however, when we turn to the parliamentary systems favored in Europe and many other countries. These systems reject the principle of separation: whoever wins the parliamentary election gains control of the executive. Since the president isn't elected, there is no need to organize different DDays for the presidency and the legislature. There is only one crucial event: Parliament Day.

In other words, parliamentarians can ignore the first part of this chapter and use our format for Presidents Day to provoke further reflection. But at this point, some distinctive design problems arise. The most important involves proportional representation. Most parliamentary systems adopt this principle; as a consequence, European parliaments typically contain four or more parties, and European governments are often multiparty coalitions.

This requires us to deal more explicitly with a form of information overload that was also lurking in the American case. In proposing our basic format, we envisioned the two major parties as the central protagonists at the National Issues Debate on television and the citizen assemblies throughout the country. But third parties have often played an important role in American politics. How to integrate them into DDay?

This may be an important question in the American case, but it becomes absolutely central issue for any system embracing proportional representation. Under PR, the ongoing coexistence of four or more parties is the rule, not the exception. How can so many spokesmen be squeezed into hourlong formats without replicating the sound-bite politics that we hope to displace?

Europeans have confronted a similar problem when distributing free television time for use during electoral campaigns. Unsurprisingly, different countries differ as to the appropriate distributional formula, but they tend toward the principle of proportional representation: if Party A has 35 percent representation in the parliament, it gets roughly 35 percent of television time, and so forth.[19]

We take a similar approach. At the televised debate and citizen assemblies, all parties in parliament will be represented on the podium, but their speaking time will be distributed according to the principle of proportional representation—a party that has 35 percent of the seats in the old parliament will get 35 percent of the speaking time, and so forth. Parties may form coalitions and give a single coalition spokesman all their combined time.

As each spokesman comes on stage, he is provided with a clock indicating the number of minutes allocated to him. When the first question is posed, the speaker with the largest time allocation is obliged to answer, but the others are free to pass, and to reserve their time for future questions. This permits the most sustained debate on the questions that engage the greatest controversy; and it avoids heavy-handed intrusion by allowing the spokesmen themselves to decide when their distinctive perspectives will most help the voters make up their mind.

The proportional principle is our baseline, but it requires modification to serve more basic purposes. Parliamentary systems sometimes create broad-based "governments of national unity," especially in times of national emergency. Deliberation Day would degenerate if such governments were entitled to use their massive parliamentary support to transform Parliament Day into a cheerleading session. Even under normal conditions, the dominant party or coalition has a great communication advantage by virtue of its control over the government. Since the point of Deliberation Day is to give the voters a well-rounded view, a modification of PR is required to limit the time of the party coalition that was previously in power. Rather than granting it the proportion of time suggested by its share of parliamentary seats, we impose a ceiling of 50 percent on its time share. This allows at least one of the opposition parties to respond to the governing coalition's analysis of each question.[20] We also modify the proportionality principle in the case of fringe parties. Most PR systems require minor parties to win a threshold percentage of the popular vote before gaining admission to parliament. But these thresholds are often very low—1 percent of the vote can sometimes be enough to send delegates to the assembly. One percent of an hourlong session is thirty-six seconds — too close to the sound-bite zone. We would advise a 10 or 15 percent threshold for representation on Deliberation Day, and invite smaller groups to form coalitions enabling them to transcend this threshold. If they are unable to find suitable conversation partners, it is better to keep them off the podium than to allow party representatives to intervene with sound bites calculated more to dramatize their presence than to contribute to the general discussion.

With these modifications, Parliament Day will look quite different from its American counterpart. On Presidents Day, each question receives only two answers, and quite a few questions can be asked within the space of an hour. On Parliament Day, a single question can generate from one to five answers — and if the latter occurs frequently, fewer questions will get asked. To enrich the agenda, it may make sense to reduce the speaking time for each participant from two and a half minutes to two — depending on the number of spokesmen who make it over the 10 or 15 percent threshold. Nevertheless, the diversity of viewpoints expressed on Parliament Day might well compensate for the smaller number of questions placed on the table. Although the parliamentary format will differ from Presidents Day, it isn't clear which one enables ordinary citizens to reach a richer understanding of the electoral stakes.

Parliamentary systems will also require revision of the run-up to Deliberation Day. In contrast to the American alternative, these systems don't operate on fixed electoral calendars. General elections often occur as a result of a vote of no-confidence, or a strategic decision by the prime minister. This means that the new holiday will cause more private and public inconvenience. Businesses won't be able to plan well in advance. Bureaucrats will find it harder to organize the schools and community centers needed for deliberative purposes. The shorter the campaign season, the greater these costs of adaptation — this may suggest the wisdom of a modest lengthening of campaign periods in some systems.[21]

Another variation will be required four weeks before Deliberation Day. Under the American model, Democrats and Republicans have the right to docket two issues of national concern for public discussion. Something more complicated is needed within a multiparty setting. Each party's power to set the agenda should depend on its voting strength in the last parliament. Parties with less than 25 percent of parliamentary seats can get their issues onto the docket by joining a coalition with the requisite voting strength. Broadly speaking, this will yield an agenda for discussion that represents a fair balance between the previous government and its critics.

Taking a more general view, prospects for Parliament Day are looking pretty bright. Lots of serious work would be required to frame a sensitive proposal for a particular parliamentary system. But there is nothing in the basic set-up that makes the project an obvious nonstarter. Except for the special problems posed by proportional representation, Parliament Day poses fewer design difficulties than those prevailing under an American-style separation of powers.

Consider, for example, the classic Westminster model of British parliamentary government. Since power is concentrated in a single assembly, we may dispense with the problems involved in organizing Congress Day. Since the Westminster parliament is not selected through proportional representation, the multiparty problem is relatively tractable. The only serious difficulty is to find a way to convince the Conservatives and Laborites to treat the Liberal Democrats fairly so long as this third party continues to have substantial support in the country.[22]

Given the recent constitutional ferment in Great Britain, perhaps it will be a leader in the movement to incorporate Parliament Day into the democratic understandings of the twenty-first century?

Referenda and Other Experiments

Deliberation Day is, of course, applicable to other democratic processes. Some of these are strategically placed to provide data and experience supporting adoption of the proposal.

Referendum democracy offers a case crying out for reform. The referendum was popularized in the Progressive Era with the hope that it would empower a thoughtful and engaged electorate and lessen the role of money and corruption in politics.[23] In fact, it has often subjected the public to rival strategies of manipulation through campaign advertising, fueled by large contributions and designed to push hot buttons for opinion change identified from focus groups.[24] The referendum confronts the voter with special problems that Deliberation Day is well equipped to solve. Referenda often lack party labels—thereby depriving many voters of a heuristic device that allows some to find their way through the thicket of campaign issues.[25]

Many referenda also contain complex and misleading verbiage, making it easy for inattentive citizens to vote differently from the way they would if they were better informed.[26] Sometimes an apparent Yes really means No, or vice versa.

At the same time, referenda are typically worded in a Yes or No fashion, and this makes them especially amenable to treatment on Deliberation Day. We can avoid the complexities of multiparty representation we confronted with Parliament Day, and the presentations can proceed more or less as in a two-candidate race. This has been our experience in organizing Deliberative Polls in conjunction with referenda, even when the group supporting the Yes or No option was a diverse ideological coalition. For example, the No side in the Australian referendum on the republic included monarchists, who wanted to keep the queen as head of state, and strong democrats, who wanted a president chosen by direct election (rather than having him elected indirectly by Parliament, as was proposed in the referendum). And in the Danish referendum on the euro, the main centrist parties were in the Yes camp, but parties farther to both the right and the left were against. Nevertheless, there wasn't a serious problem managing the dialogue with all the key supporters at the plenary sessions of the DPs. Nobody complained that they were given an inadequate opportunity to explain their positions within a framework that granted equal time for the Yes and No sides.

As these examples suggest, referenda are often employed for especially momentous changes—membership in the European Union or adoption of the euro, or creation of a new constitution on the national or state level. The issues will be complex and important, raising matters far removed from the ordinary give-and-take of politics. This makes the introduction of Deliberation Day especially appropriate. Moreover, the extraordinary character of the decision permits the ad hoc introduction of the new holiday on an experimental basis. Given the referendum's high importance and enduring consequences, doesn't it make sense to have a special holiday that will allow citizens to confront the issues in a balanced and thoughtful way?

If the ad hoc introduction of DDay establishes that a nation *can* transform a politics of sound bites into a politics of popular deliberation, this will provide a precedent for future experimentation, and ultimately, the introduction of DDay on a regular basis.

There are some places—most famously Switzerland, California, and other states of the American West—that have made referenda part of the normal process of government. Most of these referenda don't deal with momentous transformations, and voters are frequently required to cast ballots on a larger number of propositions at the same time. As we shall explain, these referenda don't seem very suitable for DDay.[27]

Nevertheless, other political sites may prove promising for experimentation. A small town or city, for example, might use a Sunday afternoon as a pilot DDay in the run-up for an especially important referendum or local election. Such a demonstration project would be relatively inexpensive, and yet would suggest the project's potential impact on levels of voter knowledge and civic engagement.

Here the exercise in public consultation begins to intersect with an agenda for social science research. Pilot DDays would be the obvious target for serious study. Different DDays could proceed under different formats, providing priceless experience for more ambitious future initiatives. Perhaps a debate is unnecessary at the beginning; small groups may do just as well without it. Perhaps more extensive briefing documents would make a difference; perhaps they would not. Perhaps the small groups would work better if they were smaller, closer to the size of focus groups than to the size of discussion groups in the DPs. While our proposals have carefully tracked the experience of Deliberative Polls, more field experiments would help in fine-tuning the design and in documenting its effects.

For example, one could readily envision a demonstration project in which small groups were randomly assigned to variations in the format (with video or without, with briefing documents or without, with large-group sessions or without). These studies could, in turn, become the basis for further demonstration projects in an ongoing process of institutional fine-tuning that would lay the foundation for larger-scale applications.[28]

No less important, these small-scale projects can test the viability of our larger vision of deliberative democracy. If DDay works in a town or city, why can't it work in a state or nation? If it works in a one-shot referendum, why can't it also work for presidential or congressional elections?

Virtual Possibilities

In the meantime, new technologies will open up further dimensions for exploration. The future development of the Internet will not only provide us with new resources for organizing DDay; it will also open up distinctive normative horizons.

Consider the analogy we have employed between the vision of a deliberative society suggested by the Deliberative Poll and the one actualized by Deliberation Day. There is, in fact, a crucial difference between the two formats. It turns on a point easily overlooked but obvious once explicitly stated — the role of place, of physical location, as people interact. In any vision of national dialogue, physical location places restrictions on the possible scenarios that can be realized through unmediated face-to-face discussion. These restrictions disappear if the face-to-face discussion can be mediated through technology. At the moment, the Internet has limitations, both in its possibilities for dialogue and in the distribution of access. But we are not far from realizing richer forms of dialogue and wider degrees of access. Now is the time to envision what might happen once restrictions of place are overcome by these developments.

Let us look more closely at the difference between DDay and DP. In the poll, the participants represent a microcosm of the entire country. People from New York are talking face-to-face to people from California or Montana, all brought together at a single location. By contrast, each DDay group is a microcosm of a local community. The many microcosms add up to a deliberating society, but one in which people talk with those physically nearby. Both offer representations of a national deliberation, but with the crucial difference concerning the relevant community of deliberators.

Put another way, DP and DDay embody two related, but distinct, visions of democracy. The DP embodies for a microcosm a normatively relevant counterfactual—what if everyone in the population could have a serious and balanced dialogue with a random sample of other citizens? But without new technology, this ideal is not realizable in practice. How could one possibly arrange for everyone in the country to deliberate in a national microcosm of several hundred? It is barely possible to imagine a repeated process of random sampling until the entire population was somehow recruited and sent on trips to sites for innumerable exercises in deliberation. Even as a thought-experiment, this strains the imagination. The counterfactual has normative relevance, in that it would allow citizens to encounter the full diversity of opinion expressed throughout the country, and not only within their locales. In contrast DDay's vision of local deliberation is perfectly achievable in the real-world.

But once we turn to technology, the DP vision begins to seem like a practical alternative. Suppose that every citizen could engage in a futuristic version of online dialogue. In this brave new world, the text-based Internet is a thing of the past, and something like two-way television makes virtual communication almost indistinguishable from the face-to-face variety. This thought-experiment allows us to imagine competing counterfactuals clearly. On the localist DDay scenario, the citizens plug in within local communities, randomly assigned to networks connecting nearby geographical areas. On the national DDay scenario, a New Yorker might be randomly assigned to talk in a small group with someone from California or Montana, and the five hundred–person assemblies would each represent a statistical microcosm of the nation as a whole.

We have in fact conducted an online experiment that suggests the promise of the national DDay. Parallel to the 2003 National Issues Convention on foreign affairs, held in Philadelphia and broadcast on PBS in January 2003, we conducted the first national Online Deliberative Poll with the same questionnaire and briefing materials. Respondents in the national sample who did not have computers were provided with them as an incentive for participation; others were given an honorarium. All participants had microphones, reducing the disadvantage of those who were less literate or less comfortable with text. Over four weeks, the respondents deliberated for two hours a week in randomly assigned small groups that, like their face-to-face counterparts, selected key questions for competing experts. The expert responses were posted weekly on the web and became the subject of further discussions. The project was conducted in parallel with a face-to-face national Deliberative Poll on foreign policy and produced broadly similar results.

The online Deliberative Poll results suggests that we should begin to view a national DDay in virtual space as a serious contender compared with traditional localist arrangements. In both the online and face-to-face experiments, balanced discussions led national samples to take more responsibility for world problems — by contributing to the solution of AIDS and world hunger in developing countries, by requiring higher gas mileage for vehicles even if it meant they would be less powerful, and by increasing foreign aid. In both experiments the public was insistently multilateralist in conditions for any war with Iraq. Even though the changes from online deliberation were less pronounced than in the face-to-face version, these parallel results suggest that online deliberations, if they continued longer, might someday produce even bigger changes than those resulting from the face-to-face process.[29]

But if a national DDay is becoming a technological possibility, this hardly implies that it should be preferred to the old-fashioned localist version. Consider Congress Day, for example: Since the vote here is for senators and representatives, a national DDay in virtual space is categorically inappropriate. Americans live in what Madison called a "compound republic."[30] We do not have unitary national elections, but state-based elections that are compounded into a national result.

Yet even for Congress Day, our Internet experiment brings new questions to light. From a constitutional point of view, the compounds in our "compound republic" are states, not local communities. To be sure, states have traditionally refused to elect their House delegations on an at-large basis, dividing representatives into smaller districts. But under modern conditions, each House member represents more than half a million people — a much bigger populace than anybody's notion of a "local community." Given this fact, the Internet of the future raises a new question: Should we take affirmative steps to encourage truly local discussion, or should the conversational circle expand to embrace citizens of the entire congressional district?

Such questions are even more pointed on Presidents Day. Formally speaking, the president is selected by the state delegates who cast votes in the Electoral College. But over the centuries, the presidency has emerged into a very different office from the one contemplated by the Founders. He (or she) is truly a national figure, regularly claiming a mandate from the American people in dealing with the Congress. Given this fact, the argument for a national DDay becomes more powerful. In deliberating during Presidents Day, perhaps it would be a good thing for the average Californian to hear the views of randomly selected Iowans and Georgians, and vice versa?

When all is said and done, Californians would still vote together to determine who should win their state's electoral votes; but under the nationalized scenario, each state's citizens would make this judgment after exposing themselves to the views of other members of the national polity.

But, of course, there are counterarguments. Constitutionalists notoriously disagree about the balance of state and nation in our federal system. Strong advocates of states' rights may plausibly insist that even in presidential races, the relevant political conversation should be restricted to citizens of the same state. Since our Internet thought-experiment will not become a reality for another generation or so, it suffices here simply to raise the issue. Someday access to the Internet (or its descendants) will be as common as access to the telephone now. In such a world, these Internet-based deliberations will become eminently feasible.

Even when practical issues are set to one side, there is another kind of concern. Call it the "localist objection," which rejects the Internet option as a matter of principle. So far as the localist is concerned, the old fashioned DDay format holds a special promise. By gathering in neighborhood assemblies, Americans will be creating "social capital" in their local communities. They will be meeting people from different walks of life, and getting a chance to form associations that will integrate them more firmly into ongoing community networks. They will thereby find modes of communal understanding that move beyond the roles of consumers in shopping malls or anonymous voters in polling booths. This accumulating social capital may well fuel further participation and a further sense of political efficacy. Even if DDay deliberations focus only on candidates for national office, the community-building effects will carry over to state and local politics. According to the localist, it is a mistake to allow Internet fantasies to blind us to these enduring benefits.

These arguments aren't necessarily dispositive. The technologist will emphasize the greater diversity of views that are likely to result in virtual microcosms created from people across the land. Doesn't this more multifaceted approach to the issues represent a greater value than the deepening of social capital promised by the traditional DP? And then there is the matter of dollars and cents. As the next chapter will show, the costs of organizing huge numbers of citizen assemblies will be substantial, and many of these costs could be avoided once the Internet alternative gets off the ground.

Before this debate can become serious, two enormous breakthroughs are required. The first involves technology. The existing text-based system not only disadvantages the less educated. It fails to provide the rich communicative repertoire familiar to all of us in face-to-face communication. Without voice and video connections, virtual deliberation is a pale shadow of a real-world DDay.[31]

A second breakthrough is also imperative. Before a democratic system could get off the ground, we must overcome the "digital divide" and achieve universal access for all citizens — not just for dial-up modems but for the broadband required for the first breakthrough. We are at least a generation away, then, from a virtual DDay. For the foreseeable future, the localist version of DDay represents the wave of the future.

Working within this "place-based" structure, we can foresee some supplementary uses for relatively primitive Internet technologies. For example, existing Internet hookups might be helpful for physically disadvantaged people who have trouble traveling to ordinary neighborhood centers. Residents of remote rural districts might also find it especially arduous to take the trip to DDay centers for face-to-face encounters. But it might be more feasible to gather in small groups of fifteen around a computer, and then organize virtual citizen assemblies for the Q and A with local political representatives.

These supplementary uses will, in turn, provide an accumulating base of experience for testing the feasibility and desirability of more ambitious exercises in virtual deliberation.

We can find out only once we begin.

6

WHAT PRICE DELIBERATION?

Deliberation Day will be expensive. But there is more at stake than totting up the dollars and cents. We must ask what the dollar signs mean. Is Deliberation Day like an enormously expensive Mercedes-Benz—which we are free to reject merely because other consumer goods better satisfy our desires? Or are the costs involved more akin to those spent on educating the young or defending the country?

We can't answer these questions with economic reasoning alone. To motivate the requisite political reflection, we focus on one of our "big ticket" items: the proposal to pay each participating citizen a stipend of $150. Such payments are hardly unprecedented; similar (but smaller) stipends are paid every day to Americans serving as jurors in criminal and civil trials throughout the nation. But these $150 payments will add up to many billions each DDay, especially if our initiative is successful and tens of millions of Americans turn out to discuss the issues.

This big budgetary item will lead us to reflect on a curious asymmetry in modern public finance. National and local governments spend hundreds of billions of dollars a year on highways and health care and other goods and services. When the state is viewed as a machine for satisfying needs and wants, our budgetary imagination knows no bounds. But when it comes to citizenship development, we spend almost nothing. Is this disparity justified? Is the $150 stipend a mere luxury or an essential aspect of our initiative?

A mature assessment of the costs also requires some economic sophistication. Basic economic theory emphasizes that dollar signs sometimes prove to be misleading indicators of real resource costs. When such a divergence occurs, good cost-benefit analysis requires us to move beyond nominal dollar values to analyze the genuine "opportunity cost" generated by our program. Within the present context, this will lead us to treat another "big ticket" item in a distinctive fashion.

From the layman's point of view, it may seem very costly to use countless school classrooms and governmental office buildings as sites for tens of millions of deliberators. But from an economic perspective, this represents an elementary analytic mistake. Recall that we are not giving Americans a new day off for DDay; we are appropriating an already existing holiday — Presidents Day — for a better civic purpose. Even in the absence of DDay, the school buildings would be empty, as the government closes for business on Presidents Day. Since the buildings would be empty anyway, there is no opportunity cost involved in using them for deliberative purposes, and we should not add billions of dollars to our cost estimates to reflect their "rental value." The same point applies to the economic production lost when half the working population takes at least one day off during our two-day holiday. Since many people currently take Presidents Day off, the opportunity cost is greatly reduced along this dimension as well, probably to zero.

This hardly implies that DDay will be cheap. Lots of work will go into preparing for the holiday, organizing its operations, and cleaning up afterward. (And don't forget the free lunch served to tens of millions of DDayers in school cafeterias throughout the land!) While these real resource costs will range in the billions, the magnitudes will seem quite manageable once placed within a suitable political and economic framework.

Or so we will argue.

The Political Economy of Citizenship

Yes, it would be nice for voters to cast more informed ballots. Who could object to such a banality? But does this consensus dissolve when it comes to *paying* people to deliberate? It is one thing for Americans to take up their responsibilities voluntarily. But does the use of money somehow profane the majesty of citizenship?

The anxiety has deep roots. It motivated an aged Benjamin Franklin to a rare intervention at the Constitutional Convention of 1787. Too sick to speak, he had his fellow delegate James Wilson deliver a lengthy diatribe against the very idea that the president or members of Congress should be paid for their labors. Franklin argued that salaries would encourage faction. Rulers would progressively try to enrich themselves, leading to the disastrous return of monarchy: "This catastrophe I think may be long delayed, if in our proposed system we do not sow the seeds of contention, faction & tumult, by making our posts of honor, places of profit." Franklin's Constitution would have contained a clear provision barring all payment to elected representatives.[1]

The old man's motion was a nonstarter. After hearing Franklin out, the delegates quickly moved on to other business without further remark. Even in that elitist era, it was perfectly clear that forcing representatives to serve the public for free would unacceptably limit participation to the elitest of the elite. If a broad range of the public were to aspire to public office, it was right and fitting for them to get paid adequately for their services. The same logic applies here. Our present practices encourage ordinary Americans to forget that *citizenship is an office* — and one that is no less crucial to the functioning of the Republic than more august positions. DDay aims to remind them that voting is not an occasion for expressing consumer-like preferences. It is the key moment for confiding ultimate coercive power to men and women who will be speaking in the name of the United States and taking actions with fateful consequences for the entire planet.

If we are right to suggest that Americans need reminding, and that DDay will help do the trick, we should keep Benjamin Franklin's mistake in mind when confronting economic realities. Most people work hard for a living — with millions working overtime to make ends meet. They will be tempted to use a couple of days off to recuperate from the stresses of ordinary life, catching up on their sleep and taking care of responsibilities at home. They may regret that they can't afford the time for DDay. But they are also too hard-pressed to enjoy many other good things in life, and they may simply shrug as others go off to debate the issues of the day.

The prospect of a cash stipend will prompt a massive reappraisal. In 1998 the median wage was $105 a day.[2] A grant of $150 will seem like serious money to most Americans. Responsible citizenship will no longer seem like a distant ideal but a practical way of spending a day off from work (especially since this will be a two-day holiday and only one will be spent deliberating). The stipend will not merely symbolize the American commitment to equal citizenship; it will help give a new social reality to this commitment by enabling ordinary people to take their citizenship seriously.

A substantial payment will be especially important to parents. Their kids won't be going to school on DDay, and somebody must take care of them if the parents are to leave home in good conscience. DDay organizers will minimize the pressure by artful scheduling arrangements. As we shall explain shortly, citizens will be strongly encouraged to reserve their place in advance at a preselected deliberative site specified by the Deliberation Day Authority (DDA). To ease the burden of child care, reservation forms will invite parents to specify a family member or friend who has agreed to take on child-care responsibilities. The DDA will make every effort to enable the parent and his designate to stagger their days of attendance—allowing the parent to reserve for day one and his designate to reserve for day two. (Computers are wonderful things!)

But this is a partial solution at best—especially for single-parent families without larger social-support networks. As a consequence, the new civic holiday will become a great market opportunity for teenage babysitters. Millions of moms and dads will need to make special informal arrangements for child care. A generous stipend will give them the wherewithal to find satisfactory solutions to their problem of civic engagement. After babysitting costs are taken into account, $150 may not seem nearly such a large number.

We do not wish to overstate our case. Even with a substantial stipend, the prospect of attendance at Deliberation Day will generate a great deal of anxiety in the hearts of millions—the poor and less-educated may be particularly wary when it comes to speaking out on policy issues in a public forum. Millions more will find the prospect of DDay insufferably boring and avoid it like the plague. Others will simply decide that they have better things to do with their time.

But DDay will not fail even if most voters stand apart from the communal goings-on. The crucial question is not how many Americans use the holiday as a convenient excuse to catch up on their sleep. It is whether enough accept its invitation to operate as a "critical mass." We shall be defining this concept in terms of three criteria—moving beyond (1) overall size to consider the turnout in terms of its potential for (2) open-mindedness and (3) representativeness. These criteria will help refine the relevant questions raised in determining whether $150 is "too much" or "too little" to pay as a stipend.

As a thought-experiment, begin by setting the stipend at zero. Following Benjamin Franklin's advice, simply invite the general citizenry to engage in DDay and then see who shows up. The overall turnout, we fear, will be too small, too closed-minded, and too unrepresentative. We shall define these three terms, and illustrate our problem, by glancing at the operation of a real-world institution that bears a remote resemblance to our initiative.

Most states run presidential primaries to pick their delegates to the national nominating convention, but a declining number use a caucus system. As on DDay, citizens are asked to attend neighborhood meetings to consider the merits of presidential candidates. But at this point the resemblance ends. While the details of the process differ from state to state, we focus on Iowa—both because the state's caucuses play a central role in the current system, and because their procedures are quite standard.

How do the Iowa caucuses differ from those we propose on DDay? For starters, Iowans don't join together at a common meeting place for the neighborhood citizenry. They attend separate meetings organized by the Democrats and the Republicans.[3] The point of these sessions is not deliberation but decision. There are short speeches in praise of rival candidates, but the main business is to demonstrate how many caucus members support each nominee.[4] Each local caucus typically sends delegates to party nominating conventions, and each candidate's share depends on the number of his caucus supporters.[5] The meeting spends most of its time determining each candidate's support and which of his supporters should be named as delegates to the statewide party conventions.[6]

DDay is also different in that it is a holiday, and this will increase attendance substantially. Nevertheless, the data from most caucus states should serve as a warning to modern-day Benjamin Franklins who question the need for a citizen stipend. As we shall see, Iowa caucuses are held under exceptional conditions which generate exceptional turnouts. But for present purposes, the crucial data come from other caucus states, where the average turnout is only about 2 or 3 percent of the party's vote in the fall election—a sharp contrast to the 20 or 30 percent of voters who participate in states holding presidential primaries.[7] Apparently, ten times as many Americans are willing to spend a few minutes casting a primary ballot than are willing to spend a couple of hours standing up for their candidates at a caucus.

Such tiny turnouts are far too small to fulfill our basic purposes. Much of our proposal's political value is generated by the law of anticipated reaction: We want incumbents to worry about DDay during the years when they are exercising the powers of government. Yet incumbents won't be concerned about the next DDay unless they expect enough voters to show up to present them with a real risk of electoral reprisal. The critical mass required to generate serious strategic concern will depend on several variables, including the anticipated closeness of the vote and the proportion of DDayers who may change their minds. But on plausible assumptions, a 2 or 3 percent turnout rate is simply too low to make DDay anything but a joke.

Turnout is much larger at the Iowa caucuses. This is where the presidential race begins, with Iowans attending Democratic and Republican caucuses on a cold Monday evening in January or February of the election year.[8] Even here, turnout has been variable.[9] When a sitting president is running for reelection or an Iowa politician is running as a favorite son, attendance plummets because the result seems foreordained.[10] But when the presidential race is open, turnouts move well beyond the norm for other caucus states.[11]

Since major candidates use an early victory in Iowa as a springboard for nationwide success, they make massive efforts to mobilize their supporters.[12] And Iowans are perfectly aware that the caucuses play a crucial role in winnowing the field.[13] The highest recent turnout was in 1988.[14] With Ronald Reagan leaving office, both party nominations were energetically contested. And the weather was less icy than usual, with temperatures rising above freezing.[15] In response to these especially favorable conditions, 234,000 Iowans attended the caucuses — 18.5 percent of the number who came out to vote in November.[16]

This is more than six times the norm in other caucus states, and we find it broadly encouraging for DDay. As in Iowa, candidates and media will be treating DDay with high seriousness. And while Iowa caucuses occur on a work night, DDay attendance will get a big boost from being held on a holiday. Nevertheless, modern Ben Franklins should beware: Apart from the obvious dangers of extrapolating the best results from Iowa, a closer analysis of the data suggests that it would be a bad mistake to dispense with the $150 citizen stipend.

For starters, suppose that 18.5 percent of Election Day voters turned out for DDay, as they do for the most contested Iowa caucuses. Even this turnout won't be good enough to make the holiday a crucial reference point for politicians as they chart their campaign strategies. This becomes especially clear when our second criterion — closed-mindedness — is brought into play. Experience with Deliberative Polls suggests that representative samples can shift their opinions substantially after talking the issues through — net changes of 10, 15, or even 20 or more points are entirely possible. Such large swings can often change the outcome of an election. But these results come from representative samples of the population, and the Iowans who turn out for the caucuses are self-selected partisans. They are more likely to be activists who strongly identify with their political parties and express more extreme ideological positions than the general electorate.

For example, 41 percent of participants at the 1988 Democratic caucus described themselves as "liberal" or "extremely liberal," in contrast to 19 percent of all Iowa Democrats; Republicans exhibited a similar skew to the right. No less remarkably, 32 percent of all caucus participants said they had been active in state politics for "more than twenty years."[17] This doesn't sound like a very open-minded bunch. Of course, the purpose of the Iowa caucuses isn't to discuss the issues but to win delegates for particular presidential candidates — so it isn't surprising that each campaign organization tries to recruit its most committed supporters to attend the meeting.[18]

But a similar dynamic will occur on DDay. Though the official purpose of the day is to explore the leading issues, rival candidates will be intensely interested in shaping the agendas discussed in the citizen assemblies throughout the land. To tilt the deliberations in their direction, they will predictably mobilize their committed followers and encourage them to push for questions that are favorable to their candidate. Grassroots groups will have a similar objective. They will want to demonstrate the breadth and intensity of their members' commitments by urging them to come out in force and shift the conversational agenda to their particular ideological concerns.

Here is where the payment of a substantial stipend becomes important. Dedicated party workers and ideological activists may attend DDay without further financial incentives, but the overwhelming majority of voters will have greater doubts about participating. The offer of a substantial stipend will prompt lots of ordinary Americans to overcome these doubts and give DDay a try. Encouraged by the stipend, the overall turnout will move well beyond Iowa levels and will greatly increase the ratio of open- to closed-minded participants.

From this vantage point, the relatively modest Iowa turnouts are a blessing in disguise. As we have seen, these caucuses are almost designed to discourage attendance by the open-minded since they insist upon a public show of support for particular candidates. If a caucus at its very best can attract only 18.5 percent of Election Day voters, it should be quite easy to dilute the impact of hard-edged partisans by designing DDay sessions that explicitly reach out to Americans of *all* persuasions.

This is, of course, the overriding point of our proposed format. DDay offers itself as common ground for all citizens, and does not authorize the political parties to hold separate caucuses for their partisans. It categorically rejects any effort to force participants to express a definite preference for a particular candidate, encouraging them to spend the run-up to Election Day in further discussion. Rather than forcing each citizen to come to a final answer, DDay emphasizes the importance of asking the right questions. These key differences in design, coupled with the substantial stipend and the day off from work, give us every reason to anticipate a vast increase in moderate and undecided voters on DDay.

A large increase will have salutary effects on political incentives via the law of anticipated reaction. Not only will turnout be much greater, but the proportion of "persuadable votes" will be far larger as well—making DDay into a powerful strategic reality for politicians to conjure with years in advance.

The expanded turnout will also have a salutary impact on the ordinary citizen's experience of the holiday. If too high a proportion of DDay participants enter the deliberations with a closed mind, they will spoil the environment for everybody else. Indeed, they can do lasting damage, since a bad initial experience might lead many ordinary Americans to steer clear of future engagements: "If DDay is simply an occasion for opinionated loudmouths to insist on their positions, who needs it?"

Once the holiday stipend dilutes the proportion of activists, strongly committed types can play valuable roles. As we have emphasized, the holiday should be a time not only for citizens to discuss the major issues framed by the candidates; they should also have a chance to expand the agenda and ask the candidates' representatives to respond to grassroots concerns. Dedicated members of the Sierra Club or National Rifle Association play a valuable role in seeking to persuade other members of their fifteen-person groups to put other issues onto the conversational agenda. Similarly, strong supporters of a particular candidate may well play a constructive role in helping define the most profitable areas of inquiry.

The crucial question is to define the point at which the presence of too many closed-minded types can create an overall atmosphere uncongenial to the open-ended exploration of the issues. This is a matter that deserves serious empirical investigation. The appropriate social science experiments resemble those used in existing Deliberative Polls, but with one big difference. In the past, DPs have sought to recruit a representative sample of the voting population—since their aim has been to determine how the general public would change its opinions after serious deliberation. In contrast, the new round of experiments should simulate unrepresentative conditions in which activists bulk disproportionately large. This will help define the tipping point at which their presence chills the open-ended spirit of inquiry that Deliberation Day, at its best, seeks to exemplify.

But for now we can only point to general trends suggesting that the problem is manageable. The past half-century has brought a significant decline in partisanship among American voters. Voting a split ticket doubled between the 1950s and the 1990s—with about 40 percent of voters refusing to support candidates from a single party for president, Senate, and House of Representatives.[19] Similarly, only one-third of voters categorized themselves as "strong partisans" in the 1990s, with the rest indicating one or another degree of political independence.[20] These global trends suggest that there is a big pool of relatively uncommitted types out there, and that a substantial stipend will serve significantly to ameliorate the problem of closed-mindedness.

The same is true for our third and final criterion: A turnout may not be too closed-minded but can still cause problems by virtue of its lack of representativeness. Once again, data from the Iowa caucuses serve a cautionary function. Without the spur of a financial stipend, Iowans who attend the caucuses were disproportionately male and were better educated, richer, and older than the average Republican or Democrat who voted in November. For example, 16 percent of Republican voters in the general election lacked a high school diploma, but only 4 percent who came to the party caucuses lacked one; 47 percent of Democratic voters earned less than $20,000, but only 28 percent of caucus participants earned such low incomes. And so forth.[21]

These disparities look especially troubling in light of the law of anticipated reaction. In framing their strategies, the candidates will naturally target the groups who show up in force. If the Iowa turnout is any guide, candidates are apt to frame issues to appeal to the interests of older, richer, educated males — so long as we are operating in a zero-stipend world. But once again, adding a significant financial incentive promises to ameliorate this problem. One hundred fifty dollars means more to the poor than it does to the rich; as the poor tend to be disproportionately young, the youth turnout should pick up as well.[22]

The payment will also help address the relatively low turnout among women at the Iowa caucuses. In 1988, for example, 43 percent of participants in the Republican caucus were women, compared with 53 percent nationally in the general election;[23] 53 percent of caucus Democrats were women, compared with 61 percent in the general election. This disparity is probably due to the disparate impact of child-care responsibilities — if only one parent can attend the caucus, it is typically the woman who stays home while her husband discharges the family's citizenship responsibilities. But as we have suggested, the provision of a stipend will help avoid this discriminatory effect by providing extra resources for babysitting alternatives.

There can be no guarantees of perfect representativeness—nothing is perfect about real-world democracy. It is enough that the grant of a stipend promises to ameliorate the problem significantly. Once again, we must content ourselves with a crude quantitative assessment: The higher the stipend, the higher the turnout from underrepresented groups.[24]

To develop the argument further, we move beyond cautionary tales from Iowa and consider a broader set of studies that assess the extent of political engagement by ordinary citizens. These tell an encouraging story. Americans may not know very much about the issues, but they do follow the course of presidential campaigns in impressive numbers.

They also massively increase their levels of political discussion as the campaign moves to its climax. At the moment we have set for Deliberation Day—two weeks before the election—more than one hundred million Americans are discussing their electoral choices with family and friends, workers, and neighbors. This social base for discussion is important for our argument. DDay isn't trying to create something out of nothing. Since there is a massive discussion already going on, we are simply creating a conversational focal point—encouraging citizens to extend and deepen already existing dialogic engagements. The organizational challenges involved in creating DDay are hardly insignificant. But the underlying data suggest that, when supported by a substantial stipend, tens of millions of Americans would accept DDay's invitation of responsible citizenship.

To make out the dimensions of civic opportunity, we focus on a recent study by the Joan Shorenstein Center at Harvard's Kennedy School.[25] As we have seen, the center polled a random sample of one thousand potential voters each week during the 2000 electoral cycle to determine how closely they were following the presidential campaign. One of the questions explicitly asked respondents whether they had discussed the campaign on the day of their interview.[26] Like other studies, the Shorenstein data suggest that around 5 percent of voting-age Americans are political activists engaged in discussion on a year-in and year-out basis.[27] From an operational perspective, these are also the people most likely to turn out on Deliberation Day without a stipend; and, if Iowa is any guide, there is a serious risk of closed-mindedness and unrepresentativeness if they

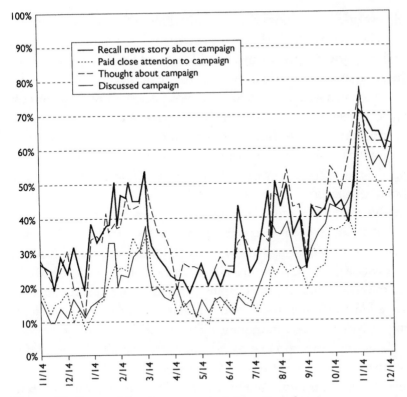

Figure 1 Voting-age citizens' awareness and discussion of 2000 presidential campaign (Source: www.vanishingvoter.org).

aren't joined by many other citizens. But happily, the Shorenstein data indicate the existence of a solid social base for attracting tens of millions more. As Figure 1 indicates, the network of political conversation expands far beyond the narrow circle of activists as the campaign progresses.

When the Shorenstein study began polling a year before the election, it found 10 or 15 percent discussing the campaign. But as the primary season broke into the news, more than 30 percent began talking politics. Once the nominations had been decided during the early caucuses and primaries, the network of political conversation contracted to activist circles, but it expanded once again as the national conventions inaugurated the fall campaign. Two weeks before Election Day—the moment we have scheduled for Deliberation Day—42 percent of Americans were discussing the presidential race. This amounts to a *trebling* of the conversational network and suggests that tens of millions of ordinary Americans may well be prepared to do their work as citizens — so long as we organize the holiday right and give them a suitable stipend for their participation.

The Shorenstein numbers are even better than they look, once we reflect on how they were generated. The survey counts a respondent only if he reports engaging in a conversation *during the past day*. This makes the data particularly valuable, since other studies typically interview people at a later point and ask them to remember the extent of their engagement — giving them a chance to exaggerate their civic involvement by "misremembering" the facts.

But this procedure also underestimates the percentage of Americans who are discussing the campaign in a significant fashion. To see the point, suppose that the Vanishing Voter Project had tracked the same group of respondents for five days in a row and found that 42 percent had discussed the campaign each day. Despite this constant figure, the particular conversationalists in the sample would differ from day to day — with some talking all five days, some four, some three, and so forth. Taking the week as a whole, the proportion of conversationalists would be a good deal higher than the 42 percent reported on any single day.[28]

This conclusion is buttressed by other leading surveys, which directly ask respondents to state the frequency with which they discuss politics. These suggest that about three-quarters of voting-age citizens are talking politics at least once a week as the presidential election reaches its climax, with about half engaging in several discussions weekly.[29]

These data provide a distinctive perspective on the oft-remarked fact that only 60 percent of voting-age citizens even register to vote in presidential elections. While this low registration rate is disheartening, turnout rates are very high for those who do register — 86 percent or 111 million Americans cast their ballots in 2000.[30] Since the nonregistrants are far less likely to discuss politics, the data suggest that the overwhelming majority of voters have engaged in rather frequent — if quite uninformed — conversations during the campaign.[31] The question is whether we can use Deliberation Day to channel these massive discussions for more constructive civic purposes.

We emphasize that there is no need for anything like a one hundred million turnout for the holiday to be a resounding success.[32] So long as we can move well beyond Iowa, and attract thirty-five million or forty million to Deliberation Day, we will satisfy our three criteria of success. Attendance by this critical mass should suffice to resolve our concerns with closed-mindedness and allow political activists to play a constructive role in the course of the day's debates. It will also serve to reduce concerns with representativeness to manageable levels. And so far as the competing candidates are concerned, the presence of such a large mass of deliberating citizens would force them to recognize that a poor performance on DDay might easily put five million votes at risk — or even more, as the consequences of DDay are felt in countless further conversations over the next two weeks in the run-up to Election Day. This grim prospect should suffice to generate a cascading cycle of virtue through the law of anticipated reaction.

Despite the encouraging data, there is no such a thing as a sure thing in politics. DDay doesn't exist, and we can't extrapolate existing evidence to "prove" that citizen turnout will achieve a critical mass. Moreover, we refuse to hedge our bets by advocating measures that will increase turnout at a price that strikes us as morally unacceptable.

Consider, for example, the way English-speaking countries have traditionally recruited citizens for jury service. For centuries the law has backed up its summons for jury duty with the threat of a criminal sanction. While fines are imposed erratically in contemporary America, the threat of punishment serves as a significant psychological prod pushing people in the direction of jury service. Some countries take a similar approach to assure big election turnouts. Australia, for example, has been successful in using the technique to achieve high turnouts — with the threat of a fine, and the accompanying moral stigma, proving itself an effective backup sanction.[33]

Nevertheless, we refuse to extend these precedents to the present case. Shy people have a *right* to stay clear of face-to-face engagements with their neighbors; and anyway, it would be absurdly counterproductive to force recalcitrant people to show up to scoff when others are making a good-faith effort at serious dialogue. Apart from its patent futility, we hate coercion, and would oppose its use even if it weren't counterproductive.

And yet our rejection of coercion doesn't affect our enthusiasm for more positive incentives. Contrast our proposed stipend of $150 with the amounts that Americans receive when serving on juries. Though jurors sometimes deliberate on matters of life and death, they are rarely paid

$50 a day for their trouble.[34] We think these sums are scandalously low, but even if you disagree, they don't serve as an appropriate benchmark here. Since it is a criminal offense to ignore a summons for jury duty, no-shows lose much more than $50 when they refuse to do their duty. They also risk getting into trouble with the law — while the fines may be modest and erratic, many job applications and other official documents ask about run-ins with the law. Most people would pay the difference between $50 and $150 to avoid telling their prospective employers about such disagreeable encounters.

Since we are rejecting all coercive measures, stipends of $50 or less won't suffice to assure the substantial turnout required to make Deliberation Day a success.[35] Such derisory payments could well be counterproductive: If somebody offered you $25 for an entire day's work, wouldn't you think that he was making some kind of bad joke? Rather than taking the offer seriously, wouldn't you refuse to cooperate just to show him that his offer was ridiculous?

Only a stipend in the range of $100 to $200 signals the serious commitment required for a new venture in citizen sovereignty. Within this range, it pays to be generous, especially in the short run. If we are to succeed, the very first Deliberation Day must attract a critical mass of citizens. If the turnout is too small, too closed-minded, or too unrepresentative the first time around, many participants won't give it a second chance. A good initial turnout will begin to generate a cycle of virtue on its own — as participants tell their more skeptical friends to give the next DDay a try.

If our experiment is successful, the role of monetary payments will decline over time. More and more Americans will develop habits of attendance, and the holiday will come to symbolize a rebirth of thoughtful citizenship in the country. But at the beginning, it will pay to be generous — there can be no guarantees, but $150 strikes us as a stipend that will give DDay a jump start and generate a critical mass of participants on the first go-round.

Lost Opportunities?

To fix ideas, suppose that fifty million Americans show up on the first run of Presidents Day. This is a vast project in citizen sovereignty, but can we really afford it? When all is said and done, how big is the bill for Deliberation Day?

We can't make sense of such questions without some basic economics. The key point is that a project doesn't incur real economic costs unless it deprives other activities of real resources. Consider, for example, the problem posed by providing the physical space for fifty million deliberators. If we actually had to build new facilities to house three-plus million small groups and one hundred thousand citizen assemblies, the costs would be astronomical. But in the real world, the opportunity cost involved in creating this space is very close to zero.

We can piggyback entirely on existing facilities to satisfy our DDay needs. In the late 1990s, there were about ninety thousand public schools in the United States, with about forty-six million elementary and secondary students.[36] This represents an average of five hundred students per building, and the schools are nicely distributed on a neighborhood basis.[37] The physical plant also looks good for our purposes: Classrooms are almost universally equipped with television sets (for the National Issues Debate); auditoriums and gymnasiums can be adapted for use by the citizen assemblies — and for lunch if the school cafeteria can't accommodate the entire crowd.[38]

There will be some geographic mismatches, and some odd-sized schools which won't be used to capacity (though Deliberation Day will work just as well if a school can only house 250 or 300 participants). Even if we conservatively assume that the schools can handle half as many deliberators as students, twenty-five million Americans could be accommodated each day. Add the twenty-three hundred public institutions of higher education (currently serving twelve million students),[39] and we already have the capacity to serve more than thirty-five million daily, or seventy million-plus during the two-day holiday. Tens of millions more could be accommodated in private schools[40] and universities,[41] courthouses,[42] nonprofit institutions,[43] and community centers. And if space gets even tighter, the Deliberation Day Authority could contract with some of the 150,000 churches with congregations of five hundred or more for the use of appropriate facilities.[44]

Of course, there will be many other costs associated with managing these facilities during Deliberation Day, and we will be considering them shortly. But our proposal would be a nonstarter if there weren't enough space, so it is important to resolve this matter first. Indeed, it probably won't be necessary to look beyond the public education sector to handle turnouts of fifty million or so. The question is how to put a price tag on the rental value of these facilities.

Here is where the economic principle of opportunity cost comes into play. To determine the real resource costs involved in appropriating all these schoolrooms, the question to ask is how they would have been used in the absence of our initiative. The answer is straightforward once you recall that the schools are already closed on Presidents Day while kids join their parents for ski weekends and holiday sales. Since the schoolrooms would have been empty anyway, the opportunity cost of devoting the space to DDay is zero.

More complexity is required for our second big-ticket item. Our proposed stipend of $150 adds up to real money when there are fifty million Americans involved. As a glance at the multiplication tables suggests, this turnout requires a payout of $7.5 billion from the federal treasury. But once again, the dollar size of this transfer payment doesn't measure its opportunity cost. The crucial point, as before, is that our new holiday doesn't replace a regular working day. If such a substitution occurred, opportunity costs would be heavy. But since we are appropriating an already existing holiday, we won't be losing a full day's economic production. To be sure, many people currently work on Presidents Day, and the loss of their current output would represent a real opportunity cost if DDay required all economic activities to cease. But such a total shutdown is no part of our proposal. To the contrary, this is one of the big reasons why DDay is a two-day holiday. While each American will be guaranteed the legal right to take one of these days off to attend deliberations, it is up to him and his employer to decide whether he will work on the other day. This means that a good deal of economic activity will still go on during the holiday—at levels roughly comparable to those prevailing on the current Presidents Day.[45]

It is an elementary mistake, then, to treat each citizen's $150 stipend as if it measured the value of the work that she would have otherwise dedicated to market production. The true opportunity cost should be measured in a different way: While most citizens currently use Presidents Day as an extra day of leisure, many will give up this extra leisure time to attend DDay activities. The key question is: How to place a dollar value on a day's leisure?

Gary Becker won a Nobel Prize (in part) for pioneering work on this issue. He estimated the economic value of leisure time at about 40 percent of the wage rate, and more recent studies are roughly in line with these early estimates, placing the opportunity cost of leisure at about $6 an hour, or $50 for an eight-hour day.[46] But there is a special problem with using such estimates here. Although economists tend to describe all nonwork activities as if they involved a homogeneous commodity called "leisure," this label begs a big question in the present case. When Joe Public decides to go fishing on DDay, he isn't merely enjoying some leisure time. He is shirking on his obligations as a citizen.

To be sure, we don't want to make him into a criminal for this lapse. And so long as a critical mass of his fellow citizens attends DDay, our fisherman's excursion won't destroy the civic point of the holiday. Nonetheless, if he chooses to absent himself, he owes it to his fellow citizens to take a comparable amount of time soberly considering his Election Day decision. If he decides to go fishing instead, he isn't engaging in some generic leisure-time activity. He is defaulting on his civic obligations. How to place a dollar value on *this* lost opportunity?

A debate between Gary Becker and George Stigler—another Nobel laureate—suggests that this is a deeply contested issue within the heartland of economics.[47] The particular question provoking the debate centered on the criminal law. When attempting a cost-benefit analysis of law enforcement, the benefit side of the equation is clear enough: Each increase in enforcement prevents some crimes from occurring, and a good economic analysis tries to put a price tag on the benefits enjoyed by people who would have otherwise been crime victims. This is tough in practice, but it doesn't raise any fundamental conceptual issues.

Measuring costs, by contrast, generates a trickier question. In addition to the expenses involved in hiring extra police, judges, and jailors, increasing law enforcement places a new burden on would-be criminals. Now that it is tougher to commit a crime and escape detection, some potential murderers and rapists will think twice and successfully control their criminal impulses. But these acts of restraint, however commendable, won't be costless — the would-be rapist may suffer intense frustration in acting like a good citizen and restraining himself.

This point leads the two economists to their disagreement. In Becker's view, one of the costs of crime control is the frustrated rapist's lost opportunity to assault his victim. If a potential rapist would pay $1,000 to engage in his crime, this should be considered a cost of law enforcement. It is true, of course, that the $1,000 represents the cash value of a lost chance to be a bad citizen; but for Becker, this is of no importance: A cost is a cost, and it is not for the economist to evaluate its moral value. Stigler disagrees: It is a good thing, not a bad thing, for the rapist to be frustrated, and a competent cost-benefit analyst should *not* count the loss of antisocial opportunities as a cost.

We agree with Stigler and generalize his point to include all other failures to live up to the obligations of citizenship. When an American lives up to these responsibilities by going to DDay, he has indeed lost an opportunity to sleep overtime, but this is a benefit, not a cost, of the program. Suppose, for example, that Deliberation Day succeeded over time in increasing its turnout from fifty million to seventy-five million participants, leading the federal treasury to increase its payout from $7.5 to $11.25 billion. It would be fundamentally misleading for an economic analyst to suggest that this success had increased real resource costs, since twenty-five million more Americans had lost the chance to catch up on their sleep! Building on Stigler's point, a normatively sensitive analyst should chalk up this increase as a sign of the holiday's success in encouraging more Americans to appreciate their civic responsibilities.

Not every flow of cash from the federal treasury represents an expenditure of real resources. When the government pays off $7.5 billion in long-term bonds, no economist would measure the real resource cost involved at the full $7.5 billion. This payment simply represents a transfer from taxpayers to creditors — with one group, rather than the other, obtaining the right to spend the money. By the same token, the citizen stipend is best conceived as a transfer from taxpayers to good citizens.[48] If fifty million Americans received citizen stipends, the real resource cost isn't $7.5 billion but the much smaller sum needed to administer the payment operation — as on Election Day, officials from the Deliberation Day Authority will be present at each site, and at the end of the day, they will authorize payment to each participant by check or electronic deposit. These costs will be quite small—for example, the Social Security Administration currently spends four cents on each electronic deposit and forty-five cents on cutting each check.[49]

There is a second potential cost. Although the citizen stipend is a pure transfer, it will appear as a significant dollar item in the federal budget—amounting to $7.5 billion, say, if fifty million Americans turn out. This money must be raised somehow—by cutting other government expenditures, raising taxes, or increasing the debt. If we eschew expenditure cuts, the alternatives can be seen as increased taxes or interest rates. But these will be very small within the context of a $2 trillion dollar federal budget. Though significant increases in taxes or interest rates can generate serious resource misallocations, the tiny changes involved here would be barely visible. Their negative impact on economic activity is problematic. And if that is a serious concern, it may be entirely avoided by cuts in other government expenditures. All things considered, these potential costs seem far too speculative for us to estimate in the abstract.[50] In contrast, we can put rough dollar numbers on a range of "out of pocket" expenditures that can give us a sense of the orders of magnitude involved in our proposal.

Real Costs

We have begun with a conceptual cost-cutting operation. Using tens of thousands of schools on DDay won't generate opportunity costs since the schools would be empty anyway. And so far as the citizen stipends are concerned, only a relatively small fraction is properly charged as a real resource cost of the program. Now that we have swept away some phantom costs, it is time to consider the real dimensions of the problem. The initial implementation of DDay will be especially expensive as new routines are developed. But once the kinks are ironed out, operational expenses will be about $2 billion for a Deliberation Day that attracts about fifty million participants. (See Appendix A for more fine-grained estimates.)

During the initial period, the Deliberation Day Authority (DDA) will be confronting a formidable management problem. We envision a familiar form of cooperative federalism guiding the overall enterprise—with the federal DDA setting guidelines and discharging distinctly national functions while state DDAs confront the primary task of implementation.

There will be challenges aplenty on both levels. State and local election boards will provide useful assistance. They possess the crucial databases on voter registration[51] and regularly confront a series of broadly similar organizational challenges — opening temporary facilities at widely scattered sites, deploying officials who confront a host of problems that require tact, common sense, and legal judgment. Nonetheless, the new holiday will raise logistical challenges that can readily outstrip the modest organizational capacities of existing institutions.

Begin with the problem of assigning citizens to sites. On Election Day, this is a pretty straightforward matter. The election board estimates the number of voting machines required at each site on the basis of past turnouts, and each neighborhood's voters are simply informed where to show up in order to cast their ballots. If there is an especially heavy turnout, voters will suffer the inconvenience of standing in line — but despite the delays, the system will discharge its basic function.

This won't be true on Deliberation Day. If a couple of thousand citizens descend on a school that can accommodate four hundred, there will be lots of frustration and very little deliberation. Unexpectedly low turnouts won't have such a demoralizing impact, but the excess operating facilities will generate unnecessary costs. To operate effectively, the DDA will have to arrange for a more sophisticated system — more like reserving a ticket on an airplane than showing up at a bus stop. Each registered voter will be encouraged to make an advance reservation at a site within easy travel distance. As sites fill up, more will be opened, and still more will be made available for last-minute arrivals on DDay. But these will be filled on a first-come, first-served basis, and there will be no guarantees for latecomers.

Modern technology will make a tremendous difference in organizing a user-friendly system. Fifty years ago, costs might have been excessive, and the resulting system would have been quite forbidding — requiring the average citizen to reserve long in advance after confronting some serious paperwork.

But this isn't true in the twenty-first century. The crucial question isn't overall cost but whether the DDA can deploy the necessary organizational savvy. Lots of big businesses and governmental institutions deal with a mass public on a day-to-day basis — from airlines to hotels to banks to the Social Security Administration, the post office, and the Internal Revenue Service. The main challenge for the DDA is to piggyback on their expertise and resources and to pay existing institutions to divert some of their capacities for DDay uses.

The principal problem is the notorious "digital divide" that separates computer haves from have-nots. Our interviews with professionals indicate that a system of Internet registration is perfectly feasible and exceptionally cheap. A voter will simply enter her Social Security number, which will serve to locate her name and address in the computerized database compiled by the election board. After some questions designed to protect against hackers, the computer will reserve a place for the voter at a randomly selected nearby site and provide a map showing how to get there.

Things will be a bit trickier on the wrong side of the digital divide. The computerless citizen can be handled quite cheaply — at a cost of a dollar a phone call — through an automated voice system that asks him to punch in his Social Security number, asks a few security questions with Yes or No answers, and provides him with an appropriate site reservation. But complexities will arise that require a talk with a real human being, and this will be more expensive.

Nonetheless, the job is perfectly doable. Big business and government already employ large call centers that respond to millions of phone calls each day from the general public.[52] And the market is big enough to respond to large but temporary increases in demand. Although no single firm could handle the tens of millions of calls that DDay might require, the federal government has already successfully confronted tasks of comparable magnitude. In 2000, for example, the Census Bureau contracted with twenty-five companies to handle sixteen million (outbound) calls.[53]

Government call centers could also be redeployed from their normal business to handle peak demand. To provide a sense of the costs involved, the market cost of an automated system is about $1 a phone call, while the rate for a telephone contact with a human reservationist is about $5 for a five-minute conversation.[54]

We shall be providing detailed estimates of these and other costs in a separate appendix, but the main point is straightforward: This is no place to economize. The poor and elderly are on the wrong side of the digital divide in massive numbers, and their turnout will be extremely sensitive to the ease of human contact. If their initial phone call is rewarded by a busy signal or an endless wait for a human voice, they may not try again. The offer of a $150 citizen stipend provides a particularly useful incentive here — since this sum will seem especially substantial to the bottom half of the income distribution, a substantial number might dial again. Nevertheless, an effective phone system is absolutely crucial for sustaining the representativeness of DDay. Without the rapid response of a human voice, DDay will be dominated by the distinctive concerns of middle-class folk on the connected side of the digital divide.

But man does not live by telephone alone. More creative forms of outreach will be required to engage those who find telephoning a daunting task — perhaps because their native language isn't English. We may ameliorate the problem by allowing citizens to select reservationists who speak Spanish and other common languages, but the DDA should move beyond merely technical solutions. The Census Bureau, for example, organized a remarkably successful outreach campaign, involving more than 140,000 local businesses and civic associations, to encourage participation in the 2000 enumeration. We propose a similar effort — with businesses and civic groups organizing sign-up sessions during workday lunch hours and at shopping malls in the evening. This will permit people to obtain a face-to-face reservation from a volunteer equipped with a computer, avoiding the telephone and Internet entirely. Based on the census experience, we have budgeted $65 million for an ambitious outreach program — a substantial sum, but well worth its price in achieving a more representative turnout.[55]

With a serious effort, the problems posed by the digital divide should prove to be manageable, and will diminish over time. Both computer literacy and computer access are on the rise: more and more Americans will find themselves in a position to log on and obtain a reservation for DDay in a matter of minutes. There will always be a need for effective supplementation, and there will always be differential burdens creating a shortfall from the ideal of representativeness. But these will be reduced to tolerable proportions by the time DDay gets off the ground. After all, it will take a decade or more before our proposal gains enough political momentum to win legislative enactment in one or another Western nation. By that time, the digital divide will seem less forbidding than it does today.

The DDA faces more traditional challenges in securing the needed facilities. While the schools and other buildings exist in abundance, each state DDA must sign many contracts with many institutions to gain access.[56] There is also the matter of arranging an official presence at each site for the holiday. Citizens will be spending an entire day—not just a few minutes—on the premises. As a consequence, the mix of talents required to run Deliberation Day will be quite different from those required on Election Day. There will be more personal flare-ups calling for tactful resolution or decisive action, and much more effort needed to prepare the facility for deliberation, supervise operation during the holiday, and return the property to normal use afterward.

No small task. As a consequence, our budget calls for a substantial staff, headed by the school's principal, that includes teachers, policemen, cafeteria workers, school bus drivers, custodial workers, and some volunteers from civic organizations. Since this is a holiday, all will be paid at overtime rates. One aspect of this complex enterprise is worth singling out—since it will call upon the DDAs to discharge a particularly delicate task. Recall the set-up of the citizen-assemblies: each five hundred–member body requires the selection of a moderator to preside impartially over the debates between representatives of the rival political parties. The appointment of these moderators is a key function—which the DDA should coordinate but not exercise on its own. If given unilateral power over the appointment of moderators, the DDA would be a tempting target for partisan takeover by a political party wishing to slant Deliberation Day in its direction. Since its credibility is at stake, each state DDA should reach out to civil society to discharge this function. Depending on the local context, the best choice might be a nonpartisan body like the League of Women Voters or a state or local bar association. That body, and not the DDA itself, should supply the need for moderators by nominating community leaders with an established reputation for fairness.

We are dealing with a major and multifaceted initiative—but not one that outstrips the operational capacities of the modern state. Everyday government involves the successful implementation of far more formidable tasks—for starters, think of schools, armies, and the Environmental Protection Agency. Other initiatives resemble DDay in requiring lots of personnel for brief periods of time—think of the census or disaster relief. There is no reason to suppose that government, in cooperation with the private sector, can't handle the distinctive challenges of DDay.

Summing Up

There will be substantial start-up costs, and some blunders in the early days. But hopefully, these will be forgiven—Deliberation Day won't get off the ground without a groundswell of popular support, and this renewed commitment to popular sovereignty should survive despite the failure of some states and localities to follow through effectively the first time around. After a couple of shakedown cruises, the process should begin to settle down as schools and other sites get accustomed to their DDay routines. Despite the novelty of the enterprise, we estimate in Appendix A the costs of each main component of the enterprise after the shakedown period. The hard-edged numbers we assign to each activity shouldn't be taken too seriously, but they do provide a sense of the orders of magnitude involved. For now, it will be enough to review the main points in our argument.

The most important is our decision to appropriate an existing holiday for Deliberation Day. This allows us to eliminate two big-ticket items from our cost estimates. Since facilities are already vacant, there is no resource cost in using them. Since Americans are already taking Presidents Day off, our invitation to deliberate does not involve a loss of the economic product of an ordinary day's work. These are crucial points— if we had proposed a brand new holiday, these items would have added up to dollar sums in the tens of billions.

The costs that remain seem much smaller, if only by comparison. Divide them into two broad categories. The first involves the management of individual facilities—preparing the buildings for DDay, running the school bus system to pick up people without cars, welcoming citizens in the morning, assigning them to rooms, intervening to maintain order, providing lunch, and checking out deliberators at the end of the day.

Some of this work might be discharged by volunteers — citizens willing to show up early and greet the crowd and stay late to help with the processing of stipends while spending 9 to 5 talking with their fellow deliberators. But we have provided for a substantial corps of paid administrators, police, and workers to get the job done.

The second set of tasks involve long-term planning: arranging for facilities and workers for the next holiday, developing the reservation system that links citizens to sites, establishing ongoing relations with the civic organizations that name moderators, and so forth. This requires the establishment of a permanent, but small, bureaucracy in each state and on the national level.

Most of the costs in the first category will increase with DDay turnout; many in the second will not. Appendix A puts them all together and suggests that a DDay with thirty million participants will cost about $1.25 billion dollars, moving to $2.5 billion as attendance reaches the seventy million mark.

To gain a sense of proportion: During the 2000 electoral cycle, the administrative costs of running national elections were about $1 billion.[57] An additional $3 billion was spent by all candidates for federal office.[58] Since most of this money is spent on sound bites, it seems only fair to spend a comparable sum to give the voters a chance to talk back — especially when DDay will also improve the way candidates spend their $3 billion dollars during their own campaigns. Or again: In 1999 the country's automakers spent $13 billion on advertising their wares. We do not begrudge their efforts to convince the public of the superior merit of Ford or Chevrolet, but the disproportion suggests the extraordinary skew of the communications stream away from politics and toward commerce — indeed, all television advertising in 1999 added up to $66 billion.[59] And these amounts are spent every year, while Deliberation Day will be celebrated (initially) only one year in four!

Or again: Reflect on the present imbalance of expenditure in existing governmental budgets, both state and national. Tucked away among trillions of dollars of expenditure are derisory sums devoted to the electoral process. As the recent election fiasco between Bush and Gore revealed, even vote counting is underfunded. From a democratic perspective, it is absolutely fundamental to identify electoral winners; and yet as a budgetary matter, it is treated as a matter of tertiary importance, far less important than upgrading roads between major cities, or even minor towns.

It is easy to work up an interest-group explanation for this sorry state of affairs. There are well-organized lobbies interested in pumping up highway budgets — construction companies, labor unions, trucking firms. But there is no similar lobby agitating for near-perfect vote counts. Before a close election, neither political party knows whether it will win or lose by a more accurate count; and after the election, heavy investments in counting technologies will never arrive in time to fix the immediate problem. And so politicians are content to muddle along without spending a lot of money. The low expenditures reflect not the status of the electoral process within the system but the absence of a compelling practical reason for serious budgetary action. Only a groundswell of public concern will change the existing calculus, but perhaps the time is coming?

The Florida fiasco of 2000 has already led Congress to authorize significant sums for a real improvement in vote-counting technology. The same Congress enacted the first significant reform of campaign finance in a generation. The new McCain-Feingold law is only a modest step, but it would never have been enacted without sustained popular support that finally overwhelmed the status quo.[60]

DDay invites Americans to take the next step. Even if the next round of campaign finance reform makes real progress in reducing the power of big money, it won't change the overwhelming role of the sound bite in American political life. At best, it will reduce the number of sound bites favored by the rich and increase those expressing the concerns of the rest of us. Only something like DDay gives the country a chance to move beyond sound-bite democracy.

Americans may well reject our initiative, but they should not do so because of its economic costs. The question is whether ordinary people can convince themselves that popular sovereignty has a future in America, and that it remains possible to take back control over politics by constructing a new place for face-to-face dialogue. If Americans retain their democratic faith, they will find the economic costs easy to accept; if they give it up, much more than Deliberation Day is at stake.

PART

DELIBERATION AND DEMOCRACY

7

THE PROBLEM OF MASS DEMOCRACY

We have been pursuing our project in a distinctive spirit — the spirit of realistic idealism. In Part I we put realism first: There we aimed to convince you that DDay was no pipe dream but an entirely doable project. Taking citizens as they are, and without revolutionizing society as a whole, it is entirely practical to build deeper foundations for a more vibrant democratic life.

Having made our pragmatic case, we turn to the idealistic side of the argument. Nothing like DDay is on the political agenda of any serious movement in the world today. Many progressives campaign for a fairer distribution of wealth and income; they insist on racial and gender equality; but not a single political party places a high priority on deepening the deliberative character of political life. If DDay is such a good idea, why hasn't anybody thought of it before?

Because our proposal challenges a historically entrenched prejudice that limits the collective imagination. Since the eighteenth century, modern political thought has declared its intellectual independence from classical Greek understandings of democratic life. So far as the ancients were concerned, democracy was a face-to-face affair of city-states. Aristotle famously doubted that a genuine democracy could survive if its citizens couldn't hear each other's voices in a common assembly.[1] If this were right, democracy would be an anachronism in the modern world, where nation-states embrace millions, even billions, within their territories. Before democracy could become a credible ideal for the modern age, there was a need for a radical reconstruction of the Greek understanding. The intellectual process was long and complex, and culminated in the eighteenth century. By this point, the classical notion of face-to-face democracy had been displaced by the Enlightenment theory of representative government.[2]

After two centuries, this idea is so familiar that it blocks creative thinking. When we speak of "democracy," we no longer expect ordinary people to deliberate seriously before delegating the task of government to elected politicians. Only these political professionals have the time and energy to weigh the complex of facts, interests, and values called into question by modern legislation.

Little wonder, then, that Deliberation Day isn't on anybody's reform agenda. At first glance, our proposal seems to recall an obsolete notion of democracy. With even the New England town meeting in terminal decline, isn't it more than a little quixotic to propose a massive new initiative in face-to-face political engagement?[3]

To frame a cogent reply, distinguish face-to-face *democracy* from face-to-face *deliberation*. Our new civic holiday does not require the people to make final decisions, as they sometimes did in ancient Athens or Renaissance Florence. It simply asks them to choose candidates for office in a more focused and considered fashion. After citizens discuss candidates on Deliberation Day, they still delegate the task of ultimate decision making to the man or woman who emerges victorious on Election Day.[4]

We are not seeking a return to the imaginary glories of the city-state. We are trying to strengthen the modern system of representative democracy. This is why we have repeatedly asked how the law of anticipated reaction shapes the behavior of politicians seeking public office. By taking up this perspective, we could explore the complex ways in which DDay reshaped political incentives — pushing politicians to move beyond sound bites in their campaigns and rewarding them for public-spirited decision making while in office. These claims did not depend on a misplaced nostalgia for the New England town meeting. They were grounded on a commonsense appreciation of the dynamics of representative government, and the way it will respond to the prospect of a more thoughtful and engaged citizenry.

In this chapter we elaborate on our basic point by placing it in historical perspective. Over the past two centuries, Americans have proposed many new schemes to engage ordinary citizens in especially focused debate and deliberation. But two stand out as especially relevant. In the late eighteenth century, the Founding Federalists made a remarkable effort to include ordinary citizens in the debate over ratification of their proposed Constitution. A century later, the Progressives made active citizen engagement a centerpiece of their campaign for constitutional reform. What can be learned from these initiatives? How does DDay build on the strengths, and avoid the mistakes, of the past?

Our argument takes a contemporary turn in succeeding chapters. We begin by locating our proposal within the growing concern, expressed by Robert Putnam and many others, with the social foundations of democratic life. Putnam is right to emphasize the importance of ongoing social networks in building up "social capital" that democracies need to function. We explore how DDay builds on his insight, but also why social capital isn't enough to assure a responsive democracy. Something more is required: DDay helps build a distinctive form of "political capital" that provides a crucial resource for political dialogue. Without this step, democratic ideals may ring hollow under twenty-first-century conditions.

We then proceed to explore our contemporary ideals more carefully. Liberal democracy is a confusing cluster of ideals and understandings. We consider three tension-ridden value clusters broadly shared in the West. To what extent might DDay contribute to the fuller realization of our democratic hopes?

The first value cluster centers on economic inequality, the second on the activist regulatory state, the third on unresolved tensions between ideals of equality, deliberation, and participation. DDay hardly provides the definitive solution to any of these problems. But it does contribute something valuable in the ongoing effort to confront them.

The final chapter marks a return from theory to practice. We have been arguing for a change in the existing system, but the system is already changing—and for the worse. We have already pointed to the rise of media marketing and opinion manipulation in our politics. We propose to fill out this sketch to clarify the real choice confronting democracies in the twenty-first century. It is one thing to reject the novel prospect of DDay if the alternative were the status quo—which at least has the virtue of familiarity. But if there is a grimmer prospect before us, the question takes on a different, and more exigent, form: Should we take self-conscious steps to deepen the deliberative foundations of contemporary politics or allow marketing experts to degrade it further through hot-button sound bites and demagogic appeals?

Normal Politics/Constitutional Politics

We are writing during a period of normal politics: a time when most ordinary people aren't spending much of their energy on their concerns as citizens. Professional politicians dominate center stage, small armies of activists campaign for one or another cause, but the mass of private citizens are content to kibitz on the sidelines, without taking the time to consider thoughtfully the major issues that divide the contesting parties. The tragedy of September 11 has generated a great deal of flag-waving but has not changed this basic reality. For the moment, at least, the terrorist attacks have unleashed a bureaucratic politics of national security, leaving average citizens in the dark about the meaning of it all.

This is undoubtedly the standard condition of modern life, but it is a mistake to project it indefinitely into the trackless future. During the past two centuries of American history, normal politics has been disrupted repeatedly by a politics of mass mobilization. Rising movements of ordinary men and women burst onto the scene to support the demands for fundamental change voiced by new leaders who challenge politics-as-usual.

There are places in the world where disruptive mass politics is abhorred as a civic calamity.[5] But this isn't true in the United States. While mass mobilizations have regularly generated vast anxieties, they have also served to energize the construction of the most enduring political achievements. America was born out of a mass revolutionary movement for independence, led by the very same men who campaigned for the Constitution. And the Framers' success in gaining popular ratification of the Constitution of 1787 established a model for later generations.

Call it the model of constitutional politics: It is one thing for a mass movement to disrupt the patterns of normal politics; it is quite another for it to gain the deliberate support of a majority for constructive new initiatives. Nevertheless, eighteenth-century Americans managed to succeed in taking this tricky second step, and succeeding generations have followed the Founders in making the awkward transition from disruptive agitation to deliberate political construction.

During the nineteenth century, the greatest example of constitutional politics came after the Civil War. There was nothing inevitable about translating the agonies of bloody battle into new constitutional commitments to racial equality. And yet Americans managed to use wartime passions to fuel an intense popular debate that ultimately generated enduring constitutional principles.

A similar pattern recurs throughout the twentieth century—though war has not been as central. Time after time, mass movements have managed to use their political energies to engage the broader public in deliberate acts of political affirmation. For example, the Women's Suffrage Amendment is unthinkable without the women's movement; the New Deal without the labor movement; the Civil Rights Acts without the civil rights movement.[6]

During these periods of heightened engagement, most Americans continue to spend the bulk of their time and energy in the pursuit of self-interest. Nevertheless, there is a perceptible shift in the balance between private and public concerns.[7] The proportion of political activists increases, and ordinary citizens are more willing to step up their levels of engagement—writing letters, organizing meetings, marching on Washington, mobilizing for decisive shows of political strength. As this dynamic proceeds, the movement's diagnosis of the leading issues will resonate far more broadly in everyday conversations—generating billions of questions, answers, and counterarguments over time.

It isn't enough, then, to consider how DDay might operate during normal politics, when most citizens are functioning at relatively low levels of interest and information. We must also consider how our new holiday might operate under the more excited conditions of constitutional politics.

Our inquiry proceeds by setting up a dialogue with two great movements of constitutional reform in American history. We begin with the eighteenth-century Founders, whose greatest texts contain valuable reflections on our problem. The Federalist Papers proposes a dualistic analysis of mass public opinion. It strongly favors affirmative steps to involve the broad citizenry in focused acts of deliberation during rare periods of constitutional politics. But it is skeptical about undertaking similar efforts during normal politics.

We turn next to the Progressives of the early twentieth century, who challenged the Founders' refusal to carve out special spaces for focused deliberation during periods of normal politics. For present purposes, the Progressives' most revealing reform was the "citizen initiative"—a procedure that enables activists to push their reform proposals onto the ballot for direct consideration by the voters. Many American states have adopted this reform, and we now have a century's experience with its operation. This history suggests that the Progressives didn't do a good job confronting the distinctive challenges of organizing popular deliberation during normal politics. They ignored the social context that might facilitate the kind of serious public dialogue that would make initiatives meaningful. At the same time, we can learn from these historical mistakes and show how DDay can more successfully realize Progressive hopes for effective citizenship during normal politics.

We then turn to the special problems of constitutional politics, characterized by excited conditions of mass mobilization. Here it is the Founders who were overly optimistic about the prospect of broad-ranging deliberation at these moments of high passion. How might DDay help fill this hole in Founding thought, and make popular deliberation a significant reality during moments of constitutional politics?

The Founders' First Step

Two centuries onward, the constitutional convention at Philadelphia is often viewed as an assemblage of bewigged gentlemen with reactionary views on race, women, and private property. All this is true, but anachronistic: the British Loyalists were no less conservative on these social and economic matters. Where the Framers stand out was in their revolutionary nationalism—they had earned their claims to leadership by standing up for America, and mobilizing a mass movement for independence over a decade of armed struggle. George Washington was reluctant to come to Philadelphia and chair the Constitutional Convention, but he was convinced that his presence was absolutely essential for success—

public endorsement by this revolutionary warrior served as a signal to his enormous following to mobilize for another round of popular agitation in support of the new constitutional initiative.

Washington's support was especially crucial because the convention was intent on a radical extension of its revolutionary nationalism. Its initiative created a powerful central government that took away many large powers from the states. Centralization not only offended local loyalties. It flouted the conventional view that large republics inevitably degenerated into bureaucratic tyrannies. The leading Framers were quite candid in confessing that their new-modeled government shattered past precedents. Here is Madison in the Federalist Papers:

> Hearken not to the unnatural voice which tells you that the people of America . . . can no longer be fellow-citizens of one great, respectable, and flourishing empire. Hearken not to the voice which petulantly tells you that the form of government recommended for your adoption is a novelty in the political world; that it rashly attempts what it is impossible to accomplish. . . . Why is the experiment of an extended republic to be rejected merely because it may comprise what is new?[8]

We are all too familiar with this kind of revolutionary vanguardism, and the disastrous consolidation of power which it has so often permitted. But here is where the Founders truly distinguished themselves. Despite Washington's status as revolutionary war hero, he didn't have the slightest interest in using force to impose the new Constitution on the general population. The Philadelphia Convention broke new ground in designing a special procedure requiring focused dialogue and sustained deliberation from the general public before its Constitution could be validated in the name of We the People of the United States.

One part of the Founding system is relatively familiar. After the Constitution was proposed in Philadelphia, the text was submitted to special ratifying conventions in each state. The Constitution would achieve legal validity only if nine conventions approved. These extraordinary assemblies understood their task in deliberative terms. They were not mere rubber stamps of the statesmen who sat at Philadelphia, nor of the voters who elected them. Each state convention put the proposed Constitution to the test of focused deliberation before voting it up or down.[9]

There was a second, and less remarked, aspect of the Founding process. Each of the states set up a special election day for selecting convention delegates — no other offices were up for consideration at the same time. As a consequence, the public mind could not be diverted to electoral races for other positions. The convention delegates were focusing on a single issue: the merits of the proposed Constitution. Rivals could not deflect discussion onto other matters. This precedent-breaking effort aimed to concentrate the public mind and focus deliberation on the great constitutional issues at stake.

It proved extraordinarily productive. Two centuries onward, judges and scholars still consult the Federalist Papers — a collection of newspaper articles by Madison, Hamilton, and John Jay written as part of the special election campaign in New York. These famous essays were a tiny part of the remarkable outpouring from the infant nation's printing presses. The massive popular literature provoked by the special elections serve as a standing rebuke to government by sound bite.[10]

Putting the two parts of the process together, the Founding procedure was doubly deliberative: the Constitution could gain ratification only if it survived first the popular debate during the campaign for delegates, and then the delegates' debate at the ratifying conventions. Not for nothing did Hamilton begin the Federalist Papers with the proud claim: "It . . . seems to have been reserved to the people of this country . . . to decide the important question, whether societies of men are really capable or not, of establishing good government from reflection and choice, or whether they are forever destined to depend, for their political constitutions, on accident and force."[11]

It's easy for twenty-first-century readers to recognize how this bold claim fell short. Hamilton's boast is mocked by the exclusion of women and slaves from the franchise. Worse yet, voter turnout was distinctly underwhelming. While the outpouring from the printing presses was impressive, voters did not come out in droves at the special election. Even the quality of deliberation at the ratifying conventions was uneven — only some states actually achieved the sustained levels of constitutional dialogue that popular myth attaches to the Founding.[12]

All these failures in execution are important, but they should not obliterate the distinctive character of the Founders' achievement. World history is littered by the efforts of revolutionary leaders to use force to impose their political will upon a reluctant nation. For all their shortfalls, the American Founders were the first to glimpse the possibility of a better way—designing novel institutions that invited ordinary voters, as well as their representatives, to join in a specially focused and sustained deliberative enterprise.

This is the thread that links the Founding to Deliberation Day. We shall be elaborating this connection further, but we begin with a key difference. We propose to make DDay a regular part of presidential and congressional elections. In contrast, the Founders believed that special efforts to catalyze a broad-based and focused debate should be relatively rare events. Here is Madison explaining why:

> Notwithstanding the success which has attended the revisions of our established forms of government, . . . it must be confessed that the experiments are of too ticklish a nature to be unnecessarily multiplied. We are to recollect that all the existing [state] constitutions were formed in the midst of a danger which repressed the passions most unfriendly to order and concord; of an enthusiastic confidence of people in their patriotic leaders, which stifled the ordinary diversity of opinions on great national questions; of a universal ardor for new and opposite forms produced by a universal resentment and indignation against the ancient government; and whilst no spirit of party connected with the changes to be made, or the abuses to be reformed. The future situations in which we must expect to be usually placed do not present any equivalent security against the danger which is apprehended.[13]

Once again, Madison is presenting himself as the proud head of a revolutionary movement. He does not fear popular agitation and mobilization. His concern is what happens in its absence. In his view, constructive popular deliberation can occur *only* after a mass movement generates "enthusiastic confidence" in revolutionary leaders, stifling "the ordinary diversity of opinion." The public mind is concentrated further by evident danger to the collective welfare—in this case posed by the British invaders. The ominous threat from the king has helped "repress the passions" and created "universal resentment" against established forms of government. Mass mobilization at a time of danger enables ordinary citizens to put aside the narrow "spirit of party" and deliberate soberly on political fundamentals. Collective mobilization + dangerous crisis = Madison's formula for broad-based popular deliberation in constitutional politics.[14]

This is the point where Madison's thinking takes a darkly paradoxical turn: If the Federalists use their constitutional moment to win deliberate consent from the People, their very triumph will make it unwise to invite further exercises in focused mass deliberation. By stabilizing political life, the new Constitution will ease the sense of crisis that suppressed passion and faction. The mass movement that fought for the revolution and endorsed the constitution will slowly disintegrate, and the citizenry will retreat from public-spirited engagement to more selfish pursuits.

To be sure, Madison recognizes that future crises may arise that will call Americans to take up the challenge of constitutional politics. But in more ordinary times, he expects the attention of ordinary citizens to waver, and factions to thrive. Rather than seeking to reengage voters in focused civic conversation, he counts on elected representatives to take up the slack. The overriding aim of the 1787 Constitution is to govern this depressing world of *normal politics,* where mass movements of concerned citizens are conspicuous by their absence. The constitutional challenge is to give representatives incentives to "refine" public sentiment, to encourage them to enact better laws than those favored by ordinary voters who haven't given the issues sustained consideration.[15]

But why does Madison think that elected representatives are up to this formidable task? Isn't it more likely that they will take advantage of their constituents' apathy and pander to their selfishness? Madison recognizes that this will happen sometimes—"Enlightened statesmen will not always be at the helm"[16]—but he remains cautiously optimistic. His principal argument relies on the enormous size of the new Republic. Each federal representative will come from a large district, and this fact alone will give civic-minded members of the social elite a powerful electoral advantage. Madison thinks that the only candidates who can win in these big districts will be gentlemen who have generated far-flung reputations for civic virtue. Although local politicos might win the votes of particular communities through their petty dealings, they can't compete effectively with the Madisons and Washingtons on the larger stage of federal politics. With notables gaining election to the nation's highest offices, the people's representatives will do a better job than their constituents in refining the popular will through public-spirited deliberation. Although sustained popular deliberation was essential in constitutional politics, Madison denies it an equivalent role in normal politics.

The omission did not go unnoticed at the time. Thomas Jefferson considered it the single greatest failing in the Founding design. His writings contain ingenious proposals for integrating a dense network of face-to-face deliberative assemblies into the Founding scheme.[17] But Jefferson was ambassador to Paris at the time of the Convention, and his concerns were never taken seriously in Philadelphia. So the Founders took no more than a first step toward creating special institutions for mass deliberation. But first steps are important — and in creating special deliberative procedures for constitutional ratification, the Founders blazed a trail for others to follow.

The Progressive Critique

During the early twentieth century, the Progressives carved out new spaces for public deliberation. In contrast to the Founders, they sought to make these new procedures available to citizens all the time and did not reserve them for the specially mobilized conditions of constitutional politics. So far as they were concerned, political developments during the nineteenth century offered new reasons to criticize Madison's faith in the "refining" capacities of elected representatives. And if Madison was wrong in relying so heavily on representatives, it only made sense to create new avenues for political deliberation by ordinary citizens.

To prepare the ground for the Progressive critique, consider that Madison's confidence in political elites was a contingent product of his own concrete experience. Modern political parties did not exist in his eighteenth-century world. Leading members of the upper class could win elections without competing with professional politicians who had the support of well-organized political parties. They could also manage their own campaigns without manipulating a complex communications system. During early elections, candidates for Congress typically stated their views in a single letter published in the local newspaper, and left the rest to their friends, relations, and economic dependents. Within this setting, Madison's confidence in the capacity of representatives to "refine" the public will made practical political sense. Each upper-class gentleman could count on his particular social network to deliver the vote within his geographic zone of influence, but something more was required to gain support in large federal voting districts. Without the support of mass media and party professionals, members of the elite with well-established reputations for public service had an advantage in projecting their names before this broader public. Once elected to office, these large-souled patricians might well take their deliberative responsibilities seriously.

But Madison's vision of representative government was dependent on special historical conditions — which were swept away by the rise of mass political parties.[18] As the nineteenth century rolled on, the political stage was increasingly dominated by professionals who owed their electoral victories to their mastery of the nuts-and-bolts of party organization. Many of them were party hacks who would respond in disbelief to the Madisonian suggestion that their principal task was to refine, rather than gratify, the desires of their constituents.

The social and economic elite did not disappear. As they were pushed to the sidelines of electoral politics, they were increasingly obliged to exercise their influence indirectly. Some public-spirited types campaigned for civil-service reform and tried to find a place in the executive branch. But most pursued their political interest through economic means — bankrolling parties, and when pressed, corrupting politicians. If Madison had been magically transported to the Gilded Age at the end of the nineteenth century, he would have had a hard time maintaining his Founding faith in the statesmanship of politicians during periods of normal politics. It is no surprise, then, that Progressive reformers mounted a frontal challenge to Madisonian premises.

They did not entirely despair of representative government. To the contrary, the early twentieth century brought a series of formidable efforts to clean up the corruption of patronage machines and replace it with a new style of reform politics. But at the same time, the Progressives proposed a series of structural changes that would allow ordinary voters to intervene decisively when their political representatives went astray.

The most significant, for our purposes, was the popular initiative. While the Progressives ultimately failed to get their proposal enacted at the federal level, it was adopted in many American states. The basic idea is simple: When citizens don't like what their representatives are doing, they can get together and place their own proposal before the voters on Election Day. If their initiative is endorsed by a majority at the polls, it gets enacted—sometimes gaining the lofty status of a constitutional amendment.

The citizen initiative poses a challenge to Madison's faith in elected representatives, but it pays to clarify the precise relation between Founding and Progressive ideas. As we have seen, the Founders were not opposed to all efforts to reach out to ordinary voters and engage them in special forms of deliberation and decision. They simply wanted to reserve such appeals to the People for rare moments of constitutional politics generated by sustained popular mobilization in response to a dangerous crisis. Only then could the public mind constructively deliberate on fundamental political choices.

The Progressives rejected this narrow view. They wanted citizens to get their proposals on the ballot whenever they could persuade a small minority of voters to sign petitions in support of their initiatives.[19] The crucial question, of course, is whether this extension from constitutional politics to normal politics has proved successful.

Experience has been decidedly mixed. One key problem has been devising an appropriate threshold that a group must satisfy before it can gain access to the ballot. The more signatures a group must collect on its petitions, the more expensive it is to leap over the threshold. With costs rising into the millions, well-organized business interests often find it easier to collect the requisite signatures than do citizen groups.[20]

This economic differential is particularly troubling, since the Progressives were trying to break the power of big business over the legislative agenda in state capitols. This doesn't render their reform entirely useless—citizen groups can also make it past the signature threshold on matters of broad concern. But it does exacerbate another big problem, and one central for our purposes.

Call it the problem of effective communication. Since initiatives are intended to operate as laws, they can't be framed in layman's language. This places great strain on the capacity of ordinary citizens to know what they are voting on. The states respond to this obvious problem in obvious ways. Before the election, they circulate official booklets containing brief arguments — pro and con — prepared by leading protagonists. And when citizens enter the voting booth, they encounter a short and simple description of each proposal's legal complexities. The simplicity is necessarily misleading — a short paragraph on the ballot cannot possibly serve as a reliable guide to the legal jungle hidden beneath the surface. As a consequence, proponents make heroic efforts to spin their voting booth "simplifications" in ways that make their initiatives seem more attractive than they really are — while opponents cry foul and try to persuade election officials and judges to make hurried efforts to police the blurry line between simplification and deception.

This bobbing and weaving is surrounded by a swirl of media hype. So far as Madison Avenue is concerned, there isn't a lot of difference between advertising a candidate and touting an initiative. Groups on both sides engage in the same kind of focus-group search for hot-button formulas that can be exploited in ten-second sound bites. All this costs lots of money — further exacerbating the economic advantage of rich business groups.

There is an even more serious problem. The resulting cacophony simply overwhelms the cognitive capacities of the most conscientious citizens. It would be tough enough to penetrate the haze if only one initiative were on the ballot; but the task becomes impossible when the ballot is cluttered with a host of proposals on a bewildering variety of subjects. Voters in Oregon, for example, were asked their opinion on eighteen initiatives at the 2000 election.[21] As if this weren't enough, voters were also asked to cast a ballot for president and other important offices. They would be foolish to divert much of their limited time and energy away from these candidate races and carefully study the complexities of proposed initiatives.

For all its deficiencies, the initiative may serve as a useful supplementary technique in the overall operation of democratic government — reasonable people can reasonably disagree on both relevant facts and values.[22]

Only one thing is clear — the great Progressive hopes for the device have been shattered by a century's experience. The reformers didn't think they were making a small improvement. They were aiming to pour new meaning into the democratic experience. They envisioned ordinary people carving out a special space for serious public deliberation, hammering out sensible solutions to pressing problems, and intervening decisively to shape the future course of politics.

They not only expected their shiny new tool to fashion better public policy. They hoped it would lead ordinary Americans to a renewed confidence in themselves as self-governing citizens, engaging in decisive action after reasoned argument. The sad truth is that, a hundred years down the line, the Progressives merely managed to create another forum for the manipulation of sound bites — generating outcomes that are sometimes better, sometimes worse, than the legislative system of lawmaking that it seeks to challenge.

The Progressives' Mistake

Where, precisely, did the Progressives go wrong?

It is easy to supply a sweeping diagnosis. On this neo-Madisonian view, the entire effort simply was blind to some obvious truths about normal politics. *Of course,* most Americans aren't paying attention most of the time; *of course,* selfish interest groups will try to exploit this fact; *of course,* the initiative will fail to express the considered judgments of ordinary citizens. Americans will awake from their civic slumber only when some large danger looms that prompts mass mobilization. Pretending otherwise won't help. It will only result in the creation of new legal forms that will invariably disappoint in practice.

We think this pessimism is overdrawn. Neo-Madisonians are undoubtedly right to emphasize that ordinary people won't spontaneously organize to deliberate successfully under normal political conditions. But it doesn't follow that nothing can be done to correct this situation. Perhaps the Progressives' mistake is less profound, more remediable. Perhaps they simply used the wrong strategy to achieve their objectives.

This is, at any rate, our view of the matter. We think the Progressives made a common mistake, especially common in America. They put too much confidence in legal formalisms to achieve their objectives. They simply created a new legal avenue to power—the "citizen initiative"—and expected ordinary people to do the rest. We are proposing something more far-reaching: not a new legal form, but a new social context. Serious deliberation will become a living reality in normal politics only within a social setting that effectively motivates ordinary people and that media merchants find tough to colonize.

This is the point of Deliberation Day. The Progressives made a very small step toward creating the right social context by requiring state governments to distribute a pamphlet to each voter shortly before the election. These pamphlets contain short statements—pro and con—that argue the merits of each proposal. When the pamphlet arrives in the mail, the hope is that people will read it and discuss it with their friends—and not throw it out with the weekly trash.

We employ a similar device on DDay—recall that participants receive a short statement presenting each candidate's position on the leading national issues. But this piece of paper plays a small part in the overall design. Our overriding aim is to provide a social context in which ordinary citizens can interrogate such "top-down" communications in ways that makes sense to them.

The real work at DDay begins after small-group members watch the initial television debate. As they define unanswered questions, and ponder the responses of local party representatives, they move beyond top-down communication and engage in the serious bottom-up enterprise of self-government. Question and answer, back and forth, hour after hour: The exercise of public reason is a social activity on Deliberation Day.

We take citizens as they are, not as they are supposed to be. We don't mail them a pamphlet and expect them to assess the countless controversial statements swirling around a bewildering variety of proposed initiatives. This is a recipe for cognitive overload. And once citizens throw the official pamphlet into the trash, they remain at the mercy of advertising blitzes that reward big money and clever phrasing.

To provide a sensible context for real political learning, DDay focuses on a relatively small number of issues. It invites ordinary men and women to ask questions without pretending that they already have the answers.

Rather than relying on sound bites, citizens mull over the responses of local opinion leaders within a framework that gives a fair chance to both sides.

Encouraging citizens to address the leading issues from different angles, this process of collective engagement can't help but have a significant impact. As we have seen,[23] many participants will come into the proceedings with little or no acquaintance with the issues under the searchlight. After their multifaceted exposure to the (contested) facts of the matter, they will be in a far better position to understand how their basic values are implicated in the concrete disputes that divide the parties in the forthcoming election. They may even come to a deeper appreciation of the other side's arguments.

We are not searching for miracles. Nor do we suppose that we can create an active citizenry out of nothing. But evidence from Deliberative Polls establishes that ordinary people *do* have the capacity and the will to engage in the deliberative enterprise. The challenge is to create a social context within which millions, and not only hundreds, have the realistic opportunity to fulfill their civic responsibilities in a thoughtful way. Without the invention of new social contexts, the Progressive ideal of active citizenship will be mocked by the countervailing dynamics of the political marketplace.

Constitutional Politics

This book has been focusing on the pathologies of normal politics — and for good reason. Major innovations like Deliberation Day make sense only when there is a serious problem in the here-and-now: "If it ain't broke, don't fix it." Our central task is to convince you that the existing system *is* broke. Without giving ordinary citizens new tools to challenge sound-bite politics, we confront a clear and present danger: Political elites, and their media merchants, will increasingly escape from real accountability at election time. We face the prospect of Election Day rituals stripped of real democratic substance. If you aren't convinced of this, you will never endorse Deliberation Day.

Nevertheless, our historical exercise suggests the limits of a presentist perspective. If the future is anything like the past, a time will come when the existing system of normal politics will once more be challenged by rising mass movements. And a sober assessment of our initiative should take this prospect into account. Although DDay may seem a sensible remedy for present-day pathologies, perhaps this evaluation changes as one looks to the longer run?

Unfortunately, this question invites lots of crystal ball gazing. Mass movements can take many shapes, respond to many problems, and struggle for radically different political visions. To fix ideas, we will elaborate variations on a single scenario that may, or may not, be in our future. Even if real-world politics take a very different turn, our thought-experiments should serve to highlight some salient institutional possibilities.[24]

So take a ride on our personal time machine: Destination, the year 2020. We are happy to report that DDay is now part of the nation's election year ritual. But a lot more has happened. The past two decades have generated a massive increase in environmental consciousness that has given rise to a broad-based and politically aggressive Green movement. As the presidential election of 2020 approaches, the Green leadership seeks to use DDay to achieve a decisive breakthrough. Leading spokesmen *demand* that the major-party candidates recognize the environmental crisis as one of the nation's leading issues.[25]

The candidates respond by doing what comes naturally: They consult with their favorite pollsters before coming up with a final answer. Given the strategic importance of the decision, neither side contents itself with the standard polls of the early twenty-first century. Instead, they conduct their own private versions of Deliberative Polls that simulate likely public reaction on DDay. At various spots in the country, Democrats and Republicans assemble five hundred-person groups and put them through DDay routines. After analyzing the data, the consultants return to their respective campaigns with grave faces and loud warnings: Both candidates run a grave risk if they focus attention on the environment. Average Americans share a growing sense of an environmental crisis, but the distribution of informed opinion poses real risks to each side's coalition. Given these dangers, it's safer to ignore the activists' superheated demands and focus DDay on other topics.

After mulling over their pollsters' reports, both candidates play it safe. When the time comes to specify the Leading National Issues for DDay,

they seek to divert the collective conversation down tracks that their consultants consider more winnable — the Democrats focusing on social security and health care, the Republicans on a tax cut and military defense.

But the candidates don't have a monopoly over the DDay agenda. Citizens have the perfect freedom to raise questions on their own, and to
require party representatives to answer them in the five hundred–citizen
assemblies held throughout the land. The next move is up to the enviro-
leadership: Should it react to the candidates' effort to shut them out by
organizing a massive movement of their followers: "Don't let the professional politicians go on with business as usual. It is time for citizens to
take charge of DDay and confront the looming environmental crisis.
After the politicos talk about *their* issues on the morning telecast, all serious citizens should insist on changing the subject and focus the rest of
D-Day on the *real* problem facing the country."

The prospect is tempting, but dangers lurk: What if the Green leadership makes a maximum effort and the movement fizzles on DDay? Won't
such a fiasco demonstrate that normal folk aren't really interested in the
so-called crisis? Isn't it safer to downplay the significance of DDay and
avoid an embarrassing failure the day after?

In weighing its options, the movement leadership will reflect on experience at prior DDays. Even during normal politics, the enviros — and many
other groups — have been trying to educate the broader public by encouraging partisans to raise questions about the environment for consideration
on DDay. As a result, environmental activists have already provoked discussion of their issues in hundreds, perhaps thousands, of citizen assemblies from time to time. By this point, however, the environmental movement has become a truly massive political reality — strong enough to
mount a broad-based challenge to the professional politicians' definition
of the leading issues. With millions of mobilized citizens raising environmental questions, the "environmental crisis" might serve as a principal
focus for community conversation throughout the land. Suppose the leadership decides that the time is ripe for a maximal effort and calls upon the
movement's partisans to focus all their energies on DDay. What next?

We have been describing a conjunction that is especially dangerous to
the long-term health of a constitutional system — the political establishment has turned its back on a rising mass movement and refuses to take its

concerns seriously. This cold response can play into the hands of hotheads among the activists: "If the powers-that-be won't listen to us, we must force them to pay attention by taking more radical and violent measures." Such steps, if endorsed by increasing numbers of the movement's leadership and followership, threaten to unleash a cycle of incivility — violence from below breeding violence from above.

DDay allows movement moderates to offer a constructive alternative: "Rather than shouting in the streets, we can move into the citizen assembly halls and effectively challenge the ongoing terms of political debate. Despite the seeming impasse, further dialogue *is* possible."

We emphasize this integrative function because it might not be so obvious on the surface of political life. DDay will be a turbulent affair during periods of constitutional politics. The rising movement's challenge to the establishment agenda may generate large increases in DDay participation, as tens of millions of relatively uninvolved citizens come to the nation's schoolhouses to learn what all this hubbub is all about. Tensions may rise if the movement's activities generate a countermovement: "These so-called environmentalists are trying to destroy the American way of life. Don't let them monopolize the conversation on DDay!"

All this energy may well lead to lots of shouting matches in small groups and citizen assemblies. Extremists may also use DDay as an excuse for organizing violent protests at the fringes. But none of this should divert attention from the integrative character of the event. For all the shouting, DDay will give an opportunity for millions of moderates in the environmental movement to claim a great victory despite the cold response of the political establishment. And it will also permit the vast center of the community to show that it *can* sustain a political conversation on issues of central concern.

The center may not hold at each and every assembly in the country — and the sensationalist media will have a field day reporting the moments of pathological breakdown. But consider the alternative: Without DDay, movement radicals will still be in a position to stage their provocations, but movement moderates will have a tougher time demonstrating the continuing possibilities of constructive dialogue.

To put the point more generally, every mass movement is a jumble of competing tendencies — some more, some less, alienated from the entire political system. A similar schizophrenia afflicts the defenders of the status quo—some will respond to the new rising movement by engaging in dialogue, some by suppressing it with force. When activists and conservatives confront one another, two dynamics are always possible. Violence breeds violence; mutual respect, respect. The friends of violence start with a strategic advantage—they can act unilaterally, and inflame the other side. The friends of mutuality desperately require forums in which both sides can show that they can reason together, even when they disagree. DDay is only one step—but not a small one—down the path toward the civilized outcome, inviting both sides to keep working at the frustrating business of solving common problems.

Of course, a rising movement's agenda may prove *so* provocative that it may utterly fracture the community. It is fatuous to suppose that all problems have institutional solutions. The slavery question precipitated civil war, leaving the talkers to despair on the sidelines. But it is equally fatuous to suppose that institutional structures, and the civic culture they support, don't matter. The Great Depression and the Civil Rights Movement might have degenerated into mindless campaigns of violence without the integrating practices and institutions that were then in place.[26] And while such large mobilizations seem quite distant as we write these words, it is overly complacent to suppose that the country will not have special needs for integrative institutions in the future.

The long-term case for DDay is enhanced by a basic feature of constitutional politics. When a mass movement of energized citizens begins to occupy the center of the political stage, it takes a good deal of time for the political system to resolve the challenges posed by their agenda. Looking back to past cases, a decade or more may elapse as rival contenders for political leadership use a series of elections to appeal for popular support.[27] To explore the implications of this basic point, we develop our scenario further to consider the potential impact of DDay over a series of elections. If the environmentalists prove moderately successful in refashioning the conversational agenda on DDay 2020, how will this affect the shape of political conversation when DDay comes around again in 2022 and 2024?

Suppose that our hypothetical movement has managed to broaden and deepen its popular support further during the interim. Then the candidates for a given office—one or both of them—will have a large incentive to nominate the environmental crisis as one of their own leading issues for the next DDay. By making this decision, the candidate(s) bring the movement's brand of constitutional politics into the very center of the citizenry's deliberations.

This will contribute further to the integration of the popular movement into the system of representative government. But the next DDay may not otherwise fulfill the movement's expectations. Tens of millions of participants will come to the proceedings with many doubts—some will believe that the entire "environmental crisis" has been greatly exaggerated; others may suspect that the proposed solutions are misguided at best, counterproductive at worst. There will be a lot of talk on DDay, and the conversational drift may not be in the movement's direction. If one, but not the other, political party has taken up the environmentalist cause, the pro-Green side may lose the election, and the entire movement may suffer a serious setback. Even if both parties select the environmental crisis as a leading national issue, they will differ on appropriate solutions, and the ensuing DDay conversation may tend to support measures that fail to satisfy many activists—who may bitterly denounce DDay if it diverts public attention away from more radical measures.

But DDay doesn't make its contribution by guaranteeing radicals or reactionaries their favorite outcome. Its focus is process, not substance. Like it or not, the future will bring sweeping transformations in the aspirations and operations of American government. The question is whether these fundamental changes occur after a barrage of sound bites managed from on high or through a broad-based conversation which encourages ordinary citizens to ask their own questions and define their own answers.

Founders, Progressives, Deliberators

We have been engaging in an exercise at historical triangulation. By juxtaposing the Founders with the Progressives, we have been locating ourselves within an ongoing tradition that insists upon active citizenship as the cornerstone of democratic self-government. This is a tradition containing lots of words but few practical ideas. How does our initiative respond to the anxieties and aspirations expressed by leading voices of the past?

Like the practical proposals made at the time of the Founding, DDay tries to channel the high-energy politics of mass mobilization into deliberative channels during constitutional politics. But like the Progressives, we aim to go further and carve out a space for focused deliberation during more normal periods of political life. We don't underestimate the difficulties. Madison was right to point them out, but he was wrong to think they were insuperable. Evidence from Deliberative Polls establishes that ordinary citizens are willing and able to take on the challenge of civic deliberation during ordinary times. But they won't do so in response merely to new legal forms, like the citizen initiative, provided by the Progressives. The challenge is to move beyond legal formalism and create a new social context in which ordinary citizens can engage in meaningful dialogue that makes sense to them, a context that facilitates genuine learning about the choices confronting the political community.

The priority of social context — that is the main contribution Deliberation Day brings to the ongoing tradition of active citizenship. This contribution cuts across other great debates. For example, the Founders treated the principle of representative government as the cornerstone of their constitutionalism. The Progressives were great champions of direct democracy — proposing a host of devices, like the initiative, that aim to give the final say to ordinary voters.[28] DDay provides both sides of this familiar debate with a new and valuable resource.

Begin on the side of direct democracy and recall the Deliberative Poll deployed in connection with Australia's referendum on its constitutional future. The results showed that deliberation made a big difference. The microcosm of Australia gathered in Canberra for a weekend of deliberations massively increased their support for a republic that was independent of the British Crown. By the end of the weekend, the Yes vote moved from 56 percent to 73 percent, a 17-point increase (and one that held up nicely in comparison to a control group that did not deliberate.)[29]

This is the kind of collective decision that will shape Australian political life for a long time — wouldn't it have been worthwhile to call a special Deliberation Day before the decisive vote? If deliberation made such a difference for a representative microcosm, wouldn't it have made a difference for the nation as a whole?

The exceptional character of major constitutional referenda makes them an especially appropriate occasion for adopting DDay on an experimental basis. Not only are the stakes especially high, but the introduction of the holiday for the referendum doesn't commit the country on a permanent basis. If the initial experiment works out well, there will be time enough to consider whether DDay should become a permanent part of the calendar.[30]

At the same time, our proposal suggests the inherent limitations of Progressive ideals of direct democracy. Although it makes good sense to hold DDays on referenda of extraordinary importance, it is absurd to take a couple of days off to debate each one of the large number of citizen initiatives that get on the ballot in California or other states in the American West. Given the costs involved, the primary focus of DDay should be on the central business of American democracy — selecting the president and Congress in an informed fashion. Rather than continuing the Progressive infatuation with the forms of direct democracy, the practical challenge is to provide a social context that will enable ordinary citizens to control representative government in a reasonable fashion.

Overall, then, DDay provides a path beyond some familiar impasses in our constitutional tradition. We cannot go back to the Founding vision of a republic guided by patrician politicians, but the Progressive demand for direct democracy is not a realistic cure for our democratic discontents.

There is a better way forward: Provide ordinary people with a social context through which they can fulfill their citizenship responsibilities in a way that makes sense to them. DDay won't work miracles, but it does provide citizens with a precious tool for holding government accountable — both at ordinary elections and at extraordinary referenda that seek to define turning points in national life.

8

RESPONSIBLE CITIZENSHIP

Having placed our proposal in historical perspective, it is time to state our case in more contemporary terms. DDay is new and unfamiliar, so the modest dimensions of our initiative are easy to forget. Each citizen gets a chance to talk with his neighbors on *one* day every *four* years—and if our experiment proves successful, the holiday may ultimately become a biennial event.

This is hardly a call for revolution. It is a rather modest effort to adapt the great tradition of republican self-government to the challenges of a new century. To clarify our reformist ambitions, we sketch two central aspects of this tradition, beginning with its distinctive notion of *private citizenship*. Although the term is familiar, it describes a rather curious political animal, and it pays to reflect on the distinctive features of the breed. We then move to a societal level, and locate private citizenship within a broader understanding of a *relatively healthy* civil society. The elaboration of these two concepts permits us to explain why a modest reform like DDay can play a genuinely important role in sustaining the practice of private citizenship within a broad range of twenty-first-century societies.

Private Citizenship

Consider two questions:

1. What's good for me?
2. What's good for the country?

It is important to keep these questions conceptually distinct. Something might be good for me and bad for the country, or vice versa. Of course, you might turn out to be lucky. After considering the question seriously, you might conclude that self-interest and public interest coincide in a particular case; but this happy state of affairs isn't to be presumed; and it would be quite remarkable if you were always so lucky.

The crucial issue is what you do when your answers to the two questions diverge—when X is bad for me but good for the country (or good for me and bad for the country). There are two conceptually easy answers. The first is offered by the *perfect privatist:* always choose self-interest. The second is offered by the *public citizen:* always choose the public good.

Both answers have long and complex intellectual histories. Modern libertarians famously insist on the first answer, but we can trace this radically self-interested stance back to Christianity's rejection of worldliness and its suggestion that personal salvation is compromised by active political engagement. The second simple answer returns us to Athens, not Jerusalem, and Socrates' famous decision to obey his city's unjust death sentence rather than go into exile.[1] Such categorical privileging of the public can also be seen in more contemporary lives—Nelson Mandela's, for example.

For the present, we won't be exploring these simple—sometimes noble, sometimes foolish—engagements with public citizenship or perfect privatism. We are more interested in the conceptually more complex response of the *private citizen.* This is a political animal who seeks to modulate his commitments to the public and private good over time—sometimes choosing self-interest, and sometimes sacrificing it to the public good. Of course, different private citizens disagree about how much, and when, to sacrifice self-interest. But this is a debate within the family: so long as you believe that you should sometimes opt for the public interest and sometimes for self-interest, you have eluded the conceptual simplicities of perfect privatism and public citizenship. You have located yourself firmly in the conceptual territory of private citizenship.[2]

Most residents of Western democracies are private citizens. They are sometimes prepared to sacrifice their self-interest to the public good. They may even be prepared to die for their country, on appropriate occasions. But most of the time—for some, almost all of the time—they bracket these public commitments and pursue their self-interest. Within this framework, the "pursuit of self-interest" shouldn't be understood as a synonym for crass selfishness (though it includes this as well). The phrase is broad enough to include love of family, commitment to religion, pursuit of learning, and countless other noble aims. The only thing it doesn't include is a commitment to the national interest, if and when it demands the sacrifice of competing values for the common good.

So understood, the private citizen is a conflicted character. A mere mortal, he has limited time and energy. Yet his private aims and public commitments easily outstrip these limits, requiring some hard choices. More time with your family may mean less for your religion; more time for your job may mean less for the public good; and so forth. Within each value domain, the result of all these hard choices may generate a good deal of personal disappointment: If only I had more time to devote to family or friends, I would be living such a good life!

Sometimes these exclamations lead to a readjustment of effort; sometimes, to a sigh and a shrug. But this ongoing process of reappraisal and adaptation is part of what life is all about.

All this seems pretty obvious, but it is time to bring it to bear on our present problem. Put yourself in the position of the typical private citizen: You think it's in the public interest for you to cast an informed ballot, but there are lots of other good things in life — serving as a Little League coach or keeping in touch with a friend who has moved to a distant city. Given finite time and energy, something has to be sacrificed: Why not economize on the time needed to deliberate on your electoral choices? Isn't it good enough to go to the polls and simply vote on the basis of concededly inadequate deliberation? Won't the Republic survive even if I cast an ignorant ballot?

In response to these reasonable questions, Deliberation Day discharges a signaling function: Though the consequences of a single uninformed vote may seem innocuous, DDay alerts each private citizen that the collective failure of deliberation seriously threatens the enterprise of self-government. This signal, in turn, can provoke private citizens to change their behavior as part of their ongoing process of reappraisal and adaptation: "I was operating under the impression that my failure to deliberate was unimportant to the effective operation of our democracy. But by establishing this new holiday, my fellow citizens are suggesting to me that I was wrong. The collective consequences of tens of millions of ignorant ballots are really very deleterious. So perhaps I should reconsider, and devote more time to responsible citizenship."

But DDay does more than operate as a signal of public need. It also provides a relatively accessible form of constructive response. After all, it takes a lot of work for a private citizen to gain a critical perspective on the relative merits of competing candidates — much more, for example, than it takes for him thoughtfully to choose his next car or buy his next computer. In making these private choices, he can ask friends who have made similar purchases in the recent past and find out about their experiences. But the public choices posed by rival candidates often require book-learning and access to expertise. Some people may have the training to take on such tasks; others may be able to discuss the matter with friends whose knowledge they respect. But most lack the knowledge and the social networks needed to organize their own critical inquiry. For them, DDay will provide the first reasonable opportunity to fulfill the ideal of responsible citizenship.

As the experience with Deliberative Polls demonstrate, ordinary citizens are entirely capable of constructive engagement with the distinctive processes provided on DDay — substantive dialogue with fellow citizens leading to the formulation of questions addressed to political representatives. As in the DP, we can expect them to emerge from their experience with far greater understanding of the public choices that they confront.

The new holiday, in short, serves both as a signal of public need *and* as a means for fulfilling the need it has identified. Of course, this won't be enough to persuade perfect privatists to attend. Since they are motivated exclusively by self-interest, the only attraction of DDay is the offer of $150. Using DDay to take a vacation for personal pursuits may be worth more than $150 — in which case, privatists will avoid the citizen-assemblies and devote themselves to better things.[3] Citizen-assemblies won't even attract everybody who answers to the name of private citizen. Many will find that they have more pressing obligations — perhaps a child or a parent needs special care. Others will find the entire exercise too intimidating or boring. They will be content to wait till their friends come home and tell them what they have learned from DDay. As we argued in Chapter 6, the key question isn't the number of no-shows but whether a critical mass of voters do respond positively to the call of responsible citizenship.

This basic point leads us beyond the theory of private citizenship to the idea of a *reasonably healthy civil society*. This notion has a quantitative and a qualitative aspect. Quantitatively, the society must contain enough people who subscribe to the ideal of private citizenship to generate a critical mass on DDay. Qualitatively, the overwhelming majority must possess the skills and social competences required for profitable group deliberation. Of course, many people will profit even if they stay silent most of the time. But at least a significant portion must be prepared to engage more actively in the process of small-group deliberation.

This is the point where our proposal makes contact with a particularly vibrant stream of social science. Robert Putnam's idea of "social capital" has inspired a great revival of interest in the sociological foundations of political life. The basic idea is neo-Tocquevillean. Vast areas of civil society serve as schools for the development of political skills. Even when organizing such humdrum affairs as bridge clubs or bowling leagues or a social evening with friends, participants are obliged to coordinate their activities without heavy reliance on hierarchic commands or cash incentives. In sustaining these social networks, they cultivate a range of social skills and moral sentiments that serve as a preparation for private citizenship—the partial sacrifice of self-interest for the good of the group, the willingness to cooperate with others in defining common objectives.

Putnam and his followers make these points through both historical studies and quantitative analysis.[4] Their conclusions intersect with DDay in three ways. First, and most obviously, they help identify societies with sufficient social capital to sustain a project like DDay. Though Putnam finds a decline in social capital formation during recent decades, he keeps his pessimism under control. The United States remains rich in social networks serving as schools for citizenship. Rather than counseling despair, he suggests the need for creative institutional designs that promise to reverse recent declines.[5]

This is where Putnam's argument intersects with DDay a second time: The new holiday is precisely the sort of new initiative that promises to reverse the current decline in social capital accumulation. From beginning to end, it will invite the participation of citizens' groups. Aside from encouraging their members to turn out, DDay will generate abundant nuts-and-bolts jobs for volunteers. School buses will be driving the carless to DDay centers, but there will be a need to organize supplementary car pools. Civic organizations will be asked to recruit volunteers to greet DDayers at each center, and help check them in and out. As nonpartisan service groups engage in these activities, more politicized organizations will also be active as they try to shape the flow of neighborhood deliberation. And DDay will force political parties to recruit local opinion-leaders to represent their side at citizen assemblies throughout the land.

All this activity will have synergistic effects. Existing social networks will interact with one another in new ways. The general hubbub will attract new people into the social web. There will be lots of meeting and greeting, especially at lunch—when all groups will be invited to set up tables advertising their own activities and soliciting new members.

Beyond all this formal activity, there will be the simple fact that tens of millions of neighbors will have the chance to break the ice, and to meet the family down the block for the first time. Perhaps they will be bowling together before long.

There is a final way DDay engages current concerns with social capital. Putnam's argument puts a distinctive emphasis on the politically constructive role of social activities far removed from politics. Even when they are merely organizing a bowling league, or inviting friends over for a game of bridge, participants are generating skills and social networks that prepare them for more political engagements. We find this claim quite plausible, but it should not divert us from a special need.

Quite simply, many traditional contexts for citizenship are dead or dying. Vietnam killed the citizen-army. Television, when combined with the spread of such democratic reforms as the direct primary, killed the political party as a popular institution. The citizen jury barely survives on the periphery of ordinary life. The only significant institution that still invites involvement by ordinary citizens is the public school, and it too is under attack.

The rituals of citizenship have been stripped down to a precious few. Besides the formal act of voting, perhaps the most significant act of citizenship occurs when Americans show their passport at the border, and thereby gain admission to the land of opportunity. But it is quite possible to live in America today without regularly dealing with others as fellow citizens — fellow workers or professionals, yes; fellow religionists or union members, yes; but fellow citizens, focusing on our common predicament as Americans? We may wave the flag, but we begin quickly to run out of citizenship activities. Significant political conversation seems reserved for TV pundits.

DDay fills this vacuum. It provides a place for ordinary Americans to reaffirm that they are fully prepared to take themselves seriously as private citizens confronting the public business.

If you forgive the jargon: DDay will not only catalyze the creation of vast amounts of social capital; it has a unique role to play in building *political capital*. A vigorous civil society undoubtedly plays a useful supporting role in the life of a democratic republic. But a vibrant democracy needs something more; it needs tens of million of private *citizens* who are comfortable interacting with one another in the special ways required to engage responsibly in the conduct of public business.

The disintegration of the mass political party is especially important here. There was a time when the party label was something more than a political abstraction of (increasingly) uncertain meaning. It was a placeholder for a complex set of face-to-face networks which participants found personally meaningful and politically important. With the decline of the mass party, democratic societies must build new interactive networks that provide the political capital required to sustain the project of private citizenship which serves as the foundation of a vigorous democratic life.

The Qualities of Deliberation

Summing up, we can say that DDay discharges three key functions: It serves, first, as a *signal* of the public need for deliberation; second, as an effective *vehicle* for private citizens to discharge this need; and third, as an *expressive mode* through which participants can affirm their identities as private citizens, seriously engaged in the public business.

Consider the last point further. Citizenship can be expressed through many different interactional modes. In contrast to the citizen-army, DDay doesn't emphasize the willingness to fight and die for the public good. In contrast to the political party, it doesn't emphasize partisan commitment to a particular programmatic vision. DDay expresses a different aspect of the citizenship ideal—thoughtful deliberation about the public good. We are dealing with a part, not the whole, of private citizenship.

But it is an important part. The basic point is obvious enough: A responsible citizen thinks before he acts. This maxim is put into practice each day in the nation's courtrooms, where citizen-juries are asked to deliberate on the fate of individuals accused of crime or civil wrong. Just as the jury provides a social space for responsible citizenship in the justice system, DDay provides an analogous space in the electoral system. The design of this space will be different, of course, since the task of choosing the best candidate is different from determining the fate of an individual. Nevertheless, the two public spaces express the same aspect of the citizenship ideal: Think before you act.

To elaborate the point further, consider the extent to which DDay incorporates basic aspects of deliberative rationality into the basic structure of the proceeding.

"Facts" and Empirical Premises

From Walter Lippmann onward, skeptics have pointed to the vast gap between the ordinary experience of normal people and the leading issues of national politics. Ordinary people simply don't have the basic facts required to assess the wisdom of a war in Iraq, or the future of Social Security, or the merits of a tax cut. And given this brute reality, Lippmann and his many successors urge us to abandon as sheer cant talk of self-rule by responsible citizens.

DDay enters as a counterargument. During the run-up to the holiday, both parties will have new incentives to flood the airwaves with infomercials containing competing views of the relevant facts, and the DDay presentations will provide balanced formats for continuing this debate— during both the television debate between the candidates and the give-and-take between small groups and local party representatives at the citizen-assemblies.

DDay will be especially useful in allowing the participants to distinguish between relatively uncontroversial facts and a range of more controversial claims about the world that we call empirical premises—points that are commonly invoked in political argument as if they were facts but which are, in fact, open to reasonable dispute.[6] That Mexican workers make much lower wages than comparable Americans is a fact. But does this mean that America will lose more jobs than it will gain if it signs a free-trade agreement with Mexico?

Ordinary reasoners may invoke this empirical premise as if it were a fact, but it rests on causal connections that are open to reasonable dispute. They are "essentially contested" in the sense that competing experts have sophisticated arguments, sincerely offered, supporting the truth or falsity of such empirical claims.

DDay will provide ordinary citizens with new tools to distinguish the relatively unproblematic from the genuinely contestable. The competing candidates will have new incentives to challenge empirical premises that will operate to their disadvantage on DDay, and citizens will be able to follow up with further questions in their small groups.

Our experience from Deliberative Polls suggests that a great deal of time and energy is devoted to these fact-based efforts at clarification of empirical premises. Should the United States make greater contributions to deal with AIDS or world hunger in developing countries? For many, the issue will turn on contested empirical questions: Would massive education efforts actually be effective in very poor countries in curbing the spread of AIDS? Would food aid actually get to the truly needy or would much of it get diverted through corruption?

Should the citizens of New Haven support expansion of the local airport? For many, the question will turn on whether an expanded airport would actually attract new development or whether people would actually use the facility, since it would still be much smaller than other airports in the region.

Contested facts are a factor in almost every major policy deliberation. In much ordinary conversation they go unchallenged. Citizens rarely stop to examine evidence about whether they might be correct. By airing competing arguments about them, deliberation permits their reexamination — opening up the possibility of opinion change after due reflection.

The questioning of empirical premises — and the introduction of a host of uncontroversial facts into the conversation — may seem like humdrum matters. But if this were all that DDay accomplished, it would be a great success. After all, each participant comes to the holiday with a host of value commitments developed over the course of a lifetime. It would be silly to expect that a single day's discussion will generate radical revisions of these basic normative frameworks. (Indeed, it would be more than silly. It would be disheartening to learn that most citizens' value frameworks were so malleable!)

But what is not silly is to suppose that ordinary people have great difficulty gaining a reasonably good sense of the way their basic values actually apply to the great national issues before them. By enriching the factual basis of their understanding, DDay vastly enhances the capacity of citizens to act responsibly.

Normative Completeness

A second criterion for good deliberation is "normative completeness." By this, we mean the extent to which arguments offered in favor of a position are answered by those with a different view, which are answered in turn by the initial proponents, and so on. This dialogue could, of course, continue for a virtually unlimited period of time so long as participants had further normative responses to the arguments previously offered. (Jürgen Habermas has something like this in mind in his famous thought-experiment of an "ideal speech situation.")[7]

DDay conversations will fall far short of such Olympian heights, but they will look very good when judged by real-world standards. Most political conversations take place among friends and family members with broadly similar political views.[8] In contrast, DDay requires a sustained confrontation with a series of different views. The rival candidates begin the discussion on the national level, speaking in ways that they hope will be persuasive to a vast audience. But their competing messages will be initially assessed in fifteen-person groups in myriads of localities — whose backgrounds will vary greatly from region to region and neighborhood to neighborhood. Questions that seem sensible to southern suburbanites will be very different from those elaborated by small groups from northeastern city centers. When citizens gather together in their larger assemblies, their questions will present a distinctive challenge to the local representatives of the competing political parties. These spokesmen will find themselves caught in the middle between the national messages of the presidential candidates and the local concerns coming up from below. Rather than simply elaborating the candidates' remarks, they will try to tailor the party's positions to resonate with the dominant concerns of their local audiences.

The resulting chorus can't help but push the overall conversation in the direction of normative completeness. Indeed, the contrast between the televised arguments and those presented at the morning session of the citizen assembly is likely to serve as an engine for further normative elaboration during the afternoon: "Mr. Local Democrat, you said X in the morning, but how does this square with what your national candidate said on TV?" And of course, the local representative of the opposing party is sure to make similar points in the ongoing sparring match.

The increasing range of normative argument will interact with an increasing appreciation of the factual context—giving the participants a deepening understanding of the stakes involved in their decision. If our experience with Deliberative Polls is any guide, this understanding will lead some participants to change their minds.[9] But the frequency of opinion change is hardly the measure of its value.

Even when participants hold to their prior views, they will be voicing their opinions in a very different spirit. After spending a day in deliberation, most will begin to appreciate the shallow basis for their prior views. Although their bottom lines may remain unchanged, they will hold their opinions in a different spirit—one befitting a responsible citizen who refuses to jump to a knee-jerk conclusion but has taken the time and trouble to think seriously about the public good.

Reason and Reasonableness

Some people at DDay will be only consumers, not producers. They will listen to the ongoing exchanges in the small and large groups, and they may learn a lot from what they hear. They may even change their mind. All this is all to the good. Call it the process of *reasoned opinion formation*.

But millions more will do something more on DDay. They will not only listen and learn but actively contribute to the ongoing flow of talk. To be effective, they must deploy *the arts of political reasonableness*.

Their principal task is to ask good questions, not to announce assertive conclusions. This requires participants to be open-minded enough to listen to what others are saying. Some of them must also be clever enough to frame appropriate questions that capture the spirit of the conversation. Almost all must be prepared to treat each other respectfully, letting each take his or her turn in the common discussion. Otherwise, they will never reach a civilized conclusion about the particular questions that should be offered up to the citizen assembly in the name of the group.

Of course, some small groups *will* fail — their course blocked by some intransigent obstructionist who refuses to cooperate. We have provided procedures to remove such provocateurs from the meetings, and have organized DDay to sustain the momentum of proceedings even when some small groups are disrupted. But the certainty of some failures shouldn't distract attention from the big picture. When given the chance, the critical mass of ordinary citizens *can* deploy the arts of political reasonableness.

This is, at least, our interpretation of Deliberative Polling, buttressed by evidence from the operation of the Anglo-American jury system.[10] If we are right, DDay will provide a new framework for a deeper realization of the ideals of responsible citizenship. Not only will it enable tens of millions of voters to cast their ballots more thoughtfully, but it will give them an opportunity to cultivate the arts of political reasonableness.

The political system will be built on a new foundation. The people who show up at DDay are secure in their political office — they are responsible citizens, nothing more, nothing less. They aren't running for reelection. They will not have campaign advisers or spin doctors. But by demonstrating their political reasonableness, they will force all the professionals to sing a different tune. There will be a lot less talk of media markets and a lot more concern with reaching political judgments worthy of thoughtful assent by responsible citizens.

Happy Holiday!

DDay is not merely an occasion for responsible citizens to gather together to exercise their political reason. It is a holiday upon which the community *celebrates* this civic commitment.

Most of our holidays have suffered greatly over the course of the past century — but we have already explained why we believe that DDay can avoid this dynamic of trivialization.[11] Now is the point to enter a more fundamental normative objection. For a democracy, our civic holidays are too aristocratic.

Nobody can deny the greatness of George Washington or Abraham Lincoln or Martin Luther King. It is right to honor their achievements. And yet our recognition of ordinary Americans is oddly truncated. Their military sacrifices are recognized on Memorial Day and Veterans Day, but their civic contributions go uncelebrated. No analogue to Labor Day marks the crucial role of responsible citizenship in the life of the republic.[12]

America is one of the few serious democracies that fails to make a holiday out of Election Day, and this compounds the problem. We shouldn't ignore the message we are sending ourselves in devoting two holidays to service on the battlefields and none to civic responsibility.

DDay would be especially effective in correcting this symbolic imbalance. It is a holiday of a very special sort. The civic ceremonies on most holidays are a pale representation of the heroic event or person to which they are dedicated. Laying a wreath before the Tomb of the Unknown Soldier is a poignantly inadequate token of a collective debt. Such celebrations are better than nothing, but they must content themselves with mere representations of the civic sacrifices involved. To fix ideas, we will say that these holidays are based on rituals of representation—in which a variety of tokens are used to recall the heroic events or persons that inspire the public celebration.

DDay is a holiday of a different kind. Citizens don't merely try to honor the ideal of responsible citizenship through rituals of representation—say, by awarding a prize to the Outstanding Citizen of the Year or by laying a wreath at her tomb. They celebrate the ideal by enacting it. They do public honor to the ideal by trying to exemplify responsible citizenship in citizen-assemblies throughout the land. In contrast to rituals of representation, DDay celebrates through *rituals of enactment*.

Such rituals provide particularly rich expressive resources for community celebration. Many DDay participants will take pride in their constructive contributions to their local assemblies—telling stories about their DDay activities for years to come. Though friends may listen skeptically when their interlocutors embroider their accounts, these millions of prideful recollections give powerful testimony to the living reality of the citizenship ideal. Moving beyond individual stories, the mass media will provide countless images of the remarkable spectacle of a nation of citizens at work— emphasizing perhaps the comical and pathological, but also the dignity of tens of millions engaged in the responsible exercise of their political sovereignty.

A faint suggestion of these symbolic possibilities is provided by the contemporary coverage of Election Day. It is easy to find fault with the television coverage on election night, but it still manages to convey the deep dignity of democratic self-government. As the election returns come pouring in, and the race is still in doubt, the drama of close races express the ultimate sovereignty of ordinary men and women in an inescapable way.

The expressive resources available on DDay will be vastly greater. After all, this is a daylong event for tens of millions to engage one another as responsible—and not-so-responsible—citizens. Election Day simply provides an opportunity for each private citizen to go into a voting booth, flick a few levers, and quickly depart from the scene. Voting on Election Day occurs in private, but citizen deliberation is entirely public—generating a remarkably rich performance for mass transmission and further reflection. And as on Election Day, the evening reports will be full of exit polls and commentary on their meaning. All this is compelling stuff for sustained civic celebration—and don't forget the fireworks!

Our emphasis on holidays may seem old-fashioned, but we take the opposite view. A holiday celebrating responsible citizenship is especially important in a modern world characterized by pluralist beliefs and an extreme division of labor. The less homogeneous the society, the easier it is to doubt whether its inhabitants retain this precious capacity. The best way to counter these doubts is to show that citizens can indeed exercise their political reason together. By celebrating this achievement, the DDay ritual of enactment will project its symbolic meaning onto all the other days of the quadrennium when the ideal of responsible citizenship is less salient in ordinary life. As they go about their lives as private citizens—occasionally casting an eye on politics, but keeping most of their attention on more private matters—people will reflect that DDay will come again, and they will once more have a chance to express more fully the public-regarding aspect of their complex identities. These moments of recognition will occur at odd times and in odd places, but they will greatly reinforce DDay's meaning as a moral reference point amid the hubbub of ordinary life.

The history of political thought has left us a legacy of familiar dichotomies—some useful, others less so. We have been struggling against a well-entrenched, but pernicious, view which juxtaposes the "freedom of the ancients" against "the freedom of the moderns."[13] Ancient freedom, it is said, is the freedom of the citizen to participate fully in public affairs; modern is the liberal freedom to pursue private interests. We do not deny that these extreme types do exist—Nelson Mandela, the public citizen, recalls the freedom of the ancients; and all of us are personally acquainted with perfect privatists who scoff at the very idea of the public interest.

But in this chapter we have been trying to bring a third conceptual type to center stage. We have called them private citizens, and DDay is for them. They are the sorts of people who want to be responsible citizens, but they want to be lots of other things as well—good parents, loyal friends, honored professionals, and effective wage earners. All of these competing hopes and aspirations distract these thoroughly modern human beings from their sense of political responsibility—but without extinguishing the appeal of responsible citizenship as one of the good things in life, worth pursuing for its own sake.

The challenge is to solve the problem of distraction, as it were, by providing a civic holiday that will focus the errant attention of private citizens and create a focal point enabling them to perform as responsible citizens in conjunction with their fellows.

It is possible, of course, that this diagnosis of the political condition of modern humanity is too benign. Perhaps, when given the chance, the overwhelming majority will reveal that they are perfect privatists after all, utterly unwilling to spend even a day reflecting on the public good. But the evidence from the Deliberative Polls does not support this view. And we will know the truth only by giving DDay a try.

9

FEARFUL ASYMMETRIES

In the previous chapter we reflected on a distinctively modern predicament. Millions of men and women may be attracted by the ideal of responsible citizenship, but they are constantly distracted by competing aims and ambitions. We aimed to show how DDay might respond to these perplexities of distracted citizenship, serving as a signal for a coordinated effort toward responsible participation in politics without too great a sacrifice of competing goals. In this chapter we turn away from dilemmas confronting individual citizens and consider how DDay responds to larger structural problems of the polity as a whole.

We have already dealt with this matter at length in Part I—showing how the introduction of DDay would change the basic incentives politicians face both when running for election and when exercising political power.[1] It didn't require much moral complexity to conclude that these sweeping changes were a good thing for the country. Very few people believe that sound-bite campaigns and poll-driven governments are wonderful things. We have learned to live with these pathologies because the effort to cure them seems far worse than the disease: While a public dialogue of ten-second sound bites is bad, government censorship is far worse; and surely it is entirely unrealistic to expect politicians to ignore the suggestions of pollsters!

This defense of the status quo is entirely convincing until DDay comes into the picture. The new holiday permits a constructive response to familiar pathologies without taking measures that are repressive, unworkable, or silly. To the contrary, the exercise of responsible citizenship by tens of millions at DDay will be another great benefit generated by the new holiday.

If you build it, they will come! And the result will be better representative government.

It took a lot of work to build the empirical side of this argument, but the moral side seems pretty straightforward. And this is a great merit, it seems to us — as a matter both of political philosophy and of democratic practice. The more complex the normative argument, the easier it is for many reasonable people to disagree with it. The more complex, the less likely to gain popular acceptance any time soon.

Nevertheless, it would be a mistake to rest our case with this no-nonsense point. The modern practice of liberal democracy actually generates a confusing cluster of ideals and understandings — most are poorly realized and many conflict with one another. Recognition of these complexities shouldn't obscure the no-nonsense case against sound-bite democracy, but it does allow for a deeper appreciation of the ways that DDay may help more fully realize the unfulfilled promises of liberal democracy.

We address three tension-ridden value clusters implicated in the standard operation of Western-style liberal democracies. The first focuses on economic inequality. The struggle between rich and poor is unending, and democratic government aims to civilize the conflict. But this is easier said than done — how, if at all, does Deliberation Day help? We turn next to the larger ambitions of the modern state. For all the talk of privatization, we continue to live in an era of pervasively activist government: How to decide which activist goals are worthwhile? And finally, there are the internal tensions within the modern ideal of democracy itself, its uneasy compromise between three dimensions of citizenship — participation, deliberation, and equality. Deliberation Day does not provide the ultimate solution to any of these problems. But it does contribute something valuable in the ongoing effort to confront them.

Inequality

At the dawn of the twenty-first century, 1 percent of Americans own almost 40 percent of the nation's disposable wealth.[2] European distributions are somewhat more equal, Latin American a good deal less.[3] But everywhere, inequalities are large and may well be growing. Are they acceptable in a just society?

We have our own views, but this isn't the place to try to convince you.[4] Opinions differ notoriously, and we don't expect the struggle over distributive justice to end any time soon. It's more important to consider the ways in which Western societies have channeled this unending struggle into civilized forms.

The democratic ethos has been central. Western governments fall short of their democratic promise, but they still look pretty egalitarian when compared to other spheres of social and economic life. Call this the *relative equality* of democratic government. And it provides a crucial element for the legitimation of inequality in other social and economic domains: "If you think the rich are too rich, the constructive way to proceed is by mobilizing a political majority for redistribution. Until you gain this majority, you must live by the democratic rules of the game, and accept the legitimacy of the status quo."

This rationale is absolutely central to ordinary understandings, but its plausibility depends on empirical facts. Suppose, for example, that big money is so dominant in campaign finance that serious politicians find it practically impossible to raise the question of distributive justice for fear of alienating their crucial supporters. Under this scenario, the relative equality of democratic government is merely a myth. Politics will have been transformed into a forum in which big money praises itself. If the deliberations of democratic citizens are crucial in the legitimation of market inequality, we cannot allow market inequalities to have an overwhelming impact on these deliberations. If this happens, we can no longer say that we, as citizens, have authorized the pervasive inequalities we experience as market actors.

This is one of the principal reasons why campaign finance is an increasingly salient issue throughout the West. But the point applies more generally: The more that political life is characterized by effective *equality* among citizens, the more the democratic ethos may plausibly legitimate the pervasive *inequalities* in other spheres.

Call this the "inverse law" of democratic legitimation, and it may seem counterintuitive at first glance. After all, partisans of greater democratic equality also tend to support greater economic and social equality. As a consequence, they don't often emphasize how increases in democratic equality can be used to legitimate inequalities in other domains. Nonetheless, a simple thought-experiment should suffice to confirm our point.

So take a ride, once again, on our time machine to 2020. As we glance at prevailing economic realities, nothing much has changed: The people in the top 1 percent continue to own two-fifths of the disposable wealth, and they remain dominant in the daily life of the business world. As we turn to politics, let's complicate the picture by considering two alternative scenarios. The first is more or less the status quo: sound-bite appeals to the public funded largely by big contributors. The second is more promising: Deliberation Day is now the order of the day, as well as an effective campaign reform that moderates—but does not end—the disproportionate influence of great wealth in the political process.[5]

Two thousand twenty is a presidential election year. In both World One and World Two, the Democratic candidate for president is campaigning on a mildly egalitarian platform—proposing new schemes of redistributive taxation, strengthening labor law, and the like. These initiatives provoke blasts of sound-bite stuff—both pro and con—in both worlds, but something more happens in World Two.

After long and anxious strategic consultations, our Demo-candidate decides to make his social justice theme his Leading Issue for DDay—using the occasion to dramatize the facts about economic inequality, emphasizing the moral and economic gains of a more equitable system. The Republican responds with a spirited defense of property rights, urging his fellow citizens to protect individual freedom and to reward the risk-taking entrepreneurship that serves as the engine of economic progress in a capitalist economy.

Election Day comes—and the same thing happens in both worlds: The Republican wins in a landslide. When the results are announced, the immediate reaction is the same: lots of joy and despair among hard-core activists, lots of hard-headed efforts to define new positions on the transformed electoral terrain. But we are more interested in the question of political morality raised by our thought-experiment: How does the introduction of Deliberation Day change the normative significance of the Republicans' victory?

Quite a lot. We aren't interested in making a black-and-white claim. We don't deny that, even in World One, the electoral victory has a moral meaning. Despite the Republicans' disproportionate access to the wealth of the rich, and despite the warring sound bites, we are assuming that the Democrats' message does get through to some extent. When most voters go to the polls, they dimly recognize that the Dems are calling for a more equal society—though they haven't seriously focused on the concrete steps proposed and considered their practical merits or moral attractiveness. Nevertheless, broad-based egalitarian appeals have sometimes enabled the Left to win electoral victories in the past, and so the Dems' failure to inspire support wasn't foreordained. As a consequence, the Republicans' victory *would* serve as a significant legitimator of the economic inequalities: "You can say what you like about 1 percent of the people owning 40 percent of the assets, but a strong majority of American voters have refused to support a self-conscious challenge to the status quo."

But this legitimating effect would be greatly enhanced in World Two. To be sure, some Democratic diehards will still cry foul even after they have been given their chance at Deliberation Day: "We've had only a few hours to make our case! In contrast, the defenders of inequality have been spending billions of dollars for decades in propagandizing for the status quo. And even if we restrict our view to the presidential campaign of 2020, the partisans of inequality have been outspending us (though, thanks to campaign finance reform, not as badly as they used to do). So all in all, we have still been laboring under overwhelming disadvantages when we put our case to the people on Deliberation Day."

All this may be conceded without disputing our main point: Democratic political morality makes the Republicans' victory a far more significant achievement in World Two. Despite the diehard critique, the Dems did get at least one chance to make their case in a *sustained* way in World Two, allowing ordinary citizens to consider the question in a sober fashion: However much egalitarians might disagree with the outcome, they can't deny that masses of ordinary men and women have taken the time and trouble to consider their case in a thoughtful fashion, and have decided that it doesn't make sense. Moreover, the Dems remain free to renew their challenge on the next Deliberation Day. What more can they reasonably ask?

If you agree, you have accepted our inverse law of political legitimation. World Two moves beyond World One by deepening America's egalitarian commitment to deliberation in the political realm. And it is precisely by moving in this *egalitarian* direction that the political system serves to enhance the legitimacy of the remaining *inequalities* haunting contemporary life.

The same point continues to apply if we change our scenario and award a sweeping victory to the Democrats. Such a victory would serve as a mandate for significant changes, but no serious leftist movement proposes the total elimination of all inequalities. And those which withstand critique on a series of Deliberation Days will seem all the more acceptable.

Whatever the political outcome, millions of voters will predictably disagree with the collective decision. And these disagreements will continue to generate a wide range of responses on all sides of the question — from passionate denunciation to philosophical refutation. Nevertheless, the provision of a political forum for ongoing argument will permit the participants to mark out the moral seriousness of the question of distributive justice — and their efforts at respectful interchange on DDay will serve as a common bond that sustains the political community despite the inevitability of continuing disagreement.

The Activist State

We have been puzzling over an asymmetric relation between democratic politics and the market economy. Since democratic politics is relatively more egalitarian, the effort to deepen democracy permits the deeper legitimation of those market inequalities that manage to gain the *considered* support of majorities on election day. Within this context, Deliberation Day promises us that we can have our cake and eat it too: a more legitimate democracy *and* a more legitimate market economy.

Deliberation Day gains further appeal when viewed against the background of another asymmetry. Broadly speaking, all Western polities have embraced a broad-ranging form of activist government — from education through retirement pensions, from health care to environmental protection, contemporary governments are engaged in an enormous interventionist enterprise. At the same time, they have remained curiously inactive when it comes to creating a suitable social context for the deliberate exercise of citizenship. On this matter, they made laissez-faire the rule. This asymmetry—massive activism on social policy but extreme inactivity on citizenship development—leads to another legitimacy gap: With citizens absent from the process, who should be setting the crucial priorities in the activist state?

The answer has been to delegate much of the burden to a rising class of technocrats, and invite elected politicians, judges, and interest groups to play a supervisory role. The resulting pattern generates the distinctive dynamics of modern administrative government. Politicians enact framework statutes, technocrats fill the gaps with regulatory solutions, and these in turn provoke criticism from interest groups, legislators, and courts in a never-ending cycle of revision.

This unending dance has profound and pervasive consequences. It affects the air we breathe, the jobs we get, the cars we drive, the health care we receive, and countless other matters. Although the administrative process has an enormous impact, ordinary people don't have much influence over its operation. They appear as passive consumers, not active citizens, in the larger story. On rare occasions, their bitter complaints may catalyze the organization of oppositional groups. But once grassroots groups get off the ground, they require sustained leadership from professionals who can take the time to master the technical issues involved. Ordinary citizens are left in the dust.

Worse yet, the system of democratic elections doesn't provide much relief from the pervasive sense of alienation. While the winners of presidential and congressional elections do shape bureaucratic outcomes, their influence on particular decisions is hard to trace. It takes an expert to explain how the election of Bush over Gore has changed concrete policies on workplace safety or environmental protection. And the ordinary voter is no expert: She is in no position to understand how her vote on Election Day may or may not be related to the bureaucratic rules shaping her everyday environment.

These sobering facts generated a rich body of reflection on public administration over the course of the twentieth century. The main line of scholarship counsels resigned acceptance of citizen passivity—for the simple reason that there isn't much of a practical remedy for the situation.

Only a know-nothing denies the importance of expert knowledge in identifying serious environmental risks, designing energy-efficient cars, and the like. This makes it tough to design systems that enable nonexperts to contribute constructively. While the passivity of ordinary citizens is distressing, it is simply utopian to invest much energy tilting at windmills.

In contrast, it *is* practical to provide elected politicians, appellate judges, and leaders of concerned interest groups with the legal tools they need to control technocrats when they go astray. Unlike ordinary citizens, these professionals may actually have the time and energy required to critique technocratic decisions. By empowering these full-timers, administrative law seeks to provide reasonable assurance that the reigning technocracy will not systematically override fundamental values.

The results are far from perfect. But according to the conventional wisdom, these failures should not call into question the larger enterprise. Surely it is better to empower generalists like politicians and judges than to leave crucial decisions entirely in the hands of technocrats. Similarly, the existing system of elite political control is far better than one that liberates capitalism from regulatory oversight. The unrestrained pursuit of profit notoriously generates massive environmental and social degradation in its wake. Although ordinary citizens may find bureaucratic operations opaque, they wouldn't find the outcomes generated by the "invisible hand" any more intelligible. But they would be stuck with far worse outcomes, as the "free market" destroyed cherished social values.

So it looks like the regulatory state is here to stay. If this implies a certain degree of citizen passivity and mystification, we will simply have to grin and bear it.

We have absolutely no interest in challenging this foundational argument for modern activist government. But we do think that Deliberation Day helps to soften its hard edges. The overwhelming majority of administrative decisions will escape review on DDay, but truly fundamental policy choices may well make it onto the conversational agenda — especially when they call for widespread sacrifice.

Suppose, for example, that the dangers of global warming become increasingly plain over the next decade. The need for a serious response becomes a potent theme of American politics, but which steps really work and who will be forced to bear how much of the cost?

These questions will provoke a host of evasive maneuvers from powerful interest groups seeking to impose the burden on others. Deliberation Day will make their task more difficult. It will create a structure enabling the general public to gain an appreciation of the basic facts and policy alternatives. This new forum will also endow agency expertise with new political value. After all, it's the job of the Environmental Protection Agency to come up with thoughtful regulatory solutions; and if it has been doing its job right, many of the candidates' proposals will have their source in agency initiatives. As a consequence, the candidates will be bringing a great deal of hard-won administrative insight to the attention of the general public.

Of course, the new holiday does nothing to guarantee that the EPA has been functioning effectively—if the agency hasn't made good on the promise of expertise, the chances for a successful response to the environmental threat are pretty dismal. But if the system of administrative law has enabled technocrats, legislators, and judges to work together as an effective team, DDay permits the general public to enter the debate in a constructive fashion. Most obviously, it permits ordinary people to put the experts in their place. When a candidate points with alarm at the impending environmental crisis, countless skeptics will be asking their small-group members: "These politicians say that there is a problem requiring real sacrifice. But why should be we believe them?" Second, insofar as these questions are credibly answered in the citizen-assemblies, DDay will give competing politicians a new incentive to back regulatory solutions that don't pander to well-organized pressure groups. With Election Day only two weeks ahead, they had better come up with programs that distribute the burdens in ways that make sense to a mass public. And finally, DDay enables ordinary citizens to consider the real-world implications of plausible alternatives: "OK, if we do have to sacrifice for the general good, should it be through a big gas tax or a big hike in the price of electricity or . . . ????"

Whoever wins on Election Day, the general public will have gained a sense that it has been constructively involved in the affair—that their claims to active citizenship have been enhanced, not depreciated, by the assistance of expert agencies of government in clarifying the stakes involved.

The point generalizes across the broad range of activist governmental policy. Suppose, for example, that the political class allows retirement pensions to operate on a fiscally irresponsible basis, and that serious problems await the pensioners of 2050. Deliberation Day makes it likelier that some brave politician will use the number crunchers to gain support for early actions that require relatively small sacrifices in 2010 so that the pensioners of 2050 can avoid big sacrifices.

Suppose, though, that no politician steps forward in a timely fashion: The fiscal deficits continue, and a serious crisis looms in the 2040s. Then, at the very least, Deliberation Day will make it possible for citizens to talk sensibly — with the aid of expert projections — about the best way of distributing the trillion-dollar burdens involved.

A painful exercise in active citizenship, but better than delegating the entire task to technocratic and political elites?

Consider, for example, the Deliberative Polls held in Texas on electric utility matters. The deliberations focused on the merits of various energy sources — natural gas, coal, other fossil fuels, and renewable energy such as wind or solar power. These energy sources were, in turn, contrasted with conservation policies that would reduce the need for more power.

In the deliberative process, the advocates of coal faced a disadvantage: Coal, while cheap, was far dirtier than natural gas or renewable energy; at the time, natural gas was comparably cheap and much cleaner. The advocates of coal made claims about new "clean coal" technology, but in the context of competing experts who advocated rival sources, it came out clearly that clean coal was still much dirtier than the other fuels — its main merit was that it was cleaner than dirty coal. In a deliberative context combining increasing information and normative completeness, coal fared less well than other sources of energy. Some DP participants preferred natural gas because it was both cheap and clean; some preferred renewable resources because they were even cleaner and not much more expensive. But at the end of the day, there was only limited support for coal — once its major attributes were knowledgeably compared to those of its main rivals.[6]

The Texas DPs concentrated on a single subject, while the DDay agenda will contain from two to four national issues. But citizen-assemblies can, if they like, concentrate most of their questions on a single topic.

We don't wish to exaggerate. As in the ongoing confrontation with the problem of equality, there can be no hope of designing a fully satisfactory system. Nonetheless, Deliberation Day does provide a new resource that may well come in very handy in the increasingly knowledge-based society of the future.

Four Democratic Possibilities

The problem of activist government suggests a more pervasive trade-off between deliberation and participation. To put the problem in its general terms, consider a very simple classification of democratic possibilities. At the most fundamental level, any institution that consults the public must answer two questions — "who?" and "what?" Who participates or has their views consulted? What kinds of opinions are solicited or expressed?

The "who" can be everyone, the mass public, or it can be a select group of some sort. This elite can be elected, appointed, or selected by lot, tradition, or whatever. The "what" solicited from this group can vary from "raw public opinion" to opinion that is the product of deliberation. Since there is no such thing as an "ideal speech situation," deliberation is always a matter of degree. Nonetheless, there is a point at which quantity turns into quality. There must be a "decent minimum" of reflection on the merits of competing arguments. Participants must have a reasonable opportunity to express views about the issue and reasonably accurate information to enter the dialogue.

Of course, there are many occasions for deliberation that occur in ordinary life, without any concerted effort at institutional design to bring it about. But since this isn't generally true on public issues, we will say that public opinion, in the form we normally find it, is an expression of "raw" political preferences.

Taking together our discussion of the "who" and the "what" yields four basic possibilities:

I. Deliberative Mass Opinion
II. Deliberative Opinion of a Select Group
III. Raw Opinion of a Select Group
IV. Raw Mass Opinion

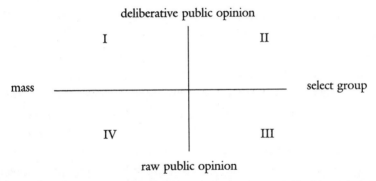

deliberative public opinion

	I		II
mass			select group
	IV		III

raw public opinion

Quadrant I represents the possibility furthered by Deliberation Day: a mass public actually forms deliberative opinions. But with the exception of the rarely realized ideal of the New England town meeting, this box is now empty, leaving us with the remaining three possibilities.

Quadrant II is realized whenever there is a select group that deliberates for the rest of us. This can be the representative group that Madison had in mind, in Federalist 10, that "refines and enlarges the public views by passing them through the medium of a chosen body of citizens." It can be the Senate, the Electoral College (in its original conception), or a "convention" in the sense meant by the Framers. Using a different method of selection, it can also be the sample in a Deliberative Poll, a select group that serves a representative function in deliberating for the rest of us.

Quadrant III, raw opinion of a select group, is filled out by the participants in poll-directed mass democracy. Ordinary public opinion polls permit select groups of citizens, chosen by random samples, to have their raw, unfiltered preferences inserted into the policy process and the public dialogue. To the extent that conventional polls influence politics and policy, quadrant III is very much a reality in public life today.[7]

Quadrant IV, raw opinion of the entire mass public, is the realization of plebiscitary democracy. This has been the long-term trajectory for democracy around the world, and has expressed itself in a wide variety of institutional forms — referenda and other modes of direct democracy, popular primaries for candidate selection, expanding the role of direct consultation in a wider range of elections. As a consequence, innumerable decisions once made in quadrant II, through a select or elite group deliberating, are now resolved by the raw political preferences of the mass public. We are bringing power to the people — but under institutional conditions that provide the people with little incentive to think about the power that they exercise.[8]

Quadrant I has special merit. It is strategically located in the array of democratic possibilities. There are reasons to move north in the diagram, to realize deliberation, and there are reasons to move west in the diagram, to realize mass consent. But the forces of history have been pushing us toward the south and the east. The twentieth century, for example, brought the proliferation of expert institutions of enormous power — ranging from the Federal Reserve Board to the Environmental Protection Agency. All these bureaucratic power centers inhabit the northeast, and express the modern belief that serious deliberation only makes sense in elite settings.

At the same time, democratic reformers keep pushing toward the southwest. We have already considered how American Progressives championed the referendum, only to have their innovation undermined by the elite manipulation of raw mass opinion. The post-1968 reforms of the system for selecting presidential candidates dramatically weakened the power of the party convention. Deliberation by a couple of thousand delegates was displaced by a system of direct primaries — increasing the level of mass consent by depriving the party professionals of their capacity to steer the system toward winning candidates in the general election.

This geographic metaphor is designed to make vivid the failure in our collective institutional imagination. We haven't figured out a way of moving north to further deliberation without also moving east to restrict the process to a select group. We haven't moved west to further mass consent without also moving south to lessen deliberation and increase the sway of raw public opinion.

Until Deliberation Day. Our proposal seeks to break out of this forced compromise in fundamental values. To some extent at least, we can avoid the choice between raw political preferences of the masses and deliberate political judgments of elites. We can take serious steps toward a democracy that is based on the *informed* consent of ordinary citizens.

We are not claiming that Deliberation Day is the only possible method of realizing quadrant I. Nor have we suggested that DDay eliminates the need to consign a host of important decisions to the other three quadrants.

Nevertheless, its introduction into the working vocabulary of modern democracy will not only enhance the overall legitimacy of the entire system. It will also provoke further efforts at institutional creativity. Perhaps DDay is only the first of many institutional inventions that will fill the vacuum presently described by quadrant I. Our description of DDay suggests — to us at least — that democracy isn't fated forever to cycle between profoundly unsatisfactory options. It emphatically doesn't imply that DDay is the only way — or the best way — to break the modern impasse in institutional design posed by the apparent forced choice between deliberation and mass participation.

We cordially invite you, then, to take up the challenge of institutional design. Perhaps you can design a better mousetrap?

We will be the first to beat a path to your door.

A Trilemma

The tension between deliberation and mass participation is part of a broader pattern of conflict bedeviling democratic institutional designs. To better appreciate the larger problem, think of it as a trilemma — a kind of dilemma with three corners implicating three central democratic values: deliberation, mass participation, and political equality. Deliberation Day is strategically located to realize all three of these values. There is a long history of democratic innovation, but the recurrent pattern has been to make progress on only two corners at a time. The strategies employed thus far have all seemed to preclude achieving all three.

But new institutional designs can overcome this pattern. Deliberation Day is our example of such a design. Consider each value-pair in turn to see why it has seemed impossible to include real progress on the third as well.

Begin with *participatory equality* — the attempt to realize both political equality and participation. Institutions aiming for political equality try to give equal weight to the views of all citizens in a mass public. This value is furthered by expanding the constituency included in the decision or by increasing the extent to which members count equally.

The first part of our trilemma is generated by introducing political participation as a second value. This involves the effort to increase the capacity of the larger public to influence, directly or indirectly, government policy. Much democratic reform has involved efforts to increase both of these values — most notably, by extending the franchise to groups previously excluded by race, ethnicity, religion, economic status, or gender. But as we have already suggested, these efforts have tended to diminish our third key value — deliberation.

We reach a similar impasse when we explore a second pairing — the attempt to combine deliberation with political equality. Call this the pursuit of *deliberative equality,* which can be achieved only at the cost of mass participation.

The Deliberative Poll expresses this ideal, of course, but this is a good place to emphasize how many other contemporary experiments in institutional design also share in this aspiration. One important line of development is the "citizens' jury." Like DPs, CJs use social science research methods to gather a sample of participants to deliberate. But the CJ is much smaller than the DP, consisting of twelve to twenty-four participants.[9] This small size brings a big benefit: In contrast to the DP, CJs can meet in a local community for an extended period. The "jurors" hear testimony, call witnesses, ask for more evidence, and finally make recommendations to some local or governmental authority.

The downside is that the small number of participants makes it impossible to establish the statistical representativeness of the deliberating group. In contrast to the DPs, CJs don't provide a scientific basis for saying that the jury's conclusions are representative of the larger society — even though this claim is often made on their behalf. Nevertheless, the extensive experience with CJs in both the United States and the United Kingdom provides additional confirmation of the competence with which ordinary people can deal with complex policy issues, once they find themselves in a social context that supports deliberation.[10]

What is more, the CJ format can be elaborated in ways that may achieve greater representativeness of the larger community. Daniel Yankelovich, for example, has been convening a series of small groups at a single location (typically San Diego) for successive weekends, each for a day of deliberation on the same topic. After seven or eight groups have met, the numbers may be large enough for statistically significant conclusions to emerge. Provided that the world does not change in some dramatic way on the issue in question during the weeks of deliberation, and provided that efforts are made to keep the experiences of the group comparable, this method has some merit as a practical alternative to Deliberative Polling at the local level.[11]

There are many other interesting experiments under way,[12] but for present purposes, Peter Dienel's work with "planning cells" in Germany is most relevant. PCs are small group discussions that employ random sampling in many decentralized locations — for example, different towns in a region. The results are then aggregated to offer statistically significant generalizations.[13] This is the format that comes closest to the vision elaborated on Deliberation Day — many separate communities having local deliberations on the same issue. Nevertheless, the number of participants remains a minuscule fraction of the population. It is only by making the leap to DDay that we can begin to resolve this dimension of the trilemma — realizing mass participation along with deliberative equality.

A final series of initiatives help us explore the third aspect of our trilemma — participation combined with deliberation, but without political equality. In recent years, there have been a number of notable efforts to pursue this strategy, which we may call *participatory deliberation*. A range of private foundations have encouraged efforts to reach out to a broader public, and provide opportunities to participate in deliberative forums.[14] Participants are provided with carefully balanced briefing materials suitable for citizen deliberation and many have also been trained as moderators for these discussions. Indeed, there is now a network of local groups who can spread the word and help organize further forums.

These conversational circles have involved tens of thousands of participants in one way or another, in contrast to the hundreds who participate in the typical Deliberative Poll or Planning Cell. But this expansion comes at a price. While DPs and PCs try to represent the way a larger community of equal citizens might deliberate, participatory deliberation doesn't have a similar aspiration.

Instead, these initiatives convene groups of self-selected participants. Empirical studies of these groups confirm many of the findings reached in Deliberative Polls, or, with smaller numbers, citizens' juries: Participants demonstrate increased knowledge, significant opinion change, increased sophistication in their political views, and increased consistency.[15]   Nevertheless, self-selection obviously limits the diversity of these groups—since no stipends are paid, there is an obvious selection bias against the poor. Self-selection also encourages the differential participation of people with special interest in the given topic. If the conclusions of these participatory deliberators were given special weight in decision making, it would come at a clear price in terms of political equality.

Once again, Deliberation Day extends these projects in a direction that promises a breakthrough. Of course, even our ambitious initiative will fall far short of ideal political equality. Despite the provisions we have made, the turnout at DDay will not be fully representative of the adult citizenry. When judged by real-world standards, however, DDay promises a real breakthrough in the system's capacity to realize simultaneously the values of equality, participation, and deliberation.[16]

Strategic Reform

There is no need to exaggerate. Even if we are successful beyond our fondest dreams, DDay will appear on the calendar only once every two years. These occasional exercises in responsible citizenship will hardly suffice to dissolve the legitimation problems posed by market inequality or the activist state—let alone the underlying tensions between equality, participation, and deliberation that haunt democratic politics.

But after the twentieth century's infatuation with great leaps forward, it is hardly a disgrace to resist the siren call of political perfectionism. The real challenge lies elsewhere. Many liberals now join conservatives in worshiping at the shrine of the status quo. Their philosophical icons may be different—liberals may prefer Isaiah Berlin, conservatives Michael Oakeshott—but the message is the same: Resign yourself to the tragic complexities of life; reformist efforts to break through the trilemmas of politics are simple-minded at best, oppressive at worst.

It is one thing to renounce the totalizing delusions of revolutionary transformation, quite another to remain satisfied with trivial variations on the status quo. In contrast to worldly-wise counsels of despair, we offer up the worldly art of strategic reform. The strategic reformer does not enumerate an endless laundry list of potential improvements. She focuses on a small number of midsized reforms and considers whether they generate large returns by constructive engagement with existing institutions. Our aim has been to convince you that DDay deserves a place on this short list, and to encourage you to devise other realistic projects which deserve serious consideration.

Liberal democracy really is an experiment, and it is far too soon to call it quits.

10

ALTERNATIVE FUTURES

In the midst of World War II, one of America's greatest social scientists had a bright idea. Robert Merton was then an up-and-coming sociologist helping out on the war effort. With the Roosevelt administration trying to build public support on the home front, Merton came up with a simple but revolutionary proposal. Why not pretest the effectiveness of "morale-building" propaganda by trying out the messages before small groups who could share their reactions in frank discussions focused on the broadcasts?[1]

And so the "focus group" was born with a distinctive rationale: "In contrast to the polling approach, it uncovers what is on the interviewee's mind rather than his opinion of what is on the interviewer's mind."[2] Merton and his colleagues quickly struck paydirt. They found that audiences repeatedly disappointed the expectations of the propaganda makers. While it might seem promising to liken the Nazis to gangsters, the technique didn't work at the test sessions. And focus groups of Irish-Americans reacted very badly to heroic portrayals of the British.[3] This process of testing and revising the message proved invaluable to the war effort. While natural scientists were laboring in secret to create the atomic bomb, social scientists were also proving their worth to the nation — by creating better propaganda!

With the coming of peace, the techniques developed by Merton and his colleagues migrated from the public to the private sector, and the motivating aim shifted as well. Focus groups were redirected to the task of selling products to consumers, rather than manipulating the attitudes of citizens. By pretesting slogans and images on small groups, advertisers gained precious insights that they could not get from more quantitative research methods. Reflecting on the rapid spread of the technique, Merton quoted, with some ambivalence, a leading authority on advertising, Leo Bogart: "The most beguiling aspect of focus groups is that they can be observed in action by clients and creative people behind a one-way mirror. Thus, the planners and executors of advertising can be made to feel that they are themselves privy to the most innermost revelations of the consuming public. They know what consumers think of the product, the competition, and the advertising, having heard it at first hand."[4] Bogart emphasized that it was easy to overgeneralize from these small groups. "While useful and provocative ideas emerge from groups just as they do from individual qualitative interviews, it is dangerous to accept them without corroboration from larger scale survey research."[5] Hence the two techniques, the qualitative and the quantitative, work best in combination. Particularly when used alongside survey research, the focus group became a powerful marketing technique for charting the most effective path to persuasion.

As the focus group industry became a big business, it was only a matter of time before it reentered the public domain. Political consultants began to offer a greatly refined version of Merton's techniques to aspiring candidates and governing politicians — but with devastating effect on the quality of democratic debate. Fine-tuning sound bites, they offered candidates pretested ways of avoiding sustained argument by pressing hot buttons with emotion-laden symbols.[6]

So we are hardly the first in the line of patriotic social scientists who have offered up to the government the idea of small-group conversations. Shouldn't the fate of Merton's contribution give us pause? Doesn't it suggest the remarkable ease with which good intentions go astray in the real world of politics?

No. Consider that we have not been telling a familiar tale of unintended consequences. Merton and his colleagues wanted to help the government manipulate the beliefs of its citizens — that's what propaganda is all about. And they achieved their aim. We do not presume to pass judgment on their initiative. Nazism was a terrible evil, and the war against it required many moral compromises. Merton's show of patriotism might be appropriate at a moment of total war, but it represented a defeat of the democratic ideals for which America was fighting in World War II. And it should be no surprise that this wartime innovation has come back to haunt American political life through the invisible hand that guides the focus group industry.

We take a different lesson from the Merton story. It suggests that idealistic social science can make a real difference to our political life — for good or for bad, depending on the nature of the ideals that motivate the enterprise. In this chapter we propose to place current focus group practice under the moral microscope. What ideals are expressed in its fine-grained structure? How do these ideals differ from those expressed by our DDay proposal?

The inquiry reveals a set of contrasting moral aspirations, suggesting that the focus group business has never liberated itself from the manipulative ideals of its founding moment during World War II. It would be a mistake, of course, to place too much weight on historical accident. Even if Robert Merton and his colleagues had not made their wartime discovery, some bright young entrepreneur probably would have invented focus group techniques a few years later.[7] But the specific historical origin of the focus group does help clarify the ultimate political question: Is it only during wartime that government can be expected to sponsor innovative techniques of small group discussion, and then for antidemocratic purposes? Now that we can see what the focus group industry has wrought, isn't it time for government to act once again to redeem the democratic potential of face-to-face dialogue and deliberation?

Some Facts

By the beginning of the twenty-first century, the focus group has turned into a big business, grossing more than a billion dollars a year.[8] This adds up to more than $4 billion on a quadrennial basis — exceeding the probable economic costs of Presidents Day. Most focus-grouping continues to involve commercial marketing. Although precise data aren't available, politics is only a small, but growing, part of the business. The aggregate figure, however, serves as a politically relevant benchmark: If the invisible hand generates a $4 billion quadrennial expenditure at focus-grouping, shouldn't we be prepared to spend a comparable sum organizing a different kind of small-group conversation?

Maybe not. It all depends on one's political evaluation of the existing enterprise. Given the size and complexity of the industry, not all focus groups are conducted in the same manner. But for present purposes, some stylized facts will help set the stage.

Focus groups are usually very small, varying in size from six to twelve. Participants are normally recruited through a variant of "quota sampling." Clients specify the demographic characteristics of their target audience, and firms try to fill these "quotas." The selection techniques are quite unscientific: People are sometimes approached at shopping malls or other areas where those with the desired demographics might be present. Since participants are paid, there is a problem with repeaters, but the better firms try to get fresh recruits. Sometimes, when qualitative and quantitative work is combined, the participants can be recruited via true random sampling as a spinoff from larger-scale research. Given the small numbers in each focus group, the results are never statistically significant, but as we shall see, they can be very suggestive.

The original idea of the "focused interview" was that the participants would concentrate their discussion on a specific stimulus — a broadcast or advertisement, for example. They then were to share their reactions with fellow members under the guidance of a professional moderator. This "specific stimulus" approach remains common, but some groups now range more broadly over a topic based on a discussion guide prepared beforehand.

In contrast to the standard opinion poll, the moderator doesn't try to get answers to predetermined questions. His job is to uncover the group's frank reactions, to draw out their views in search of unanticipated responses. A typical success involved a political ad prepared for an incumbent governor running for reelection with the message that he was "on the side of the ordinary working man and woman." Professional consultants liked the ad, but it didn't pass muster with a focus group that fastened on the candidate's flashy Rolex watch. The glint of the expensive watch undercut the message and diverted the group's entire discussion of the ad. Mission accomplished: The watch had to go before the ad could make it to the airwaves.[9]

Focus group participants are paid, in amounts ranging from $50 to $200, depending on the topic, target audience, and length of time required. A fairly typical group experience might be two hours long with eight people and a trained moderator. The moderator establishes norms of dialogue for the discussion, draws out the participants, tries to prevent anyone from dominating the conversation, but also avoids dominating it himself. The overriding aim, after all, is to discover unanticipated reactions, not to lead the group to predetermined results.

The sessions are usually recorded with observers watching from behind a one-way mirror. The dialogue is later transcribed and analyzed. Video recording permits analysis of gestures and facial reactions that put the verbal exchanges in context.

Focus groups are typically used at an early stage to help frame a message. They are used again to test reactions to that message once it is developed. Television, radio, mail, and print advertising are all put under the microscope. It is increasingly common to use "dial meter" responses to test reactions to broadcasts, second by second, to each word or phrase presented.[10] Each participant turns a dial signaling approval or disapproval and the results can be averaged on the screen. These initial reactions provide the basis for further group discussions revealing the reasons why one part of a message was embraced while another failed to connect with group concerns.[11]

Whatever one may think of such procedures, they have had a profound influence on the shape of political strategy. When he was President Reagan's media guru, Roger Ailes once remarked: "When I die, I want to come back with real power. I want to come back as a member of a focus group."[12] Ailes has lived long enough to find an even more influential job. He is now president of Fox News. But he wasn't exaggerating too much. Despite the tiny samples of unscientifically selected participants, focus group results are religiously scrutinized by consultants and candidates of all political persuasions.

FGroup versus DDay: Structural Comparisons

So in assessing our proposal, you should not be supposing that we are proceeding on a blank slate. Small groups of citizens are already being asked their opinions on large political matters — only the existing frame-works of inquiry differ quite radically from the ones we are proposing. Our task is to reflect upon these differences, with an emphasis on the micro-organizational structures that distinguish the DDay experience from the typical focus group. While these nuts-and-bolts details may seem mundane, they express very different visions of the aim of political con-versation. By elaborating the normative premises implicit in the compet-ing micro-organizations, we will be in a better position to glimpse the competing political futures that open before us.

Homogeneous Groups?

As campaign adviser Frank Luntz explains, "The composition of the focus group must be selected strategically, with homogeneity as the key to a successful session. . . . If your goal is to study the real, in-depth feelings of whites and blacks toward affirmative action, welfare, or crime, you cannot have an integrated focus group. Similarly, women will not talk freely and emotionally about abortion if men (including a male mod-erator) are present."[13]

"Freely and emotionally": the point is to create a narrow social space for people from similar backgrounds. The six or twelve people around the table may be strangers to one another, but they are insulated from a host of other Americans with different backgrounds and beliefs. They don't have to worry about the reactions from the "outsiders" who have been conveniently excluded from their face-to-face conversation. They are free to ignore their interests, or belittle their status, so long as doing so doesn't meet with the disapproval of the "insiders" in the room.

Within this setting, the moderator can explore the emotions and sym-bols that lie behind in-group sympathies and antipathies. The hot buttons revealed in these settings can serve as the basis for campaign slogans and images that will appeal to key demographic groups in the larger popula-tion. Focus groups can then be used again to test particular ads or cam-paigns. After making sure that the material pushes the right buttons, the next challenge is scientific marketing: Choose media outlets that beam the right messages to the right demographics, with different media pushing different buttons at the same time.[14]

Deliberation Day generates a different dynamic. The typical neighborhood center in an urban area will draw its participants from a three-to-five-mile area, predictably destroying the careful barriers constructed around focus groups: Men and women, young and old, will come from a variety of religions, ethnicities and economic classes. They will encounter one another as citizens confronting common problems, not as tight-knit solidarities invited to vent their distinctive hopes and fears.

When people engage with a diverse group, they focus on shared concerns and interests. In face-to-face discussions, they will attempt to find reasons that will move those from different backgrounds and social locations. They may or may not agree in the end, but they seek to isolate areas of common ground — opening the way to a dialogue of public reasons, not the expression of private anxieties. This has been the consistent finding of Deliberative Polling and other experiments with diverse groups.

DDay opens the door to a dialogue across social divisions rather than one intended to entrench or exacerbate them.

To put this first contrast in a single line: The homogeneity of FGroups encourages the emotional expression of in-group solidarities, while the heterogeneity of DDay encourages the elaboration of public-regarding reasons.

Impression Management?

As the presidential primary season was coming to an end in 1996, Bob Dole had emerged as the Republican choice to challenge Bill Clinton in the Fall. Naturally enough, CBS invited him to *Face the Nation* and present the leading issues of his campaign. For example, what did he mean by repeatedly asking whether ordinary citizens would rather leave their children with him or Bill Clinton? What precisely was he trying to say about "President Clinton's character"?

Dole responded, "I'm just repeating what the focus group said." The puzzled CBS interviewer pressed further:

> CBS: Does that mean he's not a good person?
> SENATOR DOLE: I don't know what — you'd have to ask the people in the focus group.
> CBS: No. We're asking Bob Dole.
> SENATOR DOLE: But I'd — I wasn't in the focus group.[15]

The interview caused a storm of commentary—with pundits predictably condemning Dole for dealing in unsavory innuendos, rather than confronting Clinton's family policy.[16]

It is easy to dismiss this affair as a tempest in a teapot. Unsavory innuendo is as old as politics: Politicians have been disparaging their opponents for millennia. But this has always been a dangerous game. Slyly suggesting that a rival is a child molester may easily generate a backlash, doing grievous damage to one's own character in the popular mind.

Here is where the focus group enters. By pretesting innuendos, the small-group conversations make mudslinging seem more like a manageable science, rather than a dangerous art. There are always risks in casting innuendos, but surely they are minimized when a few focus groups move their dials into positive numbers as they see Bob questioning Bill's integrity?

This is not a rhetorical question: Focus group results fail the most elementary tests of scientific reliability. Nevertheless, as Bob Dole's remarks indicate, they are given enormous credit by contemporary politicians. The only thing surprising about Dole's remarks is their candor. He is speaking for a host of politicians who are avid consumers of pseudoscientific reports from focus group gurus. By pretesting alternative verbal formulations, the focus group industry encourages politicians to think of character assassination as a scientifically controllable technique—and the more scientific the methods become in the future, the more frequently politicians will replace debate on the issues with pretested mudslinging.

DDay will have the opposite effect. When sharing the podium with Bill Clinton, Bob Dole would never think of slyly suggesting that his rival might be a child molester. Such a breach of elementary norms of civility would generate a terrible backlash. Mudslinging simply isn't the way to win the televised debate between the leading candidates on Presidents Day. Indeed, we expect these high-stake encounters to have a sharper substantive edge than the television debates that currently serve as the climax of the campaign. These are often remembered for some salient blunder in a candidate's management of his visual impression—Nixon's heavy beard, Gore's disdainful snort. Such gaffes will always matter, but they will have less of an impact on an audience charged with the task of preparing serious questions for further discussion at the citizen assemblies: "You're right that Mr. Republican has gained a lot of weight on the campaign trail, but I'm not sure that Mr. Democrat really responded to his point about taxes. He waffled badly on the question whether he was going to raise the rates. We really have to get a better answer from Mr. Local Democrat."

Politics is about people as well as issues, and voters will always be looking for hints about a candidate's underlying character. To be sure, focus groups, and other stage-managing techniques, will make it tougher for voters to obtain reliable cues. Nevertheless, we won't see an end to this great game any time soon. The challenge, instead, is to prevent the politics of personality from crowding out all other conversations from the public square.

Uninformed Opinions?

But focus groups don't merely content themselves with the management of innuendo and physical appearance. They also seek to explore the substantive issues, but in a manipulative spirit. As we have seen, pervasive mass ignorance is one of the defining features of modern political life. But focus groups don't try to remedy this basic problem. Instead, they explore the qualitative context of uninformed opinion, its motivations and vulnerabilities to further manipulation.

Small-group discussions on DDay couldn't be more different. They provide participants with the tools they need to confront their own ignorance. Candidates and their representatives can no longer count on exploiting the prejudices of a passive audience. From the televised debate that begins the proceedings, each effort at top-down persuasion encounters a bottom-up effort to define the questions for the next round of debate. By defining questions, not answers, small-group members don't merely gain more information, but even more crucially, they define priorities for inquiry. Instead of drowning in a sea of data, they can define the particular facts they need to make sense of the most pressing areas of common concern.

The result of this ongoing effort at self-education can lead citizens to focus on issue dimensions that go unrecognized in focus groups. Consider the Danish Deliberative Poll held before the country's referendum on the euro. The political protagonists had used polling and focus groups extensively as they prepared for the national campaign. But they were taken by surprise when the public reframed the relevant issues at the Deliberative

Poll. As the exchange between small groups and plenaries proceeded, the participants learned that entering the euro zone might have a negative impact on Danish pensions. Once they glimpsed this possibility, they gave it great importance—exploring its complexities in question after question raised at the plenary meetings. This barrage took the major political actors by surprise, although they had been fully briefed with the results of prior focus groups. Even the prime minister was notably unprepared when confronting the pension question at the plenary session. The incident illustrates the difference between focus group sessions that probe the contours of uninformed opinion and a DDay conversation encouraging participants to define the dimensions of their own concerns, and to demand the information they think they need for a thoughtful decision.

The recent American DP on foreign policy tells a similar story. Before they began deliberating, participants believed that foreign aid represented one of the biggest parts of the federal budget. Once they learned the truth during the conversational give-and-take, there was a dramatic increase in the level of support for additional foreign aid.[17] Contrast the likely result of focus group discussion. Moderators would content themselves with uncovering public resentment about the government sending large sums abroad when the money could be put to better use at home—sentiments based on the mistaken notion that the Marshall Plan was somehow still in effect. The ensuing expressions of righteous indignation could then be used as the basis of ever more effective political ads exploiting public ignorance on the matter, further clouding public debate.

Put aside your own views about foreign aid: Is this the kind of public dialogue we really want?

One-Sided?

Besides exploring the contours of ignorance, focus groups also help refine the shape of effective political argument—but once again, in a manipulative spirit. Effective campaign messages are strategically incomplete. Positive ads portray the selling points and leave out the downside. Attack ads focus on key disadvantages, never mentioning the offsetting benefits. Focus groups help identify the most compelling pluses or minuses, permitting the formulation of compelling sound bites—which are tested once again before they hit the airwaves.

But won't the whole political debate be larger than the sum of the sound bites? One campaign's positive ads may compete with another's negatives, enabling citizens to gain perspective. The marketplace of ideas is a genuine reality, but it is easy to exaggerate its impact. Media marketers seek to target their ads to those most responsive to their positive or negative messages — the same audience may not receive both sides. What is more, viewers tend to learn the information that supports their preexisting partisan positions, reducing cognitive dissonance by ignoring opposing factual presentations.[18]

Negative ads have an especially pernicious effect. While they may polarize and mobilize partisans, they tend to demobilize and disempower the uncommitted. Stephen Ansolabehere and Shanto Iyengar summarize the implications of their carefully controlled experiments: "Political advertising — at least as it is currently practiced — is slowly eroding the participatory ethos in America. In election after election, citizens have registered their disgust with the negativity of contemporary political campaigns by tuning out and staying home."[19]

Contrast DDay. The holiday provides a new social context for the thoughtful consideration of both sides of an argument. DPs consistently show that people don't merely learn the facts that support their predispositions. They become immersed in the ebb and flow of balanced arguments, and learn something about the other side.[20] They may not change their minds, of course. But they emerge with a better grasp of their opponents' understanding of the relevant facts.

By the same token, our proposal is designed to attract millions of Americans who are currently repelled by the negative turn of sound-bite campaigning. The point is to bring out the vast middle, provide it with the tools for public dialogue and thereby force both parties to address the concerns of average Americans. And once they have spent time deliberating, Americans are very likely to carry through and vote. At least this has been the experience of Deliberative Polling.[21]

Top-Down?

To sum up: The focus group is a place where tiny samples of like-minded Americans express "in-group" hopes and fears without the need to talk matters over with the general citizenry. Organizers are perfectly aware that group members don't know very much about the issues, but they do nothing to correct this problem. Professional moderators work hard instead to see how pervasive ignorance may be exploited by manipulating images, innuendos, and one-sided arguments to generate partisan support and to demobilize undecided voters.

A sordid business, mocking centuries of democratic aspirations. And yet the focus group remains a rather positive symbol in today's political culture. Politicians who slavishly follow the advice of focus group gurus are, of course, condemned as lacking in "leadership." But so long as they avoid Dole-ish gaffs, they aren't condemned for making substantial use of the technique in refining their political appeal.

To the contrary, focus-grouping may seem a relatively benign form of political strategizing. In contrast to interest-group lobbying, it offers a way for politicians to break through Beltway babble and hear the opinions of Real Americans. In contrast to the brute numbers of public opinion polls, the focus group promises more nuanced insights into the motivations of swing voters. Despite the predictable disdain of critics from the ivory tower, these may seem very significant virtues: When all is said and done, focus groups do enable real Americans to talk in a way that real politicians find compelling. Surely, there are worse things that can happen in the world!

From one perspective, we find this reaction quite encouraging. It suggests the enduring attraction of democratic ideals, and an almost desperate eagerness to discover their traces in our present practices. And yet, despite the attractive imagery of citizen engagement, focus-grouping is designed to facilitate top-down mechanisms of elite control. Its only redeeming virtue is the woefully unscientific way in which the industry currently does business. But as the generations pass, focus-grouping will become more scientific: It will be ever more closely coordinated with surveys of scientific random samples, becoming an even more powerful tool of elite manipulation.

Of course, DDay also contains top-down elements. The candidates have a privileged place in setting the agenda for discussion. They appear at the start, answering questions from a Deliberative Poll representing the national public. But the set-up for the holiday doesn't allow politicians to treat ordinary people as ill-informed consumers of political propaganda.

DDay gives ordinary people the tools they need to think through the issues and give voice to their conclusions — in conversations in their small groups, in exit polls reported to the nation, in continuing dialogue with their friends and fellow workers during the run-up to the election. Our new holiday is hardly enough to guarantee wise answers. But it will enable citizens to ask some of the hard questions as they ponder the future of the nation, and give new weight to the voice of a thoughtful and empowered public.

Two Futures

Representative democracy is a resolutely complex affair — involving top-down and bottom-up elements. So let us conclude by conceding a great deal to the top-down dimension. Most obviously, ordinary citizens can't hope to keep tabs on the complexities of ordinary government. They have no sane choice but to delegate the lawmaking business to paid politicians — who themselves delegate vast powers to a host of bureaucracies.

This steady flow of top-down decision making profoundly shapes the social world — and many consequential decisions will forever elude serious efforts at citizen control. The fate of any country depends in large measure on the moral seriousness and high intelligence of its political and professional elite — and nothing we have said should be taken to deny this very fundamental point.

Nevertheless, it is the enduring aspiration of democratic theory to find a serious place for ordinary men and women in this ongoing affair — a serious place, not merely a symbolic one. Voting is key, but it can't be better than the quality of deliberation that lies behind it.

Nobody denies this, but civil libertarians tend to consign it to the background. The American constitutional tradition, for example, celebrates the glories of the "marketplace of ideas" in the abstract without confronting the concrete political marketplace that is emerging in the twenty-first century. This refusal to look reality in the face is not altogether unworthy. It is motivated by the fear that realism will only provoke heavy-handed regulation. For example, it would be sheer folly to respond to the manipulative potential of the focus group by trying to shut the industry down or by intensively regulating its operation. Such remedies would be far worse than the disease itself. Like more traditional forms of censorship, top-down control will only end up enhancing the power of the powerful to suppress dissent and opposition.

Nor is much to be gained by preaching to the public about the evils of focus-grouping. No serious politician will renounce the use of a powerful tool when his rivals remain free to use it to gain a competitive advantage at the next election. Such preachments will certainly encourage politicos to avoid the blunders of the hapless Dole, who publicly confessed his dependence on his media gurus. But the savvy politico of the future will continue to spend heavily on focus groups while regularly proclaiming his independence from the conclusions they have reached. No true leader should admit to being the slavish follower of public opinion — and if you have any doubts, you need only ask a few focus groups!

But happily, moralistic preaching and top-down control do not exhaust our available options. Let the focus-groupies ply their trade, and let the politicians continue the age-old agon of competitive politics. But by all means, let ordinary people carve out a new forum for expressing their considered judgments on the leading issues of the day.

For all our talk of the "marketplace of ideas," we should not trust the invisible hand to guide us to our political future. We can, through an act of political imagination, create new institutions for redeeming the ancient promise of democratic citizenship. Ordinary men and women need not be the hapless playthings of the powerful. They can and must find new ways to hold their leaders to account, and redeem their dignity as human beings by responsibly shaping their collective destiny.

ESTIMATED COSTS FOR DELIBERATION DAY

with Eric Tam

We divide our estimate into three parts. First, DDay will require a small permanent bureaucracy on both national and state levels—these costs are incurred every year, even when the holiday doesn't occur. Next, as DDay approaches, a much larger bureaucratic effort will be required. And finally, the biggest share of the costs will occur on the holiday itself, at each of the DDay sites.

We do not try to estimate the extra "start-up" costs that will be incurred during the first couple of DDays. These will be significant.

Permanent Administrative Costs

A permanent bureaucracy will engage in long-range planning and provide the necessary institutional memory. Though the bureaucratic start-up for the first holiday will be substantial, the national and state governments will require only a small permanent staff over the longer run. We estimate that the federal government will hire two hundred full-time equivalent employees (FTEs). Each state will hire three FTEs plus one for every million residents, or a total of 430 FTEs. The average base annual salary of a federal civil servant in 2001 was $53,959;[1] multiplying by 1.35 for the costs of benefits,[2] we arrive at a cost of approximately $73,000 per FTE. A rough estimate of the labor costs for state and federal oversight would therefore be $47,450,000 per year. We estimate that the nonlabor costs would total around 50 percent of the labor costs, bringing our total estimate of permanent administrative costs to $71,175,000 per year.[3] All this is speculative, of course, but provides a sense of the order of magnitude involved.

Off-Site Costs Incurred During Deliberation Day Years

As the holiday approaches, staff must expand to deal with a massive increase in coordination and management activities. It must also discharge three basic operations: operating a reservation system, organizing an advertising campaign, and creating a system for the payment of citizen stipends.

Temporary General Administration

Many of the needed personnel would be seconded from other state and federal agencies, and others will be hired on a temporary basis. As a rough guess, we assume that one FTE will be required for every four venues and that each official will work an average of sixty days.[4] For the scenario envisioning fifty million participants, this generates $228,125,000 for the payment and support of 12,500 FTEs, each working for sixty days. (We use the same formula as the one previously employed for estimating the costs of the permanent bureaucracy.) For a turnout of thirty million, the cost would be $136,875,000; for seventy million, $319,375,000.

Reservations Coordination

Besides organizing and coordinating activities at the individual sites, the most significant task confronting federal and state authorities will be the construction of a reservations system for DDay participants. The three primary methods for processing these reservations, listed in order of ascending cost, are (1) online web interface, (2) interactive voice response (automated "phone maze"), (3) live operator. We assume that the FDDA provides the electorate with a sixty-day window for making their reservations and that the fifty million projected participants divide themselves evenly among the three reservation methods.[5] As we need only eight pieces of data from each participant (name, Social Security number, address of residence, venue, date of participation, whether transportation is required, and the name and Social Security number of a child-care provider who wishes to participate in the Deliberation Day session held on the other day), the cost of setting up a web reservation system for 16.6 million users would be quite low — an initial cost of under $200,000 and one or two full-time staff members to maintain the site.[6]

Reservations by IVR and live operators are much more expensive, requiring the authorities to contract much of the work to private firms. Although no single firm could handle the 33.3 million telephone reservations hypothesized under the fifty-million scenario, such massive phone operations are not unprecedented. For example, in 2000 the Census Bureau contracted with twenty-five private firms to handle sixteen million (outbound) calls over eight days.[7]

Competitive rates in the industry are $1 per IVR call and $5 per live call;[8] assuming that each successful reservation requires two calls, the cost of contracting out 16.6 million IVR and 16.6 million live reservations would be $200 million.[9] Under the same assumptions, the costs for contracting out the calls handled in the thirty-million- and seventy-million-participant scenarios would be $120 million and $280 million, respectively.

Advertising

The Census Bureau spent $324 million during 1999 and 2000 on promotional campaigns — including an outreach effort to more than 140,000 businesses and local politicians and volunteer organizations.[10] A much smaller campaign would be required for DDay, since the candidates, parties, and news media would already be focusing on the event. Nevertheless, there will be need for census-style outreach to business and civic organizations encouraging their cooperation and support. Based on the successful census experience, we estimate this cost at $65 million. Our budget also includes the cost of a media blitz during the run-up to the holiday, encouraging the public to make early reservations, providing phone numbers and Internet site addresses.[11] We estimate a budget of $20 million for these additional media expenditures, generating a total price tag of $85 million for the outreach effort.[12]

Distribution of Payments

The U.S. Social Security Agency's distribution costs are $0.04 for each electronic payment and $0.45 for each paper check (including labor and all fixed costs).[13] Currently, the SSA sends out 78.4 percent of its payments electronically and 21.6 percent in the form of paper checks.[14] This ratio implies $0.129 per payment, generating an estimated cost of reimbursing fifty million participants of $6,450,000. The costs for thirty million and seventy million participants are $3,870,000 and $9,030,000 respectively.

On-Site Costs

The largest share of the costs will, of course, be incurred at the local DDay sites throughout the nation. These include on-site administration, compensation for facility maintenance and operations, security, food, and transportation. We shall be assuming that the typical site is a local public school.

One site manager and four staff members will be hired for each DDay site. These administrators would coordinate the on-site activities and supervise the activities of volunteers, police, and food service and custodial staff.

Site Manager

The typical senior administrator will be a principal or vice principal of the school used as a Deliberation Day venue, whose annual mean wage in 2001 was $70,890 per year.[15] Assuming a lower limit of 190 eight-hour school days produces a mean hourly rate of $46.64. Staffing fifty thousand venues with two such senior administrators who would each work a six-hour shift[16] at a 150 percent holiday premium for each of two days would cost an estimated $83,952,000. An additional ten hours of training for each supervisor before the event would cost $46,640,000, for a total cost of $130,583,000. Staffing thirty thousand or seventy thousand venues would cost a total of $78,350,000 or $182,817,000, respectively.

Staff

The typical staffer will be a teacher at the school serving as a DDay site. The annual mean wage of a secondary school teacher is $44,247 per year.[17] Assuming a lower limit of 190 eight-hour school days produces a mean hourly rate of $29.11. Staffing fifty thousand venues with two crews of four such administrators, each of whom would work a six-hour shift (the shifts would be the same as the administrators' shifts, as noted in note 15) at a 150 percent holiday premium for each of two days would cost an estimated $209,580,000. An additional five hours of training would cost $16,070,000, for a total estimated cost of $236,367,000. The total estimated costs for staffing thirty thousand and seventy thousand venues, including training, would be $141,820,000 and $330,913,000, respectively.

Volunteers

We estimate a budget of $500 to cover clerical, supplies, food and other hospitality items for the approximately fifteen volunteers present at each venue. With this budget, the costs associated with volunteers for fifty thousand venues would total $25,000,000; the costs for thirty thousand and seventy thousand venues would be $15,000,000 and $35,000,000, respectively.

Miscellaneous On-Site Administrative Costs

We estimate a budget of $500 per venue to cover the cost of stationary, signage, travel, and other miscellaneous expenses. Computer costs will be trivial, since the average student-to-computer ratio in the United States in 2001 was 5.4:1.[18] Uploading the registration data to a central database will not add any significant cost: more than 99 percent of U.S. public schools have computers with access to the Internet.[19] With this budget, the miscellaneous administrative costs for fifty thousand venues would total $25,000,000; the costs for thirty thousand and seventy thousand venues would be $15,000,000 and $35,000,000, respectively.

Facilities

Maintenance and Operations

The average nonlabor portion of school maintenance and operating costs in the United States is $331.51 per student annually for schools with a capacity of one thousand or fewer students.[20] This figure includes expenses for basic utilities, telephone, trash collection and disposal, maintenance and groundskeeping equipment and supplies, travel expenses, equipment repair and rental, and insurance. Because the audiovisual needs for Deliberation Day (a computer in each classroom with a feed to the Internet capable of broadcasting the debate,[21] three microphones, and a speaker system) are well within the standard audiovisual complement of the average school, we assume that the use of this equipment is also covered by this figure. Dividing by 365 days provides us with an estimate of $0.908 per participant; we therefore estimate the maintenance and operations costs for the use of local facilities by fifty million participants to be $45,417,000. Our estimates for thirty million and seventy million participants are $27,250,000 and $63,583,000, respectively.

Adult Seating

Since we will be relying heavily on elementary and middle schools to serve as deliberation centers, there may be a shortage of sufficient adult seating, requiring the rental or purchase of folding chairs to fill the gap. The standard weekend rental fee is $1.50, including delivery, and the purchase price on a bulk order is less than $9.00.[22] We will be using each chair twice, so we shall be assuming a rental cost of $.75 per deliberator and a purchase cost of $4.00 per deliberator.

We haven't obtained an exact sense of the size of the chair gap, or the extent to which it can be filled by the rental market. But since elementary and middle schools will play a large role, it is a mistake to ignore the problem entirely. To provide a sense of the orders of magnitude, we assume that each elementary and middle school will need 250 adult chairs. Based on NCES figures, high schools account for 18.9 percent of the schools or approximately 8.28 million seats.[23] This leaves a gap of around 8.36 million chairs for the fifty-million-participant scenario, and gaps of approximately 3.36 million and 13.36 million chairs, respectively, for the thirty-million- and seventy-million-participant scenarios.

This need will be filled by rental and purchase, with the proportion of the gap filled by purchase increasing as participation increases. To fix ideas, we assume that 50 percent of the chairs will be purchased for thirty million participants, 67 percent for fifty million participants, and 75 percent for seventy million participants. We assume that 20 percent of the purchased chairs will be replaced after the typical DDay, and it is this cost that will be reflected in our estimates. (The cost of filling the "chair gap" will undoubtedly be higher for the first DDay, but this is one of the many "start-up" costs that we do not attempt to estimate.)

Given these assumptions about the rental and purchase requirements, we estimate the additional cost for adult seating to be $15,909,000 for fifty million participants, and $5,456,000 and $27,534,000, respectively, for thirty million and seventy million participants.

Custodial

The average salary of a custodian is $9.42 per hour,[24] and we shall be providing holiday pay (at a 150 percent premium). Some of the necessary work will occur before and after DDay, but we handle this by providing for a generous contingent during the holiday itself. Our budget covers the cost of three full-time custodians working two six-hour shifts at each venue on both days. Total cost of the fifty million–participant scenario is $50,867,000. The costs for thirty million and seventy million are $30,520,000 and $71,213,000, respectively.

Security

We would hire two shifts of three local patrol officers to provide security for each site, serving for six hours each. The average national salary of a police officer is $20.07 per hour,[25] so twelve hours of holiday pay (at a 150 percent premium) for three officers at fifty thousand venues for each of two days would cost an estimated $108,383,000. The estimated costs for thirty thousand and seventy thousand venues would be $65,030,000 and $151,737,000, respectively.

FOOD The U.S. General Accounting Office's most recent report on meal costs in the National School Lunch Program conducted in 1993 (using data drawn from the 1987–89 school years) estimated a national average cost of $1.67 to produce a school meal.[26] This figure includes the cost of raw food, production, labor, tableware, storage, transportation, food preparation equipment, utilities, and maintenance. Updating this figure to account for the CPI increase gives us a cost of $2.50 per meal. Assuming that labor costs (which make up 40.7 percent of the estimated cost) are 50 percent higher due to holiday pay, we arrive at an estimate of $3.01 per meal. We increase the total cost by an additional 50 percent to $4.50 per meal to account for any miscellaneous expenditures and to ensure that the food's quality is sufficient for adult consumption. The estimated cost of providing lunch for 50 million participants and 2,400,000 staff and local representatives would therefore be $235,800,000. Lunch for 30 million and 70 million participants and corresponding staff would cost $141,480,000 and $330,120,000, respectively.

TRANSPORTATION Deliberation Day Authorities would arrange for free transportation via school bus to all venues. Our estimate for the cost of providing this transportation is based on figures supplied by the Department of Education, which indicate that in 1998–99, 57.6 percent of public school students rode publicly funded busses to school at an average annual cost of $482 per student.[27] Assuming an average of 190 school days and converting to 2001 dollars, this works out to $2.71 per student for one day's worth of transportation. If we assume that the same proportion of Deliberation Day attendees would require transportation assistance and that labor costs make up 40 percent of the costs (to account for the holiday premium), then the total estimated cost for transportation is $93,650,000 for fifty million participants, $56,190,000 for thirty million participants, and $131,110,000 for seventy million participants. These represent significant overestimates, as a far greater proportion of the electorate than of public school students would choose to provide their own transportation.

Summary

Our estimated budget for permanent (off-site) administrative costs at the federal and state for years during which Deliberation Day does not occur is $71,175,000, regardless of the level of participation.

Our rough estimate of the additional off-site administrative costs incurred during a year in which Deliberation Day occurs with fifty million participants is $520 million, or $10.40 per participant. Our estimate of on-site costs is $967 million, or $19.34 per participant, if fifty million citizens participate. Off-site costs for a thirty-million turnout are $346 million or $11.53 per participant; for seventy million, $694 million or $9.91 per participant. On-site costs are $576 million and $1.36 billion, respectively ($19.20 per participant in if thirty million participate and $19.43 per participant if seventy million participate).

During the year the holiday occurs, then, total costs are roughly $1.558 billion for fifty million participants, $993 million for thirty million participants, and $2.124 billion for seventy million participants.

Table A. The Costs of Deliberation Day
All cost figures are reported in thousand dollar units

		Number of Participants		
		30 million	50 million	70 million
Permanent Administrative Costs (all levels annually)	General Administration			
	Labor	47,450	47,450	47,450
	Non-Labor	23,725	23,725	23,725
	Total Annual Permanent Administrative Cost	71,175	71,175	71,175
Costs Incurred Only During Deliberation Day Years	Off-Site Costs			
	General Additional Administration	136,875	228,125	319,375
	Reservation Processing	120,200	200,200	280,200
	Advertising/Marketing	85,000	85,000	85,000
	Distribution of Payments	3,870	6,450	9,030
	Total Off-Site Costs	345,945	519,775	693,605
	On-Site Costs			
	On-Site Administration			
	Site Managers (includes training)	78,350	130,583	182,817
	Site Staff (includes training)	141,820	236,367	330,913
	Volunteer Supplies and Hospitality	15,000	25,000	35,000
	Miscellaneous Administrative	15,000	25,000	35,000
	Facilities			
	Maintenance and Operations	27,250	45,417	63,583
	Adult Seating	5,456	15,909	27,534
	Custodial	30,520	50,867	71,213
	Security (Police Officers)	65,030	108,383	151,737
	Food (includes preparation)	141,480	235,800	330,120
	Transportation	56,190	93,650	131,110
	Total On-Site Costs	576,096	966,976	1,359,027
	Total Deliberation Day Year Only Costs	922,041	1,486,751	2,052,632
Total Cost of Deliberation Day Year		993,216	1,557,926	2,123,807
Total Cost of 4-Year Cycle		1,206,741	1,771,451	2,337,332

APPENDIX B
THE IOWA EXPERIENCE

There is nothing like DDay at present, but the Iowa caucuses provide some distant illumination. We analyze the significance of the turnout data in Chapter 6, but it seemed more sensible to display the data in this appendix.

Table B. Iowa State Turnout Data by Party 1988–2000

Election Year	Special Circumstances	General Election Turnout[1]	Republican Caucus Turnout[2]	Democratic Caucus Turnout[3]
1988[4] Bush-Dukakis	Open race after incumbent Reagan's departure	**1,225,614** (*75% of registered voters*) Bush (R): 545,355 Dukakis (D): 670,557	**108,824** —22% of total registered Republicans —20% of Republican-candidate voters participating in November's general election	**110,000** —20% of total registered Democrats —16% of Democratic-candidate voters participating in November's general election
1992[5] Clinton-Bush-Perot	Republican Party caucus canceled; incumbent Bush's win considered inevitable. Leading Democratic candidates opted out of Iowa caucuses after favorite-son Sen. Tom Harkin entered race.	**1,354,607** (*80% of registered voters*) Bush (R): 504,891 Clinton (D): 586,353 Perot (Ref.): 105,159	**N/A–no caucus held**	**25,000** —4% of registered Democrats —4% of Democratic-candidate voters participating in November's general election
1996[6] Clinton-Dole	Democratic caucuses featured an unopposed incumbent, President Bill Clinton	**1,234,075** (*70% of registered voters*) Dole (R): 492,644 Clinton (D): 620,258	**96,451** —20% of Republican-candidate voters participating in November's general election	**ca. 50,000** —*party did not provide actual caucus attendance figures in 1996* —8% of Democratic-candidate voters participating in November's general election

| 2000[7] Bush-Gore | Open race after incumbent Clinton's departure | 1,315,553 *(registered voter data unavailable)* Bush (R): 634,373 Gore(D): 638,517 | 85,276 | −13% of Republican-candidate voters participating in November's general election | 60,760 | −10% of Democratic-candidate voters participating in November's general election |

1. Sources: Iowa State Office of the Secretary of State (http://www.sos.state.ia.us/elections/turnout.html) (providing total voter turnout figures); Federal Election Commission, Congressional Research Service (providing total votes per candidate).

2. Both Republican and Democratic party caucus turnout figures are self-reported by Iowa state party officials. Since 1988 concerns over the accuracy of these self-reported figures have increased, as officials from both parties have been accused of "gaming" the self-reporting of caucus attendance numbers for political advantage. See, e.g., Hugh Winebrenner, "Attendance at the Iowa Precinct Caucuses," *Iowa Political Hotline* 8 (February 2000). Percentages of general election voters who previously participated in Iowa state caucus meetings were obtained by dividing the absolute number of self-reported party caucus attendance figures into the total number of actual votes cast for each party's candidate in the November general election, rounded to the nearest percentage point. Note that our methodology, based on available verifiable data, is far from perfect, as it yields a percentage that is only a rough approximation of the actual percentages of party caucus participants ultimately participating in the general election. Consider, for example, that votes cast for individual general election candidates do not map perfectly onto voters' party affiliation; for example, a Republican voter who participated in the Republican caucuses might vote for another conservative candidate or even an independent or Democratic candidate appearing on the general election ballot. Our methodology assumes that Republican caucusgoers probably voted for the Republican candidate when casting their ballots in the general election, and that Democratic caucusgoers voted for the Democratic candidate. Second, our numerator's caucus attendance data may not have been reported accurately by each party, which self-reports these numbers. See id. at n. 2. Finally, our formula's denominator does not include votes cast by Republican and Democratic voters for candidates running on tickets other than the dominant Republican and Democratic tickets. This assumption might distort our figures, particularly for 1992, when Reform Party candidate Ross Perot took votes from both parties' candidates.

3. Id.

4. Tom Seery, "Record Turnout at Iowa Caucuses," Associated Press, February 9, 1988 (providing self-reported 1988 Republican and Democratic party caucus turnout figures and percentage turnout of total registered party members).

5. Dave Lesher and Ronald Brownstein, "Harkin Scores Record Victory in Iowa Caucus," *Los Angeles Times*, February 11, 1992 (providing self-reported 1992 Republican and Democratic party caucus turnout figures and percentage turnout of total registered party members).

6. James W. Davis, *U.S. Presidential Primaries and the Caucus-Convention System: A Sourcebook* 265 appendix B; http://www.sos.state.ia.us/publications/archive/register/rro/rro_cauc.htm (providing self-reported 1996 Republican and Democratic party caucus turnout figures).

7. Iowa Democratic Party, http://www.gwu.edu/~action/states/iademresults.html (providing self-reported 2000 Republican and Democratic party caucus turnout figures).

NOTES

1. Imagine

1. These projects go under many names — "Citizen Juries," "Consensus Conferences," "Study Circles," "National Issues Forums," and "Planning Cells," among others. For a good overview of the National Issues Forums and related practices like the Study Circles, see John Gastil and James P. Dillard, "The Aims, Methods, and Effects of Deliberative Civic Education through the National Issues Forums," 48 *Communication Education* 179 (July 1999). For other practices see Anna Coote and Jo Lenaghan, *Citizens' Juries* (1997); Peter C. Dienel and Ortwin Renn, "Planning Cells: A Gate to 'Fractal' Mediation," in *Fairness and Competence in Citizen Participation: Evaluating Models for Environmental Discourse* 117 (Ortwin Renn et al. eds., 1995). Finally, two National Deliberation Days for youth between the ages of eighteen and thirty-five have been organized by FIRST (the National Foundation for Individual Responsibility and Social Trust). We discuss some of these initiatives at greater length in Chapter 9.

2. Or more precisely, the best realizations approach the design of a "quasi-experiment" with a "post-test only control group" (although some Deliberative Polls have had other comparison groups as well). See Donald T. Campbell and Julian C. Stanley, *Experimental and Quasi-Experimental Designs for Research* 34–63 (1963). Deliberative Polling® is a trademark of James S. Fishkin. Any fees from the trademark are used to support research.

3. In the citizens' jury and the consensus conference, for example, the opinions are solicited by consensus. In the Deliberative Poll, the opinions are solicited in anonymous questionnaires. For more on the Deliberative Poll see generally James S. Fishkin, *The Voice of the People: Public Opinion and Democracy* (1995); Robert C. Luskin, James S. Fishkin, and Roger Jowell, "Considered Opinions: Deliberative Polling in the UK," 32 *Brit. J. Pol. Sci.* 455 (2002); Maxwell McCombs and Amy Reynolds eds., *The Poll with a Human Face: The National Issues Convention Experiment in Political Communication* (1999).

4. Larry Bartels, "Uninformed Votes: Information Effects in Presidential Elections," 40 *Am. J. Pol. Sci.* 194, 194 (1996). Bartels goes on to say, "but the political significance of this political ignorance is far from clear." He believes that ignorance is significant—an issue to which we return in Chapter 4.

5. Robert C. Luskin, "From Denial to Extenuation (and Finally Beyond): Political Sophistication and Citizen Performance," in *Thinking about Political Psychology* 284 (James H. Kuklinski ed., 2002).

6. Robert Erickson and Norman Luttberg, *American Public Opinion: Its Origins and Impact* 25 (1973) (quoting American Institute of Public Opinion [Gallup]). We are grateful to Robert Luskin for bringing this example to our attention.

7. Martin Merzer, "Americans Oppose Attacking Iraq Alone: Most in Poll Want Allies' Support, Proof," *Knight Ridder/Tribune News Service,* January 12, 2002, available at LexisNexis News Library. The article reports on a poll of 1,204 Americans conducted between January 3–6, 2002, by Princeton Survey Research Associates. The survey asked, "As far as you know, how [many] of the September 11 [2001] hijackers were Iraqi citizens?" More than one-fifth (21 percent) believed that "most of them" were Iraqi, another 23 percent answered "some of them," and 6 percent answered "at least one of them." Only 17 percent of the respondents said that that none of the hijackers were Iraqi—the correct answer.

8. Thomas E. Patterson, *The Vanishing Voter* 124 (2002).

9. Id. Even here 8 percent mistakenly thought that Gore had taken the opposite position, and 11 percent misidentified Bush's stand. This suggests that a substantial percentage of the "correct" answers were also generated by guesses, implying that these "high salience" issues actually had broken the cognitive barrier only for a minority of the electorate.

10. One commentator joked that "don't know" is really the correct answer, given the complexity of Britain's constitutional tradition. This question comes from the initial round of the British Deliberative Poll on the future of the monarchy in 1996.

11. Michael Delli Carpini and Scott Keeter, *What Americans Know about Politics and Why It Matters* 101–2 (1996).

12. See id. at 103.

13. In different ways, this is the theme of much recent work ranging from Samuel Popkin, *The Reasoning Voter* (1991) to Paul Sniderman, Richard A. Brody, and Philip Tetlock, *Reasoning and Choice: Explorations in Political Psychology* (1991).

14. The classic statement is Philip Converse, "The Nature of Belief Systems in Mass Publics," in *Ideology and Discontent* (David Apter ed., 1964). While some of the response instability may be due to measurement error (see Christopher Achen, "Mass Political Attitudes and the Survey Response," 69 *Am. Pol. Sci. Rev.* 1218 [1975]), it is widely granted that many apparent opinions are either nonattitudes or very much "top of the head." For a good overview of the current state of this discussion, see generally Donald R. Kinder, "Opinion and Action in the Realm of Politics," in 2 *The Handbook of Social Psychology* 778–867 (Daniel T. Gilbert et al. eds., 4th ed., 1998), esp. 795–96.

15. For a good overview of this work by George Bishop and the replication by the *Washington Post* under the direction of Richard Morin, see "What Informed Public Opinion?" *Society,* July–August 1995, at 5.

16. For a model that attempts to account for variations in non-attitudes, see generally John R. Zaller, *The Nature and Origins of Mass Opinion* (1992). For reflections on the significance of the "softness" of public opinion for democratic theory, see 1 Bruce Ackerman, *We the People,* 240–43 (1991).

17. John Brehm, *The Phantom Respondents: Political Surveys and Political Representation* (1993), especially chapter 5.

18. Robert C. Luskin, "Political Psychology, Political Behavior, and Politics: Questions of Aggregation, Causal Distance, and Taste," in *Thinking about Political Psychology* 217, 230–231 (James H. Kuklinski ed., 2002).

19. For classic discussions, see generally Anthony Downs, *An Economic Theory of Democracy* (1957); Mancur Olson, *The Logic of Collective Action* (1971).

20. See Thomas E. Patterson, *The Vanishing Voter* 90 (2002).

21. See Thomas E. Patterson, *Doing Well and Doing Good: How Soft News and Critical Journalism Are Shrinking the News Audience and Weakening Democracy—And What News Outlets Can Do About It* 3–4 (2000).

22. For an account of early informal attempts to assess public opinion before the modern science of polling see Claude E. Robinson and Robert E. Chaddock, *Straw Votes: A Study of Political Prediction* (1906).

23. See Bruce Ackerman and Ian Ayres, *Voting with Dollars: A New Paradigm for Campaign Finance* (2002).

24. See Walter Lippmann, *Public Opinion* (1922); Walter Lippmann, *The Phantom Public* (1925).

25. Id. at 13–14.

26. Joseph Schumpeter, *Capitalism, Socialism, and Democracy* (1942).

27. Schumpeterian skepticism has been reinforced more recently by the rise of social choice theory, which has questioned the conceptual coherence of the very idea of majority rule. See generally William H. Riker, *Liberalism against Populism: A Confrontation between the Theory of Democracy and the Theory of Social Choice* (1982). This is not the place for a considered assessment of the conceptual paradoxes elaborated by social choice theorists, most notably Condorcet and Arrow. See generally Dennis Mueller, *Public Choice II: A Revised Edition of Public Choice* (1989). But we are entirely unpersuaded by Riker's use of social choice theory as a blunderbuss against any and all alternatives to Schumpeterian minimalism. Depending on the distribution of preferences, social choice theory can undoubtedly defeat simplistic notions of majority rule, but it hardly suggests that democrats must content themselves with Schumpeterian minimalism and renounce any affirmative effort to make sense of popular self-government.

28. See generally David Truman, *The Governmental Process* (1951); Louis Hartz, *The Liberal Tradition in America: An Interpretation of American Political Thought since the Revolution* (1955); Robert Dahl, *Who Governs?* (1961).

2. The Holiday

1. There may also be a need for special exemptions from service for emergency personnel who cannot be replaced, even for a single day. But such irreplaceables are few and far between.

2. See generally, Leigh Eric Schmidt, *Consumer Rites: The Buying and Selling of American Holidays* 34–35 (1995).

3. Id. at 32–37

4. See Len Travers, *Celebrating the Fourth: Independence Day and the Rites of Nationalism in the Early Republic* (1997); David Waldstreicher, *In the Midst of Perpetual Fetes: The Making of American Nationalism, 1776–1820* (1997).

5. See Chapter 6 and Appendix A for further discussion of cost issues.

6. See Chapter 6 for further discussion of the space that could be made available for community deliberation throughout the nation.

7. In framing legislation, it would be wise to provide that Congress Day would automatically come into existence after the first two Presidents Days are conducted, thereby placing the burden on opponents to convince a majority that the initial experiments with deliberation had been such failures that an extension of the initiative would be unjustified.

8. In a poll conducted by the Census Bureau of a sample of the nineteen million registered voters who did not participate in the 2000 elections, the most frequent reason (20.9 percent) given by respondents for not voting was that they were "too busy or had conflicting work or school schedules." See U.S. Census Bureau, *Voting and Registration in the Election of November 2000* 10 (2002), available at http://www.census.gov/prod/2002pubs/p20-542.pdf.

9. Deliberative Polls have resulted in consistent increases in political participation and civic engagement. See Robert C. Luskin and James S. Fishkin, "Deliberation and Better Citizens," Presentation at the Annual Joint Sessions of Workshops of the European Consortium for Political Research (March 22–27, 2002) (unpublished manuscript, on file with authors).

10. The National Commission on Federal Election Reform, *To Assure Pride and Confidence in the Electoral Process* 40–42 (2001), available at http://www.reformelections.org/data/reports/99%5Ffull%5Freport.php.

11. If a third-party candidate is winning the support of 15 percent or more of the voters in leading opinion polls, he or she would qualify for Deliberation Day, and we would modify the format appropriately. See Chapter 5.

12. Before 1992 candidates responded to questions posed by leading journalists, but this became unpopular with the public when journalists used their privilege to ask embarrassing "gotcha" questions. See The Twentieth Century Fund, *Report of the Twentieth Century Fund Task Force on Presidential Debates: Let America Decide* 74 (1995). Since 1992 all debates have been chaired by a single "neutral" moderator or have relied on the "town meeting" format discussed in the text. Id. at 95; Thomas Patterson, *The Vanishing Voter* 171 (2002).

13. If the first round of conversation takes longer than planned, the foreman should

respond by making an appropriate reduction in the ninety-second speaking period generally allowed to each speaker.

14. This system is called "approval voting." For further consideration of its properties, see generally Steven Brams and Peter Fishburn, *Approval Voting* (1983). Before the final vote, proponents of particular questions should be allowed to withdraw their proposals if they believe that alternative formulations have a better chance of gaining the requisite support.

15. See Chapter 6 for a more elaborate discussion of the reasons why we think this payment is justified.

16. Given the oversupply of lists, why not invite the small groups to submit only a single question, rather than two? This will require the moderator to draw more lists, on average, and therefore give more groups a sense of participation at the citizen assembly. This point is significant, but it is outweighed by other factors. Restricting the group to a single question might encourage additional tension as different members strive to "win" the privileged top spot in the voting. This would undermine the core value of small-group deliberation: to enable small-group members to explore different frameworks for evaluating the election. It is far more important for small-group members to discuss the issues intelligently than for a group representative to pose a single question at the plenary session.

17. We will be discussing questions related to turnout further in Chapter 6.

18. Some 8 out of 10 work in local government. Most of the rest work in State governments. Bureau of Labor Statistics, *1998–99 Occupational Outlook Handbook,* available at http://stats.bls.gov/ocohome.htm.

19. Depending on logistics, it will often be necessary to use facilities with many classrooms but few auditoriums. A large high school, for example, may only have one large auditorium and one gymnasium that could be fitted out for an assembly. In such a context, it may be necessary to stagger lunch periods—scheduling one cluster of small groups for food at 11:40 while another cluster is holding its assembly, and so forth. Many other compromises will also be required by the size of individual facilities. For example, there is nothing sacrosanct about citizen assemblies' suggested size of 500 people. A facility containing an auditorium that accommodated only 250 citizens would work just as well, or maybe even better.

20. Even if some of the issues raised by candidates have been slighted, and if no citizens' questions have initially made it to the floor, this does not suggest that anything has gone seriously awry. To the contrary, it probably means that a portion of the candidates' agenda has gripped public interest to the exclusion of everything else. As a consequence, it is right to devote at least half of the agenda to a further exploration of themes raised previously.

21. This is consistent with our experience in all the Deliberative Polls. In fact, we have experimental evidence that substantial opinion change can be accomplished in only one morning of discussion. See Cynthia Farrar, James Fishkin, Don Green, Robert Luskin, and Elizabeth Paluck, "Experimenting with Deliberative Democracy: Effects on Preference and Social Choice," Paper presented at the Annual Meeting of

the International Society of Political Psychology (July 2003) (unpublished manuscript, on file with the authors).

22. See John Stuart Mill, *Considerations on Representative Government* (1861), in *On Liberty and Other Essays* 353–63 (John Gray ed., 1991).

23. Id. at 354.

24. James Mill, "The Ballot" (1830), in *Political Writings* 227, 227 (Terence Ball ed., 1992).

3. From Thought-Experiments to Real Experiments

1. 2 James Bryce, *The American Commonwealth* 267 (Macmillan 1933) (1888).

2. Although forty million viewers represent a remarkable response, these numbers are down from the heights of prior years. The modern era of presidential debates began in 1976, when an FCC ruling allowed the major-party candidates to confront each other without requiring equal participation from minor candidates. During the first two electoral cycles, more than half of all television households tuned in, but the percentage then began to decline in the 1980s — from 46 percent in 1984 to 29 percent in 1996 and 2000. The third Bush-Gore debate hit an all-time low of 26 percent. Thomas Patterson, *The Vanishing Voter* 122 (2002). This drop is symptomatic of a larger decline in citizen engagement in the electoral process in response to the disintegration of political parties and the rise of media manipulation. Patterson provides a thoughtful survey of the electoral data, id. at chapter 1.

The estimate of forty million viewers is, of course, only a first approximation of voter engagement. On the one hand, Bush and Gore staged three debates, so many more than forty million tuned in to at least one of them. On the other hand, not all viewers were voters, and some were not even eligible to vote. Nevertheless, these complexities don't change the orders of magnitude involved.

3. Id. at 232–33 n. 74.

4. Id. at 123. This finding is supported by earlier research, which has consistently found a correlation between presidential debates and an information gain among the electorate. See Sidney Kraus, *Televised Debates and Public Policy* (2d ed., 2000); Marion Just et al., "Thirty Seconds or Thirty Minutes," 51 *J. Comm.* 120–32 (1990).

5. For the exceptions, see Patterson, supra note 2, at 125–26.

6. Id. at 123.

7. Id. The response rate after the second and third debates was almost as high.

8. Id.

9. Kathleen Hall Jamieson and David S. Birdsell, *Presidential Debates: The Challenge of Creating an Informed Electorate,* 198–99 (1 New York: Oxford, 1988).

10. B. Carlin, "Watching the Debates: A Guide for Viewers," in *Televised Election Debates: International Perspectives* 157, 162 (Stephen Coleman ed., 2000).

11. Id. at 162.

12. Robert Luskin of the University of Texas has been a key collaborator on almost all the Deliberative Polls. Other key colleagues include Norman Bradburn (NORC), Roger Jowell (National Centre for Social Research, London), Pam Ryan (Issues De-

liberation Australia), Dennis Thomas and Will Guild (on the electric utility polls), Kasper Hansen and Vibeke Normann Andersen (Denmark), Ralitsa Peeva and Boriana Dimitrova (Bulgaria) and others.

13. See Robert C. Luskin, James S. Fishkin, and Dennis L. Plane, "Electric Utility Issues in Texas," Paper Presented at the Annual Meeting of the Association for Public Policy Analysis and Management (November 1999) (unpublished manuscript, on file with authors).

14. See Cynthia Farrar, James Fishkin, Don Green, Robert Luskin, and Elizabeth Paluck, "Experimenting with Deliberative Democracy: Effects on Preference and Social Choice," Paper Presented at the Annual Meeting of the International Society of Political Psychology (July 2003) (unpublished manuscript, on file with the authors).

15. The DDay format also envisions each candidate providing a written 1,500-word statement on the issues, which is distributed to citizens on the day of the meetings. While this allows for ready reference during DDay, these statements don't really compare to the more elaborate briefing documents — often 30,000 words long — that are characteristic of DPs.

16. Recall that some of the DPs have been conducted in highly charged media environments. The DPs for the Australian referendum on the republic, the Danish referendum on the euro, and the British general election were all conducted at the height of national campaigns immediately before a national vote. The 1996 National Issues Convention took place at the start of the presidential nomination process, but it involved considerable candidate coverage. In these cases, respondents were in a better position to inform themselves through mass media, and not only through the specialized briefing-book process.

17. Details have varied somewhat, but this is the basic format. The 1996 National Issues Convention was a day longer, beginning on Thursday evening.

18. Note that seventy-five minutes on DDay are occupied by the television debate, leaving four hours and forty-five minutes for face-to-face discussion. One might also divide the time between the more active engagement required during small-group sessions and the relatively passive engagement required of members of an audience listening to opinion-leaders responding to questions in the plenary sessions. Under this breakdown, DPs split their nine hours into equal components of relative activity and passivity; DDay is relatively active for two and three-quarter hours, relatively passive for three and one-quarter hours.

19. See Farrar, Fishkin, Green, Luskin, and Paluck, supra note 14.

20. For these results in the British Deliberative Poll, see James S. Fishkin, *The Voice of the People: Public Opinion and Democracy* 221 (expanded ed., 1997).

21. The numbers are relatively large when compared to focus groups or other mechanisms of deliberative consultation such as citizens' juries or consensus conferences.

22. Deliberative Polling employs random sampling, in contrast to virtually all other mechanisms of face-to-face deliberative consultation.

23. See Robert C. Luskin, James S. Fishkin, and Roger Jowell, "Considered Opinions: Deliberative Polling in the U.K.," 32 *Brit. J. Pol. Sci.* 455, 466–74 (2002).

24. 67.3 percent of the fifty-two policy items showed statistically significant net change at the .05 level. The calculations about gross change include movements to and from neutrality among the possible changes of position. See id. at 467–74 for a detailed discussion.

25. See Steven H. Chafee, "The Interpersonal Context of Mass Communication," in *Current Perspectives in Mass Communication Research* 95, 98 (G. Gerald Kline and Phillip J. Tichenor eds., 1972).

26. See Kasper M. Hansen and Vibeke Normann Andersen, "The Deliberative Poll: Opinion Formation in the Experimental Context of Deliberative Polling," Paper Presented at the Annual Meetings of the American Political Science Association (September 2001) (discussion of "selective learning").

27. See Luskin, Fishkin, and Jowell, supra note 23, at 474–83 for the application of a model connecting true information gain with attitude change. The same model works in other Deliberative Polls for which we have good information measures.

28. Robert C. Luskin, James Fishkin, et al., "Information Effects in Referendum Voting: Evidence from the Deliberative Poll," Paper Presented at the Annual Meetings of the American Political Science Association (September 2000) (unpublished manuscript, on file with authors).

29. See Robert C. Luskin, James Fishkin, et al., "Learning and Voting in Britain: Insights from the Deliberative Poll," Paper Presented at the Annual Meetings of the American Political Science Association (September 1999) (unpublished manuscript, on file with authors).

30. See Richard Sinnott, "European Public Opinion and the European Union: The Knowledge Gap," Working Paper no. 126, *Barcelona, Institut de Ciències Polítiques i Socials* (1997).

31. See Hansen and Andersen, supra note 26.

32. See Luskin, Fishkin, and Plane, supra note 11.

33. See Farrar, Fishkin, Green, Luskin, and Paluck, supra note 13.

34. Henry E. Brady, James S. Fishkin, and Robert C. Luskin, "Informed Public Opinion About Foreign Policy: The Uses of Deliberative Polling," 21 (*Brookings Review* 16–19 (2003).

35. John Stuart Mill, "Considerations on Representative Government," in *On Liberty and Other Essays* 255 (John Gray ed., 1991) (1861).

36. Id.

37. See William H. Riker, *Liberalism against Populism: A Confrontation between the Theory of Democracy and the Theory of Social Choice* (1982). ("The unavoidable inference is . . . that, so long as a society preserves democratic institutions, its members can expect that some of their social choices will be unordered or inconsistent. And when this is true, no meaningful choice can be made.")

38. This is essentially the argument of "structure induced equilibrium." See Kenneth A. Shepsle and Barry R. Weingast, "Structure Induced Equilibrium and Legislative Choice," 37 *Public Choice* 503 (1981).

39. This kind of shared dimension is called single-peakedness. For the classic account, see generally Duncan Black, *The Theory of Committees and Elections* (1958).

40. See Riker, supra note 37, at 128. ("If by reason of discussion, debate, civic education and political socialization, voters have a common view of the political dimension [as evidenced by single-peakedness], then a transitive outcome is guaranteed.")

41. For an overview of these results, see Christian List, Iain McLean, James Fishkin, and Robert C. Luskin, "Deliberation, Preference Structuration, and Cycles: Evidence from Deliberative Polls," Paper Presented at the Annual Meetings of the American Political Science Association (September 2000) (unpublished manuscript, on file with authors). It might be argued that the issue of collective consistency comes into play only with more than two options and that our serious presidential candidates in the United States are likely to be no more than two in number (although three-way races will sometimes be possible and some applications of Deliberation Day will be in a multiparty context; see Chapter 5). However, even in the two-party context, the candidates are positioning themselves in an issue space that is likely to have multiple options that will receive serious consideration by the public and the various constituencies within it. The meaning of the public will and the mandate of an election will be far more amenable to coherent interpretation if that issue space turns out to be collectively consistent.

42. See Luskin, Fishkin, and Jowell, supra note 23, at 478–79 for results supporting this conclusion from the first British Deliberative Poll. It is consistent with evidence from other Deliberative Polls.

43. Samuel Popkin, *The Reasoning Voter: Communication and Persuasion in Presidential Campaigns* 44–95 (1991).

44. See Arthur Lupia, "Shortcuts versus Encyclopedias: Information and Voting Behavior in California Insurance Reform Elections," 88 *American Political Science Review* 63 (1994).

45. See generally Benjamin I. Page and Robert Y. Shapiro, *The Rational Public* (1992).

46. See Fishkin, supra note 20, at 84–86.

47. See generally Larry M. Bartels, "Uninformed Votes: Information Effects in Presidential Elections," 40 *American Journal of Political Science* 194 (1996).

48. See Cass R. Sunstein, "Deliberative Trouble? Why Groups Go to Extremes," 110 *Yale Law Journal* 71, 75–80 (2000) (describing these polarizing mechanisms).

49. See Irving Janis, *Victims of Groupthink* (1972).

50. See Chapters 5, 7, and 8.

51. For this analysis applied to the first British Deliberative Poll, see Luskin, Fishkin, and Jowell, supra note 23, at 135–36. In that Deliberative Poll, about half of the groups increased what Sunstein calls polarization, and about half decreased; with respect to group conformity, the variance decreased in about half the small groups and increased in about half.

52. See Sunstein, supra note 48, at 116–18.

53. Sunstein cites cases of balanced group composition where the tendency was not polarization but movement toward the center. See id. at 93. ("One reason may be the existence of persuasive arguments in both directions.")

54. Cass R. Sunstein, *The Naked Emperor: Why Societies Need Dissent* (forthcoming 2003) (manuscript at 157, on file with authors).

55. See Reid Hastie et al., *Inside the Jury* 79 (1983) (explaining the greater social pressure produced by the requirement of unanimous verdicts).

56. For further reflections on the centrality of this value in liberal theory, see generally Bruce Ackerman, *Social Justice in the Liberal State* (1980); James Fishkin, *Tyranny and Legitimacy: A Critique of Political Theories* (1979).

57. Phoebe C. Ellsworth, "Are Twelve Heads Better Than One?" 52 *Law and Contemporary Problems* 205 (1989).

58. Id. at 224.

59. Id. at 223.

60. See our discussion of information gains above.

61. See generally Harry Kalven Jr. and Hans Zeisel, *The American Jury* (1966).

62. Id. at 149.

63. Id.

64. Saul M. Kassin and Lawrence S. Wrightsman, *The American Jury on Trial: Psychological Perspectives* 121 (1988). See Kalven and Zeisel, supra note 61, at 153.

65. See generally Phoebe C. Ellsworth, "Psychology and Law," in 2 *The Handbook of Social Psychology* 684 (Daniel T. Gilbert et al. eds., 4th ed., 1998) (especially 701).

66. While this is only common sense in today's world, in Chapter 6 we consider how the evolution of the Internet might permit alternative organizations of DDay in the future.

67. Pamela Johnston Conover et al., "The Deliberative Potential of Political Discussion," 32 *Brit. J. Pol. Sci.* 21, 33, 35 (2002).

68. See John Gastil and James P. Dillard, "The Aims, Methods, and Effects of Deliberative Civic Education through the National Issues Forums," 48 *Communication Education* 179, 189 (1999).

69. When first interviewed, 45 percent of respondents had the most favorable position on a scale of questions on revenue sharing. After only a morning of discussion, 69 percent took that position (a statistically significant difference and one that holds up in comparison to the control group level of 58 percent, among those who had not yet discussed the issue but had otherwise prepared for the weekend). See Farrar, Fishkin, Green, Luskin, and Paluck, supra note 14.

4. Cycles of Virtue

1. We will ask a similar question later when we consider the systemic impact of our proposal to extend Deliberation Day to the midterm congressional elections. But since we have not yet described the format for Congress Day, it is best to postpone this issue.

2. The aim of such a poll would not be to represent the views of all voters in a politician's district, but only those whose views will be influenced by Deliberation Day. This will require a judgment call from the pollster, and further deliberation by the politician.

3. For a more elaborate discussion of Founding political science, see 1 Bruce Ackerman, *We the People: Foundations* (1991) (chapter 7).

4. For some classic reflections on this theme, see generally Murray Edelman, *The Symbolic Uses of Politics* (1964).

5. See James Buchanan and Gordon Tullock, *The Calculus of Consent: Logical Foundations of Constitutional Democracy,* 283–95 (1962).

6. Of course, one or another extremist group may make it their aim to disrupt Deliberation Day through systematic violence. The criminal law is the only answer to such conspiracies. While we oppose the use of criminal sanctions to discipline disruptive individuals, we would make an exception here (see Chapter 2). We continue our discussion of ideological groups in Chapters 7 and 8.

7. The problem of civility should be distinguished from a second issue. Call it "crowding out." It is conceivable that so many groups will seek to organize on Deliberation Day that they numerically overwhelm the uncommitted citizens. "Crowding out" might indeed become a problem, and we will return to it in Chapter 6.

8. See Chapter 6.

9. See Chapter 3.

10. There was a late surge of support for the Yes position in the Australian referendum on the republic in the period following the Deliberative Poll's broadcast and widespread publication of the sample's move toward Yes. See, for example, "Support for Republic Surges," *AAP Newsfeed,* October 30, 1999; Malcolm Farr, "Yes Swing Too Little Too Late," *Daily Telegraph,* November 6, 1999. While such media polls are suggestive, we do not yet have the kind of systematic evidence that would decisively establish a DP's *ex post* effect on public opinion.

11. The Center for Media and Public Affairs compared the 1996 and 2000 primary campaigns and found that the percentage of substantive stories on policy issues or candidate records dropped from 44 percent to 22 percent, and the percentage of horserace stories rose from 37 percent to 45 percent (comparisons from January 1 through Super Tuesday). See Center for Media and Public Affairs, *Campaign 2000: The Primaries, Media Monitor* (2000). For a similar report from the general election period see Center for Media and Public Affairs Election Watch, *Campaign 2000: More News, Less Filling* (2000).

12. In the 2000 elections, more than 61 percent of eligible white voters cast ballots, whereas the turnout rate for minorities was just over 50 percent. Class disparities were even more pronounced: Fewer than 45 percent of eligible voters in the lowest income quintile participated, whereas almost 75 percent of those in the highest income quintile voted. See U.S. Census Bureau, *Current Population Survey: Voting and Registration in the Election of November 2000,* table 2, Reported Voting and Registration, by Race, Hispanic Origin, Sex, and Age, for the United States: November 2000 (2002), available at http://www.census.gov/population/socdemo/voting/p20-542/tab02.pdf.

13. See generally Stephen Ansolabehere and Shanto Iyengar, *Going Negative: How Political Advertisements Shrink and Polarize the Electorate* (1995).

14. Voters between the ages of eighteen and twenty-four turn out at a lower rate than any other major social group except the extremely poor. Only 34.1 percent voted in the 2000 elections, while turnout was above 50 percent in the 1964 and 1968 presidential elections. See United States Census Bureau, *Voting and Registration Data, Current Population Survey, Voting and Registration in the Election of November 2000* (2002), available at http://landview.census.gov/population/www/socdemo/voting/p20-5 42.html.

15. The relatively high rates of participation during the 1960s seem to have been anomalous. See Paul Allen Beck and M. Kent Jennings, "Political Periods and Political Participation," 73 *American Political Science Review* 737 (1979). Generally speaking, those under thirty lack both the community ties and the stable political interests that predispose citizens to take the trouble to vote. See Norman H. Nie, Sidney Verba, and Jae-on Kim, "Political Participation and the Life Cycle," 6 *Comparative Politics* 319 (1974).

These factors, however, are exacerbated by poor civic education, and it is at this point that DDay promises to make a constructive contribution. Not only does the holiday invite the young to make good use of their superior educations, but we also imagine that schools will be running mock DDays for students as part of their normal curriculum, thereby encouraging later participation as adults. For the role of civic education, see Stephen Bennett, "Why Young Americans Hate Politics, and What We Should Do about It," 30 *PS: Political Science and Politics* 45 (1997).

16. See Chapters 6 and 8.

5. Extending the Paradigm

1. See Chapter 3; see also Robert C. Luskin and James S. Fishkin, "Deliberation and 'Better Citizens,' " Presentation at the Annual Joint Sessions of Workshops of the European Consortium for Political Research (March 2002) (unpublished manuscript, on file with authors).

2. See Norman J. Ornstein, Thomas E. Mann, and Michael J. Malbin, *Vital Statistics on Congress* 57–58 (2000). These statistics overstate the invulnerability of incumbents, since they don't take into account that some "voluntarily" retire from office in response to likely defeat at the polls. It is hard to take this factor into account in a hard-edged statistical way, but we don't think that it is substantial enough to change our basic point.

3. We are among them: see Bruce Ackerman, "The New Separation of Powers," 113 *Harv. L. Rev.* 633 (2000). On the prospects of mitigating these pathologies through institutional reform, see generally James Sundquist, *Constitutional Reform and Effective Government* (1992).

4. The following chart indicates voter turnouts since 1990:

Year	Percent of Voting Age Population
1990 (off-year)	36.5
1992 (presidential)	55.1
1994 (off-year)	38.8
1996 (presidential)	49.1
1998 (off-year)	36.4
2000 (presidential)	51.1
2002 (off-year)	39.3

Sources: Federal Election Commission, *About Elections and Voting,* available at http://www.fec.gov/elections.html (last accessed May 14, 2003) (providing turnout data for all years except 2002); Edward Walsh, "Election Turnout Rose Slightly, to 39.3%," *Washington Post,* November 10, 2002 (estimating 2002 turnout).

5. Jonathan D. Salant, April 29, 1999, available at www.cnn.com/all politics/stories/ 1999/04/29, estimates that 114 incumbents in 1998 encountered only "nominal" opposition. Of the seventy-six uncontested races in 2002, seventy-four involved incumbents. In one of the others, "Kendrick Meek won a primary to succeed his mother, Rep. Carrie T. Meek (D-Fla.). In Alabama, Artur Davis is the other non-incumbent without a major-party challenger." Manuel Roig-Franzia, "Politics," *Washington Post*, November 5, 2002. See also Benjamin Ginsberg and Martin Shefter, *Politics by Other Means: The Declining Importance of Elections in America* 3–4 (1990).

6. According to a set of studies based on voter interviews soon after the 1988, 1990, and 1992 elections, basic voter knowledge about congressional candidates is extremely poor. Fewer than 30 percent of voters could successfully identify the name and party of both major party House candidates in the election that had just occurred; voters did a little better with Senate candidates—fewer than 40 percent were able to correctly identify the name and party of both major candidates. When asked, "What issue did the candidates [in the voter's state] talk about most during the campaign for the Senate?" 34 percent of respondents answered "don't know." The results for House races were even worse: more than half of the respondents could not identify the issue most frequently discussed by their district's candidates. Steven J. Rosenstone et al., *National Election Studies, American National Election Study: Pooled Senate Election Study, 1988, 1990, 1992* (distributed by the Inter-university Consortium for Political and Social Research, 1993) (datasets).

7. See David W. Brady, John F. Cogan, and Morris P. Fiorina, "Epilogue: 1998 and Beyond," in *Continuity and Change in House Elections* 238–39 (David W. Brady, John F. Cogan, and Morris P. Fiorina eds., 2000). ("In the incumbency and isolation equilibrium that extended from the late 1970s to the early 1990s members of the House held their electoral fates in their own hands. Electoral defeat was a rarity, reflecting laziness, scandal, or an avoidable political mistake. Consequently, retirement had replaced elections as the principal source of turnover in House seats. . . . In 1994, 90 percent of all incumbents who ran, won. . . . Statistical estimates of the incumbency advantage were actually higher than in 1990, the previous midterm election. . . . In 1998 . . . of 401 incumbents seeking reelection, only five lost for an all-time record incumbent reelection rate of 98.5 percent.")

8. At present, negative advertising is widely used for strategic demobilization of voters who are not already strong partisan supporters. The game currently is to mobilize your base and discourage the vast middle. However, this game will change if DDay mobilizes and engages the less partisan. Then there will be a strong incentive to inform the inattentive so far as possible. For an overview of the current uses of campaign advertising, see Stephen Ansolabehere and Shanto Iyengar, *Going Negative: How Political Advertisements Shrink and Polarize the Electorate* (1995).

9. In late September 1996 MacNeil/Lehrer Productions organized PBS Debate Night, which featured two unique elements: first, a national debate about the congressional election with the major-party leaders in Congress (the speaker and minority leader of the House and the majority and minority leaders of the Senate), and second, local debates among House and Senate candidates in nearly one hundred separate

broadcasts around the country. This basic format was repeated in 1998 and 2000. We are grateful to Dan Werner, president of MacNeil/Lehrer Productions, for information about this innovative project.

10. In 1996 PBS estimated that the national broadcast reached 3.2 million viewers. Of course, the nearly one hundred additional local and statewide debate broadcasts greatly increased the total audience for the initiative.

11. Things will get tight on the rare occasion when both of a state's Senate seats are open. This occurs only when one Senate seat has been vacated through death or resignation. Because there is no incumbent in this seat, Congress Day will be particularly important—since elections are particularly contested when seats are "open."

And yet the information overload problem will become particularly exigent. There are two choices here: eliminate the candidates for the House from the television debate and concentrate all attention on the two Senate seats, or provide for very short debates for the candidates for all three races. This is a close call, but we prefer the first option. Senate seats are too important to permit such limited attention, and since House elections are biennial, it is almost certain that the House race will return to the agenda during the next Congress Day.

12. The six states were Alaska, Kansas, Massachusetts, Mississippi, Nebraska, and Virginia. "The Races for Senate," *New York Times,* November 5, 2002, available at http://nytimes.com/ref/elections2002/2002senateindex.html.

13. Of the seventeen states that employ commission-based redistricting, four—Hawaii, Iowa, Montana, and Washington—redistrict their congressional as well as their state legislative seats by commission. Haw. Const. art. IV, 2; Iowa Code Ann. 42.3 (West 1991 and Supp. 1996); Mont. Const. art. V, 14; Wash. Const. art. II, 43; see also Jeffrey C. Kubin, "Note: The Case for Redistricting Commissions," 75 *Tex. L. Rev.* 837, 843 (1997). The Hawaii and Montana commissions' final redistricting maps become law without formal legislative action; the Washington commission's redistricting plans can be amended by a two-thirds vote of both houses of the legislature, although the plans themselves become law without official legislative approval. See Haw. Const. art. IV, 2; Mont. Const. art. V, 14(3)–(4); Wash. Const. art. II, 43(7). In Iowa the redistricting mechanism is a bit more complex and iterative. First, Iowa's Legislative Services Bureau proposes draft district maps. The LSB then submits its maps to the legislature for approval, with only minor corrective amendments permitted. If the Iowa legislature fails to approve the plans by a majority vote, the LSB then prepares a second set of plans for resubmission to the legislature under the same procedural rules. Finally, should the Iowa legislature again reject the plans, the LSB prepares a third and final set of plans. The Iowa legislature then has the right to make any changes to the maps deemed necessary to secure final passage. See Iowa Code Ann. 42.3(1)–(3) (West 1991).

14. See generally Bruce Ackerman and Ian Ayres, *Voting with Dollars* (2002) (arguing for mitigating incumbency advantage through campaign reform).

15. Since a good deal of lead time is required to arrange for schools and other deliberative sites, the decisive polling must take place a good deal before Congress Day—though pains should be taken to keep the necessary lead time to a minimum.

16. See James Buchanan and Gordon Tullock, *The Calculus of Consent* (1965); John Ferejohn, *Pork-Barrel Politics* (1974); Kenneth A. Shepsle and Barry R. Weingast, "Political Preferences for the Pork Barrel: A Generalization," 25 *Am. J. Pol. Sci.* 96 (1981); David P. Baron, "Majoritarian Incentives, Pork Barrel Programs, and Procedural Control," 35 *Am. J. Pol. Sci.* 57 (1991).

17. Since these leaders will themselves be engaged in debates in their own districts on Congress Day, the debate may have to take place a few days in advance. This is also true of the night-before debate involving all four Congressional leaders.

18. See Chapter 4 for the parallel analysis of Presidents Day.

19. Rough proportionality is more or less the rule in Belgium, Greece, Spain, and the Netherlands. See Library of Congress Law Library Staff, *Report for Congress: Campaign Financing of National Elections in Selected Foreign Countries* 103–4, 159 (1995). The British give their two main parties, Labour and Conservative, equal shares, and give the third party, Liberal Democrats, a smaller allocation, but one that is larger than its share of parliamentary seats. See The Lord Chancellor's Department, *Procedures at a General Election* §9.21 (2001), available at http://www.lcd.gov.uk/elections/ge2001/procedures/01.htm#expenses (last accessed May 14, 2003).

20. There are complexities lurking here. Given this 50 percent ceiling, how to treat a party that was formerly a member of the governing coalition but chooses to leave the government, thereby precipitating the fall of the government and the calling of a new election?

Reasonable people can differ, but we would not want to reward such conduct by giving the departing party more time than it deserves under the 50 percent ceiling. So long as the party was part of the government during most of the last parliament, it should be counted as a coalition party and should not be allowed to pretend that it is part of the opposition for purposes of reducing the amount of time the parties who have been consistently opposed to the government can launch their critique.

This position may, however, generate unfairness to minor parties that are members of governing coalitions but may be excluded from the government the next time around. If this is thought to be a problem, the ceiling can be redesigned to guarantee a larger share of the governing coalition's time to the minor parties. This will leave the previous prime minister a bit short, but he already has had more than enough previous opportunities to present his case.

21. The longest period for a British parliamentary election since World War II was six weeks: from mid-March through early May 1997. The shortest periods were twenty-one days in February 1974 and twenty-two days in October 1974. See The Lord Chancellor's Department, *Procedures at a General Election* §1.2 (2001), available at http://www.lcd.gov.uk/elections/ge2001/procedures/01.htm#timetable (last accessed May 14, 2003).

Snap parliamentary elections have also occurred quite often, for example, in the history of the French Fifth Republic. The length of campaigns following presidential dissolutions were: thirty-eight days in 1962; twenty-four days in 1968; twenty-one days each in 1981 and 1988; and thirty-three days in 1997. Bruno Cautrès, "The Electoral Campaign," in *How France Votes* 42 (Michael S. Lewis-Beck ed., 2000).

In contrast, snap elections in Germany have occurred only twice since the Second World War, and there has been a longer pause between the dissolution of parliament and the election. In 1972 the vote of no-confidence occurred in April, and elections were held in November. Barbara Marshall, *Willy Brandt: A Political Biography* 83 (1997). In 1982 a vote of no-confidence occurred at the end of the year and elections were held in March 1983. German Bundestag, *Organization, Motions,* available at http://www.bundestag.de/htdocs_e/orga/04plenar/02itembusi/itembus2.html.

22. Deliberation Day for the selection of members to serve in Britain's new regional parliaments would, of course, require the participation of regional political parties that gain substantial support in these assemblies.

23. See generally, Thomas E. Cronin, *Direct Democracy: The Politics of Initiative, Referendum, and Recall* (1989). We are using the term *referendum* here broadly to include the initiative, in which citizens place a measure on the ballot through a petition process.

24. Id.

25. See David Butler and Austin Ranney, *Referenda around the World: The Growing Use of Direct Democracy* 19 (1994).

26. Id. at 18.

27. See Chapter 7.

28. Such a field experiment could be combined with a televised Deliberative Poll — with the face-to-face discussions following the broadcast. We would like to thank Robert Luskin for this suggestion.

29. See generally http://www.by-the-people.org (last accessed May 14, 2003); http://www.la.utexas.edu/research/delpol (last accessed May 14, 2003) (detailing the online experiment and its results).

30. See *The Federalist* nos. 51, 62 (James Madison).

31. Note, however, that the first Online Deliberative Poll used voice but not video and produced statistically significant changes in the same direction as those produced in the face-to-face version.

6. What Price Deliberation?

1. 1 *The Records of the Constitutional Convention of 1787* 83 (Max Farrand ed., 1911).

2. The median gross weekly wage for full-time workers over 16 was $525. Bureau of Labor Statistics, *Usual Weekly Earnings of Wage and Salary Workers-Press Release,* available at http//stats.bls.gov/news.release/wkyeng.to6.htm.

3. While the caucuses are formally open only to party loyalists, one may declare oneself a Democrat or Republican at the meeting. E-mail from Steve Mandernach, general counsel, Iowa Democratic Party, to Bruce Ackerman (July 31, 2002) (on file with authors); e-mail from Marlys Popma, executive director, Republican Party of Iowa, to Bruce Ackerman (July 30, 2002) (on file with authors); William G. Mayer, "Caucuses: How They Work, What Difference They Make," in *In Pursuit of the White House: How We Choose Our Presidential Nominees* 105–29 (William G. Mayer ed., 1995) (summarizing states' Republican and Democratic party caucus participation eligibility policies).

4. According to William G. Mayer, "caucuses are less an opportunity for citizens to 'come and reason together' than an occasion in which candidate enthusiasts come together to be counted." Mayer, supra note 3, at 129. Participants often arrive at the meeting already committed to a particular candidate. Telephone interview with Dr. Sheila McGuire Riggs, Iowa Democratic Party chairwoman (July 26, 2002); Popma, supra note 3. Candidates typically send campaign representatives to the caucus meetings, where they make speeches to the caucus participants. Individual participants may also make speeches, though this isn't as common. Meetings typically run between forty-five minutes and two hours, though longer meetings are not unusual. Mandernach, supra note 3; McGuire Riggs; Popma, supra note 3. See also Mayer at 105 (providing extensive discussion of how typical Republican and Democratic caucuses are structured in Iowa and elsewhere).

5. Democratic National Committee rules require proportional representation, but Republican rules do not. Occasionally, a majority at a Republican caucus shuts out the minority, with the caucus chairman choosing to follow a winner-take-all delegate allocation strategy. See generally McGuire Riggs, supra note 4; Popma supra note 3; Mayer, supra note 3, at 105–29 (discussing Republican party caucus policies).

6. Mandernach, supra note 3; McGuire Riggs, supra note 4; Popma, supra note 3. Local caucuses in Iowa elect delegates to ninety-nine county conventions, which in turn elect delegates to the statewide nominating convention. Id. See also *The Iowa Political Hotline* (January 2000), available at http://www.iowapoliticalhotline.com/ newsletters/Januaryoo/ooo16 .htm (last visited July 21, 2002).

7. See Mayer, supra note 3, at 126–28 (tables 4.4 and 4.5). Note that Mayer's turnout data are based on the expected number of voters turning out for a particular party on Election Day rather than the larger number of registered voters in the population. For a discussion on Iowa's turnout rates, see infra notes 14–17 and accompanying text.

8. Iowa's status as "first in the nation" evolved as a tradition, but it is now entrenched in state law, which provides that precinct caucuses must be "held no later than the fourth Monday in February of each even numbered year; and shall be at least eight days earlier than the scheduled date of any meeting, caucus, or primary which constitutes the first determining stage of the presidential nominating in any other state." Iowa Code Sec. 43.3. Both Democratic and Republican parties have set 7:00 P.M. as their caucus meeting time, and meetings are never held on weekends. Since New Hampshire is the next state that selects delegates, the Iowa caucuses have normally been exactly eight days prior, on a Monday, so as not to push the season any earlier. Mandernach, supra note 3. In 2000, for example, the Iowa caucuses took place on Monday, January 24; in 1988 the caucuses were held as late as Monday, February 8.

9. See Table A, Iowa State Turnout Data by Party: 1988–2000, in Appendix B.

10. The percentages of Republican and Democratic voters participating in Iowa caucuses can vary significantly. See id. (summarizing Iowa state caucus turnout data by political party and presidential election year circumstances.) The decision of favorite son Senator Tom Harkin (Dem.-Iowa) to run for the presidency in 1992 caused the leading Democratic candidates—Jerry Brown, Bill Clinton, Bob Kerrey, and Paul

Tsongas—virtually to ignore Iowa. Interview with David Yepsen, political reporter, *Des Moines Register* (July 2002). No more than twenty-five thousand attended. Since George Bush was running for reelection in 1992, the Iowa GOP canceled its straw poll and caucus. Rod Granger, "Candidates Sidestep Iowa," *Crain Communications,* February 17, 1992.

11. See Appendix B. Open presidential contests took place in 1988 and 2000. In 1988, 108,824 Republicans and 110,000 Democrats participated in party caucuses—representing 20 percent of the vote the Republican candidate won in the fall election and 16 percent of the Democratic vote. The 2000 turnout was also substantial, but smaller than in 1988: 85,276 Republicans and 60,760 came to the caucuses—about 13 percent of the Republican vote in November's general elections and 10 percent of the Democratic vote.

12. In 2000, for example, the presidential candidates campaigned tirelessly, cumulatively spending more than six hundred days crisscrossing Iowa. Bob von Sternberg, "Who Will Get the Presidential Boost From Iowa Caucuses?" *Iowa Star Tribune,* January 23, 2000. Campaigns routinely hold "caucus training" programs, send brochures to participants' homes, offer rides to supporters on snowy caucus evenings, make thousands of phone calls, and buy massive amounts of TV, radio, and newspaper space in advance of the event. See, e.g., Judy Keen, "Republican Race Not Free of Suspense," *USA Today,* January 21–23, 2000; Grace Shim, "Iowa Caucus-Goers Play 'Inside Game,' " *Iowa City Press-Citizen,* January 22, 2000.

13. Historically, the top three finishers in the Iowa caucuses become the top three presidential contenders in the national contest. See Michael Knock, "Iowa Caucuses Shift Focus," *Iowa City Press-Citizen,* January 16, 2000. But Heartland polls conducted during the past two presidential elections suggest voter demobilization, with participation by weaker partisans and ideological moderates dropping at a faster rate than engagement by stalwart Democrats or Republicans. University of Iowa Social Science Institute, *Iowa Caucus Campaign Dynamics,* January 21, 2000. Many would-be caucusgoers increasingly believe that caucus outcomes are a foregone conclusion. On the Republican side, the August straw poll has partially preempted the actual caucuses in weeding out some candidates; on the Democratic side, the lack of salient issues or an incumbent presidential contender have had a similar effect. Richard L. Berke, "Iowa, 'Polled to Death,' Is Set for Real Thing," *New York Times,* January 23, 2000.

14. See Mayer, supra note 3, at 105; Appendix B.

15. Tom Serry, "Record Turn-out at Iowa Caucuses," *Associated Press,* February 9, 1988. ("A cold snap was broken Monday and temperatures reached the upper 30s in some parts of the state. . . . It was almost like springtime in Iowa today.")

16. See Table A, supra note 9 and Appendix B.

17. Mayer has elaborated on the relatively unrepresentative character of the caucus participants. We condense his data into a single chart:

Selected Demographic Traits of Caucus Attendees and General Election Voters, 1988

| | Iowa Caucus Participant | | General Election Voters | |
	Democrats (%)	Republicans (%)	Democrat-leaning (%)	Republican-leaning (%)
Education				
No high school degree	10	4	25	16
High school graduate	31	28	37	32
Some college	21	25	21	26
College graduate	18	25	11	19
Graduate school degree	20	18	7	6
Income				
Under $9,999	10	5	23	14
$10,000–$19,999	18	15	24	20
$20,000–$29,999	21	23	19	18
$30,000–$39,999	20	18	15	15
$40,000–$59,999	22	24	14	18
$60,000 or more	8	15	6	15
Gender				
Male	47	57	39	47
Female	53	43	61	53
Age				
17–29	4	2	20	23
30–39	16	10	24	24
40–49	17	15	17	16
50–64	33	40	20	19
65 and over	30	32	19	18
Ideology				
Extremely Liberal	6	0	4	0
Liberal	35	1	14	1
Slightly Liberal	22	3	20	7
Moderate	22	13	34	25
Slightly Conservative	8	24	15	28
Conservative	6	52	10	31
Extremely Conservative	1	7	2	6
Party Identification				
Strong	56	67	n/a	n/a
Weak	26	27		
Independent member of party	13	4		
Pure Independent	2	1		
Independent member of opposite party	2*	0		

	Iowa Caucus Participant		General Election Voters	
	Democrats %	Republicans %	Democrat- leaning %	Republican- leaning %
How long active in state party politics				
0–5 years	22	9	n/a	n/a
5–10 years	22	25		
10–20 years	25	27		
More than 20 years	3	39		

*Both the Iowa Republican and Democratic parties allow caucus participation by citizens who register on the same night as the caucus meetings.

Source: Mayer, supra note 3, at 131–35 (tables 4.6, 4.7 4.9, citing various data sources).

18. Caucuses tend to give a special advantage to a presidential candidate supported by a highly motivated ideological faction. For example, Jesse Jackson and Pat Robertson ran more successful campaigns in caucus states than in presidential primary states. See id. at 145–46.

Nongovernmental organizations are already involved in Iowa and other states. For example, the Campaign Against Cancer, organized by the American Cancer Society, launched a highly effective media and volunteer campaign to sway Iowa caucus and New Hampshire primary voters during the 2000 presidential campaign. See "American Cancer Society Launches Campaign Against Cancer, Urges Presidential Candidates to Address Cancer," *U.S. Newswire,* January 13, 2000.

19. See William G. Mayer, "Mass Partisanship, 1946–1996," in *Partisan Approaches to Postwar American Politics* 209 (Byron Shafer ed., 1998) (table 5.6).

20. See Mayer, supra note 3, at 196 (table 5.1). If we average data from 1988 through 1996, 31 percent of the voters call themselves "strong partisans," 33 percent are "weak partisans," 25 percent are "independent" but leaning toward one of the major parties, and 11 percent are pure "independents."

21. See supra note 17.

22. Youthful voters between eighteen and twenty-six have the worst turnout of all groups, except for households earning less than $5,000. Only 34 percent of these young voters cast a ballot in the 2000 election. We have already pointed to other aspects of the holiday that should encourage a large increase in youthful turnout. But every little bit helps when it comes to building the civic culture of the next generation. For more data and discussion on this critical issue, see Chapter 4.

23. See supra note 17.

24. There is also some evidence suggesting that DDay will tend to attract a more representative selection of the voting public than many other forms of political activity. For example, McLeod et al. found that age, education, and income strongly affect rates of participation in traditional forms of engagement (voting, campaigning, and the like) but had virtually no effect on willingness to attend a public

forum on a local issue. See Jack M. McLeod et al., "Understanding Deliberation: The Effects of Discussion Networks on Participation in a Public Forum," 26 *Comm. Research* 743, 760 (1999) (table 1.3) [hereinafter McLeod et al., "Understanding Deliberation"]; see also Jack M. McLeod et al., "Community, Communication, and Participation: The Role of Mass Media and Interpersonal Discussion in Local Political Participation," 16 *Pol. Comm.* 315, 330 (1999) [hereinafter McLeod et al., "Community, Communication, and Participation"]. Other researchers have made similar findings. See, e.g., Steven J. Rosenstone and John Mark Hansen, *Mobilization, Participation, and Democracy in America* 234–45 (1993) (noting that those political activities least skewed toward the wealthy and well-educated include local meetings attendance and efforts to persuade others to vote a particular way).

25. Joan Shorenstein Center on the Press, Politics, and Public Policy, *The Vanishing Voter: A Project to Study and Invigorate the American Electoral Process,* available at http://www.vanishingvoter.org (last visited April 15, 2002).

26. Specifically, half of all respondents were asked in a telephone survey, "Now we'd like you to think about the past day only. During the past day have you discussed the presidential campaign with anyone?" See http://www.vanishingvoter.org/data/standard-series.shtml (last visited April 15, 2002). Respondents were U.S. citizens over eighteen years of age; each weekly survey interviewed more than one thousand respondents by telephone over a five-day period covering both weekdays and weekends. See http://www.vanishingvoter.org/methods.shtml (last visited April 15, 2002).

27. See Russell Neuman, *The Paradox of Mass Politics: Knowledge and Opinion in the American Electorate* 33, 170 (1986) (arguing on the basis of many distributions that the American public is really "three publics": 5 percent activist, 20 percent politically inert, and 75 percent episodically engaged with politics). Older studies have made similar findings. See generally, Bernard R. Berelson et al., *Voting: A Study of Opinion Formation in a Presidential Campaign* (1954); Norman H. Nie, Sidney Verba, and John R. Petrocik, *The Changing American Voter* 16–17 (1979) (describing this assessment of the public as part of the dominant paradigm).

28. It's true, of course, that a similar sort of underreporting will occur during the "low-interest" periods when the study picks up only 10 or 15 percent of conversationalists on a daily basis. But a substantial percentage of these respondents are activists who talk politics practically every day. In contrast, the proportion of frequent-but-not-daily conversationalists probably increases as Election Day approaches.

29. During the month following the election, the 1996 and 2000 National Election Studies asked respondents two questions: "Do you ever discuss politics with your family or friends?" and (if so) "How many days in the past week did you talk about politics with family or friends?" Unsurprisingly, conversational engagement is higher during the first week of the interviews than the rest of the period. We provide data for both post–election week and post–election month. Note, however, that it is only the entire sample that is statistically sound:

Year	Never	1–2	3–6	7	Daily	Discussion Rate
1996	20%	16%	31%	23%	9%	30%
1996 (week after)	17%	2%	26%	34%	20%	44%
2000	21%	1%	14%	24%	40%	57%
2000 (week after)	16%	2%	8%	22%	52%	68%

Source: 1996 and 2000 National Election Studies.

See Nancy Burns, et al., *National Election Studies, American National Election Study, 2000: Pre- and Post-Election Survey* (Inter-university Consortium for Political and Social Research version, 2001) (datasets); Steven J. Rosenstone et al., *National Election Studies, American National Election Study, 1996: Pre- and Post-Election Survey* (distributed by the Inter-university Consortium for Political and Social Research, 2d release, 1997) (datasets). These data indicate that around the time of the election, 65–80 percent of voting-age citizens are discussing politics at least once a week, and 30–70 percent are engaged three times or more per week.

Other studies suggest that the text may understate the extent to which Americans discuss politics outside the peak campaign season. In March or early April of 1980, 1984, 1989, 1991, 1992, and 1994, the Roper Organization gave respondents (adults nationwide) a card with various activities listed and asked them to "read down that list and call off each one you personally have done in the last week, either at home or at work." One of the list items was "Discussed politics with someone." In each year between 31 percent and 52 percent reported discussing politics in the past week, for an overall average of 41 percent. Henry E. Brady et al., *Roper Social and Political Trends Data, 1973–1994* (2000) (datasets). Similarly, between February and June 2000 (but mainly February through April), the 2000 General Social Survey asked a nationwide random sample of adults, "In the last twelve months . . . have you discussed your views about political or social policy issues, current affairs, or political campaigns with other people?" While 44 percent of the sample said no, 19 percent reported discussing such topics "once or twice," and 37 percent reported discussing "3 or more times." James A. Davis et al., *General Social Surveys, 1972–2000* (distributed by the Roper Center for Public Opinion Research, 2000) (datasets).

Some studies are somewhat less encouraging. The National Election Studies always ask, "During the campaign, did you talk to any people and try to show them why they should vote for or against one of the parties or candidates?" This probably leaves uncounted a lot of people who discuss politics without openly urging others to vote in a particular way. Still, 27–37 percent of respondents in election years say they did, depending on the closeness of the election and other factors. (In 1996 the figure was 28 percent; in 2000 it was 34 percent.) The National Election Studies, Center for Political Studies, University of Michigan, *The NES Guide to Public Opinion and Electoral Behavior,* available at http://www.umich.edu/~nes/nesguide/nesguide.htm (last visited April 15, 2002).

All of these data corroborate our central thesis: There is a substantial segment of the nonactivist population that engages in significant amounts of political conversation. Similar data from smaller surveys can be found at Polling the Nations, available at http://www.orspub.com (last visited April 15, 2002).

30. Amie Jameson, et al., *U.S. Census Bureau, Voting and Registration in the Election of November 2000* 2 (2002), available at www.census.gov/prod/2002pubs/p20-542.pdf (last viewed August 17, 2003).

31. In 2000 fewer than 15 percent of voters interviewed in the weeks following the elections had not discussed politics in the past week (compared with 40 percent of nonvoters); in 1996, 30 percent of voters had not discussed politics in the past week (compared with 57 percent of nonvoters). If one looks only at the week after the election, the results are even more striking: In the week after the election, only 13 percent of 2000 voters and 13 percent of 1996 voters had not discussed politics in the past week. Eighty-two percent of 2000 voters and 61 percent of 1996 voters discussed politics at least three days of the week. See Burns et al., supra note 29; Rosenstone et al., supra note 29 (2000 and 1996 National Election Studies).

32. Our expectations gain further support from other studies. A growing literature suggests that frequency of discussion is correlated with and contributes to increased political participation and increased willingness to attend a public forum. See Joohan Kim, Robert O. Wyatt, and Elihu Katz, "News, Talk, Opinion, Participation: The Part Played by Conversation in Deliberative Democracy," 16 *Pol. Comm.* 361, 372, 378 (1999) (tables 1 and 5); Jack M. McLeod et al., "Understanding Deliberation," supra note 24, at 760 (table 3). The latter study asked respondents in the Madison, Wisconsin, area, "If you were called to a local forum [about an issue the respondent had previously selected as the most important one facing Madison] where citizens discuss local or community problems, would you attend?" While there are any number of reasons for doubting the direct relevance of this question for Deliberation Day turnout, it is nonetheless significant that more than 60 percent of respondents expressed willingness to attend — even without any payment. Id. at 766, 768.

The National Election Study also allows us to determine the percentage of American voters who not only (1) discussed politics at least three times a week during the presidential election but (2) have attended a political meeting or a meeting on a local issue in the past year. On the surface, this seems like a very conservative base for predicting DDay turnout. Nevertheless, no fewer than 26 percent of all voters claim to have satisfied both these conditions in 2000. Of course, respondents notoriously exaggerate the extent of their civic participation, and we should take these self-descriptions with several grains of salt. At the same time, respondent exaggeration should be counterbalanced by the $150 citizen stipend obtained at DDay — by how much, is anybody's guess. Taking the NES percentage as a basis for calculation yields a DDay turnout of 28 million, 26 percent of the 106 million voters casting ballots in 2000. We can derive another estimate by determining the number of NES respondents who say they (1) have attended a political meeting or a meeting on a local issue in the past year, and (2) discuss politics at least three times a week. In 2000 more than 38 million adult citizens (20 percent) satisfied these requirements; among self-reported voters, the percentage was 26 percent. See Burns et al., supra note 29 (2000 National Election Study).

33. Compulsory voting in Australia has had little impact on the level of political knowledge or political engagement of citizens. More people go to the polls, but without an institutional context for discussion, they are not demonstrably more informed. See Ian McAllister, "Civic Education and Political Knowledge in Australia," 33 *Australasian Journal of Political Science* 7 (1998).

34. This is the daily rate paid jurors in Connecticut and Massachusetts after a short initial period of service, during which the employer is legally obliged to continue paying the juror's wage; the same rate is paid to jurors in Colorado after the first three days of service. Jurors in the federal courts receive $40 a day. Most states pay less, often much less. See J. Clark Kelso, "Final Report of the Blue Ribbon Commission on Jury System Improvement," appendix H, 47 *Hastings L. J.* 1433, 1557–58 (1996).

35. "To make entry pay rates more competitive in an all-volunteer force [army], the Act of September 28, 1971, . . . provided a substantial increase in basic pay rates for members with less than two years of service. A slight increase was also made in some pay grades for personnel with more than two years of service." Department of Defense, Office of the Secretary of Defense, Military Compensation Background Papers: Compensation Elements and Related Manpower Cost Items 9 (2d Ed. 1982). The cited act increased total average military pay by 14.2 percent; this was in addition to an earlier pay increase of 6.8 percent also approved that year. See An Act to Amend the Military Selective Service Act of 1967, Pub. L. No. 92-129, 85 Stat. 348, 255–357 (1971).

36. U.S. Department of Education, National Center for Educational Statistics, *Statistics in Brief: Overview of Public Elementary and Secondary Schools and Districts, 1997–98,* at http://nces.ed.gov/pubs99/1999322 (last visited May 15, 2003). ("Among the 87,631 public schools with students in membership during the 1997–98 school year, about 58.5 percent spanned the traditional primary grades, typically beginning with prekindergarten or kindergarten and going no higher than grade 8. About half (50.1 percent) of the nation's public school students were enrolled in these schools. An additional 17.3 percent of the schools covered the upper elementary and middle grades, and offered instruction to 19.6 percent of public school students. High schools represented 18.9 percent of the schools reported, and enrolled 27.1 percent of the total number of students. About 5.3 percent of schools followed some other grade configuration, including schools that spanned all of grades kindergarten through 12 and those that were ungraded.")

37. In an NCES survey in 1993–94, the average public school in cities and the urban fringe was found to have six hundred students and the average public school in rural areas had four hundred students. Id.

38. To the extent we rely on elementary schools, a few million adult-sized chairs may be required—this is a real, but relatively modest, cost. See Appendix A.

39. "In 1998–99, there were 2,279 public post-secondary institutions in the 50 states, District of Columbia, and outlying areas. Of the 2,279 institutions, 645 offered bachelor's or higher degrees, while 1,269 offered programs of at least 2 but less than 4 years' duration." U.S. Department of Education, National Center for Education Statistics,

Post-Secondary Institutions in the United States, 1998–99, available at http://nces.ed.gov/ pubs2002/quarterly/fall/q4-6.asp (2002) [hereinafter *Post-Secondary Institutions*] (citing data from the Integrated Postsecondary Education Data System *Institutional Characteristics Survey*). We may also be able to recruit institutions that participate in Title IV federal aid programs: "In 1998–99, IPEDS collected data from over 9,600 postsecondary institutions, with more than 6,500, or 68 percent, of the institutions having a Program Participation Agreement (PPA) with the Department of Education and thus eligible to participate in Title IV programs." Id. This would add space for a few million more. And, notably, 12.1 million of the 15.5 million students projected to be enrolled in postsecondary institutions in 2005 will be in public institutions. U.S. Department of Education, National Center for Education Statistics, *Digest of Education Statistics* 11 (1998) [hereinafter *Digest*].

40. Private elementary and secondary schools numbering 27,402 accommodate another five million students: "Approximately 56 percent of private school students were enrolled in elementary schools, 16 percent were enrolled in secondary schools, and 29 percent were enrolled in combined schools." U.S. Department of Education, National Center for Education Statistics, *Private School Universe Survey, 1997–98,* available at http://nces.ed.gov/pubs99/1999319.pdf (last visited on May 15, 2003) (1999).

41. There are at least 9,653 postsecondary institutions in the United States; the NCES thinks it may be underestimating by 13 percent, so this is a lower bound. *Post-Secondary Institutions,* supra note 39. There were 14.3 million students enrolled in postsecondary education in 1997. *Digest,* supra note 39, at 1. In 2005, a projected 3.4 million students will be enrolled in private postsecondary education. Id. at 11.

42. The Public Buildings Service, in charge of finding more room for the judiciary, claims that there are 731 federal courthouses, all of which can house at least an average of five hundred people. General Services Administration, Public Buildings Service, *Federal Courthouse Building Program,* available at http://www.gsa.gov/pbs/centers/ courthouse/ctprg.htm (last visited May 15, 2003). The National Center for State Courts does not provide a number (or even an estimate of the number) of state courthouses. We might, however, estimate on the basis of the number of judges: Since we know there are seventy-eight thousand judges, we might be able to assume a roughly equal number of courtrooms. (This number will, of course, be different from the number of courthouses.) Bureau of Labor Statistics, *1998–99 Occupational Outlook Handbook,* available at http://stats.bls.gov/ocohome.htm. Alternatively, see Elizabeth Petty Bentley, *County Courthouse Book* (2d ed., 1995). The author sent questionnaires to 4,700 counties, cities, and towns. She got a 65 percent response rate and provides information on 3,125 courthouses. Neither of these measures, however, provides information about capacity.

43. The nation's 2,283 YMCAs are the largest not-for-profit community service organizations in America, working to meet the health and social service needs of 16.9 million men, women, and children in ten thousand communities. World Alliance of YMCAs, *National Profile: YMCA of the USA,* available at http://www.ymca.int/ymcas

_country/national_profile/USA.htm (last visited May 15, 2003). Three hundred twenty-six YWCAs operate across the country, representing approximately two million women, girls, and males in their families. And Junior Chambers of Commerce now serve a membership of one million individuals at 275 centers and camps.

Adding all these non-profits together yields 2,884 more facilities. Underestimating that each can only hold five hundred people, we accommodate another 1.4 million deliberators.

44. "Churches, congregations, synagogues, temples and other places of formal religious worship (hereinafter called churches) [includes] 257,648 . . . organizations . . . listed in the Yellow Pages published by the nation's telephone companies. While this universe is nearly 100,000 fewer than the generally accepted number of 350,000 churches, those without telephone listings were unavailable for inclusion in the sample." Virginia Hodgkinson, *Independent Sector, from Belief to Commitment: The Community Service Activities and Finances of Religious Congregations in the US, 1992* (1993), summarized at American Religion Data Archive at http://www.thearda.com/archive/ CRUTCHFD.html (last visited May 15, 2003). About 44 percent of "churches" have congregations of five hundred–plus. Id. Assuming that churches can hold the capacity of their congregants, that gives us room for seventy-seven million deliberators as long as we (and the churches) are willing to blur the separation between church and state just a little. We may, however, need to set up dividers or screens in the sanctuaries to facilitate the small-group deliberations if no Sunday School classrooms can be found.

45. Unfortunately, there are no good estimates of the economic costs of holidays in general or Presidents Day in particular. The Bureau of Labor Statistics does not estimate the costs of individual holidays when making seasonal adjustments. According to the bureau's Handbook of Methods, it lumps economic costs of holidays into a single variable including other seasonally dependent phenomena, such as patterns due to weather, production, employment, and consumption preferences that regularly vary according to the season. U.S. Bureau of Labor Statistics, *Handbook of Methods,* chapter 2, "Employment, Hours, and Earnings from the Establishment Survey," available at http://www.bls.gov/opub/hom/homch2_e.htm# Estimating Procedures. The bureau estimates only the impact of moving holidays like Easter, Labor Day, and the Thanksgiving-Christmas period, and even here, the best estimates indicate that the effects of these shifts are "rather negligible." W. R. Bell and S. C. Hillmer, "Modeling Time Series with Calendar Variation," 78 *J. Am. Stat. Ass'n* 530 (1983).

The Congressional Budget Office has also refused to make dollar estimates in connection with proposals for Martin Luther King Day and the Family Medical Leave Act. It considered such matters much too speculative. Telephone interview by Eric Tam with Matt Pickford, analyst, Congressional Budget Office, (November 4, 2002).

46. See Gary Becker, "A Theory of the Allocation of Time," 65 *Econ. J.,* 492 (1965); Douglas Larson, "Recreation Choices and Values of Time," 69 *Land Econ.* 270 (1993).

47. Compare Gary Becker, "Crime and Punishment: An Economic Approach," 76 *J. Pol. Econ.* 169 (1968), with George Stigler, "The Optimum Enforcement of Laws," 78 *J. Pol. Econ.* 526 (1970).

48. A thought-experiment might serve to clarify this point further. Imagine that DDay succeeded beyond our fondest dreams and that every single American who paid more than $150 in taxes showed up at the event. Under this scenario, each taxpayer would be paying himself $150 as a reward for being a good citizen! No real resources would be expended other than the ancillary costs enumerated in the text.

49. E-mail from Kurt Czarnowski, Social Security Administration Regional Communications Director, Boston, to Eric Tam (October 7, 2002) (on file with authors). Of course, it will also cost a good deal to pay the official personnel stationed at each site. We will be estimating this expense shortly.

50. Our reluctance to speculate is bolstered by the notorious failure of economists to agree on the deadweight costs of increased taxation or debt. See, e.g., Joseph Stiglitz, *Economics of the Public Sector* 470 (2d ed., 1988). ("There is no consensus concerning whether the deadweight loss [of increased taxes] is large or small.") More recent work only confirms the existence of sharp disagreement. Compare Martin Feldstein, "Tax Avoidance and the Deadweight Loss of the Income Tax," *NBER Working Papers* (1995) (NBER Working Paper 5055) (estimating a deadweight loss of 165 percent), with Jean-Jacques Laffont, *Incentives and Political Economy* 23 (2000) (estimating a deadweight loss of 30 percent).

51. Under a recent federal law, voter registration databases will shortly be computerized in all states. Help America Vote Act of 2002, 42 U.S.C.A. §§15301, 15483 (West 2002).

52. There are more than twenty-five hundred call-center companies operating in the United States, ranging from a few hundred operators to fifteen thousand employees. Telephone interview by Eric Tam with John Anton, director of the Center for Consumer Driven Quality, Purdue University (October 19, 2002).

53. Id.

54. See Appendix A for further discussion.

55. Telephone interview by Eric Tam with Steve Jost, associate director of communications, Census 2000 (January 8, 2003).

56. Rather than renting the schools for DDay, the federal government should make its education aid contingent on willingness of the local school board to open its facilities to the public on DDay. For reasons we have explained, the school boards should not charge for this service, so long as the DDA pays the marginal costs of operating the facilities.

57. This is only a rough estimate. There are ten thousand election jurisdictions in the United States, and no one adds up their election costs. Many local governments do not even calculate their own election costs. See National Commission on Federal Election Reform, *To Assure Pride and Confidence in the Electoral Process* 68 (2001). We rely on the "best guess" provided by the CalTech/MIT Voting Technology Project's

final report of July 2001. Its estimate of "approximately one billion dollars" includes spending by counties both on primaries and final elections. This does not include the relatively small funding amounts from states and cities. *CalTech/MIT Voting Technology Project* 50 (2001). Nor does it include the $50 million annual budget of the Federal Electoral Commission.

58. See Bruce Ackerman and Ian Ayres, *Voting with Dollars* 247, n. 3 (2002) ("contributions to federal candidates and parties of federal 'hard' monies were in excess of $2.9 billion," citing www.fec.gov/finance).

59. See id. at 85.

60. For an analysis of McCain-Feingold and a consideration of alternatives, see id. at 12–54 (especially 45–54).

7. The Problem of Mass Democracy

1. See Aristotle, *The Politics* 172–73 (Steven Barnes ed., Jonathan Barnes trans., 1996) (circa 350 BCE) (1326a6–b25)

2. See Bernard Manin, *The Principles of Representative Government* 42–93 (1997).

3. See Jane Mansbridge, *Beyond Adversary Democracy* 128–30 (1980).

4. We will be discussing the special case of referenda further. See also Chapter 6.

5. See Bruce Ackerman, *The Future of Liberal Revolution* (1992) (chapters 1 and 2).

6. Bruce Ackerman has developed the theory of constitutional politics, and its historical development in the United States, in a series of books: 1 *We the People: Foundations* (1991) [hereinafter 1 *We the People*], 2 *We the People: Transformations* (1998). See also, Bruce Ackerman and David Golove, *Is NAFTA Constitutional?* (1995); Ackerman, supra note 5.

7. For some thoughtful reflections on this cycle, see Albert Hirschman, *Shifting Involvements* 62–91 (1982).

8. *The Federalist* 14, at 72 (James Madison) (Clinton Rossiter ed., 1999).

9. See generally Jack Rakove, *Original Meanings: Politics and Ideas in the Making of the Constitution* (1996); Ralph Lerner, *The Thinking Revolutionary: Principle and Practice in the New Republic* (1987).

10. Bernard Bailyn provides a useful compendium in *The Ideological Origins of the American Revolution* (1992). See also, 1 Herbert Storing, *The Complete Anti-Federalist: What the Anti-Federalists Were For* (1981).

11. *The Federalist* 1, at 1 (Alexander Hamilton) (Clinton Rossiter ed., 1999).

12. See Bruce Ackerman and Neal Katyal, "Our Unconventional Founding," 62 *U. Chi. L. Rev.* 475, 514–39 (1995).

13. *The Federalist* 49, at 283 (James Madison) (Clinton Rossiter ed., 1999).

14. See Ackerman, 1 *We the People*, supra note 6, at 167–79.

15. See id. at 179–99.

16. *The Federalist* 10, at 48 (James Madison) (Clinton Rossiter ed., 1999).

17. See Hannah Arendt, *On Revolution* 252–59 (1963) for some perceptive commentary on Jefferson's aspirations.

18. For a brilliant analysis of the decline and fall of elite politics, see Robert H.

Wiebe, *Opening of American Society: From the Adoption of the Constitution to the Eve of Disunion* (1984).

19. For representative samples of Progressive opinion, see Charles King et al., "Merits and Limitations of the Initiative, Referendum, and Recall," 43 *Annals* 1 (1912); Herbert Croly, *The Promise of American Life* (1909); Charles Beard and Birl Shultz, *Initiative, Referendum, and Recall* (1912).

The Progressives, in turn, were profoundly influenced by their interpretation of the Swiss experience. See Henry Demarest Lloyd, *A Sovereign People* (John Hobson ed., 1907). For more recent studies of the Swiss experience, compare Benjamin Barber, *The Death of Communal Liberty* (1974), with Kris Kobach, *The Referendum: Direct Democracy in Switzerland* (1998).

20. For a graphic description by a leading journalist, see David Broder, *Democracy Derailed: Initiative Campaigns and the Power of Money* (2000).

21. See Dave Hogan, "Fewer Initiatives Expected on the Fall Ballot," *Oregonian*, May 25, 2002 (anticipating ten initiatives in fall 2002, down from the eighteen during the previous election). In the 1990s, for example, there were fifty-six statewide initiatives in Oregon placed on the ballot during the five elections held during the decade. Richard Ellis, *Democratic Delusions: The Initiative Process in America* 36 (2002).

22. For a recent critique, see id. For a thoughtful defense, see Ian Budge, *The New Challenge of Direct Democracy* (1996). For measured assessments tending in the negative direction, see Thomas E. Cronin, *Direct Democracy* (1989); David Magleby, *Direct Legislation* (1984).

A recent study usefully emphasizes the fact that "direct" democratic initiatives must still be implemented by state bureaucracies — which often exercise great discretion in the process. So "direct" democracy isn't quite as direct as some rhetoric would suggest. See Elizabeth Gerber et al., *Stealing the Initiative* (2001). All of these books contain useful bibliographies.

23. See Chapters 1 and 3.

24. For a broadly similar use of hypothetical scenarios that we find illuminating, see James Sundquist, *Dynamics of the Party System* 11–25 (1973).

25. The environmental activists might also respond by forming a new political party and qualifying it for sufficient support to allow the Green candidate for president to compete on equal terms with the Democrats and the Republicans. But to keep the scenarios simple, we ignore this possibility in the text.

26. In 1 *We the People,* supra note 6, Ackerman emphasizes this institutional theme in his treatment of the constitutional crisis of the 1930s. He is planning a similar study of the 1960s.

27. See id.

28. Even when it came to ratifying the Constitution, the Founders left the final decision to a select group of representatives sitting in special ratifying conventions. In contrast, the French Revolutionaries used the referendum to ratify their Constitution of 1793, although it was ultimately stillborn. Americans were well aware of the referendum, which the Swiss had pioneered. See Benjamin Barber, supra note 19.

Indeed, Anti-Federalists used the referendum as part of their campaign against ratification in Rhode Island. See Bruce Ackerman and Neal Katyal, "Our Unconventional Founding," supra note 12, at 527.

29. See Robert C. Luskin, James S. Fishkin, Ian McAllister, John Higley, and Pamela Ryan, "Information Effects in Referendum Voting: Evidence from the Australian Deliberative Poll," Paper Presented at the American Political Science Association Meetings, Washington, D.C. (August–September 2000) (unpublished manuscript on file with authors).

30. For further discussion, see Chapter 5.

8. Responsible Citizenship

1. Plato, *Crito* (G. M. A. Grube trans., 1981) (c. 380 BCE).

2. For more on the theory of private citizenship, see 1 Bruce Ackerman, *We the People: Foundations* chapter 9 (1991).

3. Some perfect privatists will be attracted to DDay by the $150 but may get into the spirit of the proceedings, and at the end of day find that they have become private citizens, genuinely interested in the public and its problems.

4. See generally Robert Putnam et al., *Making Democracy Work* (1994); Robert Putnam, *Bowling Alone* (2000).

5. See Chapters 3 and 6 for our concrete arguments suggesting that America qualifies as a "relatively healthy" civil society, in both qualitative and quantitative senses of the term.

6. As in many other parts of this analysis, we are indebted to Robert Luskin for this term. He developed it for analysis of opinion change in Deliberative Polls.

7. 1 Jürgen Habermas, *The Theory of Communicative Action: Reason and the Rationalization of Society* (Thomas McCarthy trans., 1984) (1981); 2 Jürgen Habermas, *The Theory of Communicative Action: Lifeworld and System: A Critique of Functionalist Reason* (Thomas McCarthy trans., 1987) (1981).

8. When the 2000 National Election Study asked eligible voters to identify their political discussion partners, about 16 percent of those identified were spouses, 29 percent were other relatives, 27 percent were coworkers, 15 percent were neighbors, and 7 percent were coreligionists. Only 13 percent of discussion partners did not fall into these five categories. See Nancy Burns et al., *National Election Studies, American National Election Study, 2000: Pre- and Post-Election Survey* (2001), available at http://www.umich.edu/~nes (dataset). More localized studies of the 1984 and 1992 elections found almost exactly the same distribution of political discussants. See Robert Huckfeldt and John Sprague, *Citizens, Politics, and Social Communication* 110 (1995) (table 6.1); Robert Huckfeldt et al., "Political Environments, Cohesive Social Groups, and the Communication of Public Opinion," 39 *American Journal of Political Science* 1025, 1031–32 (1995).

These social contexts do not often invite broad-ranging political debate. To use one crude measure from the 2000 National Election Study, spouses agreeing on a presidential candidate outnumbered those who disagreed by a ratio of 7 to 1; discussion partners among relatives and church members agreed with one another by a ratio of almost 3 to 1. See Burns et al. Work and neighborhood environments are slightly less homogenous, with agreement-disagreement ratios closer to 2 to 1, see id.

This means that only a minority of potential voters ever engage in a dialogue with a representative of a different point of view. According to the 2000 National Election Study, only 28 percent can clearly identify at least one of their discussion partners as having an opposing candidate preference; only 24 percent said that they discussed politics with such a person "sometimes," and only 6 percent "often" engaged with a contrary-minded discussion partner. See id. Even in the three-candidate 1992 election, about half of the voting-age populace spoke "rarely" with someone they thought preferred another candidate; only 42 percent spoke with such a person "sometimes"; and 16 percent spoke "often." See Paul Beck et al., *Inter-university Consortium for Political and Social Research, Cross-National Election Studies: United States Study, 1992* (1993), available at http://www.icpsr.umich.edu (datasets). Similarly, in a classic study of a New York community in the 1948 election, only one-quarter of respondents thought that one of their discussion partners belonged to the opposite political party. See Bernard Berelson, Paul Lazarsfeld, and William McPhee, *Voting: A Study of Opinion Formation in a Presidential Campaign* 98 (1954). See also Pamela Johnston Conover, et al., "The Deliberative Potential of Political Discussion," 32 *British Journal of Political Science* 21 (2002).

9. See Chapter 3.

10. See Chapter 3.

11. See Chapter 2.

12. We principally celebrate the signers of the Declaration of Independence on July 4, but perhaps one may catch a glimpse of the mass of ordinary citizens in the background. In any event, the Declaration of Independence happened a long time ago.

13. The originating source of this dichotomy is Benjamin Constant. For a good recent study, see Stephen Holmes, *Benjamin Constant and the Making of Modern Liberalism* (1984).

9. Fearful Asymmetries

1. See Chapter 4.

2. See Bruce Ackerman and Anne Alstott, *The Stakeholder Society* 95 (1999) (the precise proportion in 1995 was 38.5 percent). See generally Edward Wolff, "Recent Trends in the Size Distribution of Household Wealth," 12 *J. Econ. Persp.* 131, 133, 136 (1996).

3. See *The Luxembourg Income Study* at http://www.lisproject.org/keyfigures/ineqt-able.htm (last visited May 14, 2003). This is the leading source of comparative data, but it reports on the distribution only of income, not of wealth in a broad range of countries. No source of comparable quality exists that seeks to compare wealth distributions on an international basis.

4. See Bruce Ackerman, *Social Justice in the Liberal State* (1980); James Fishkin, *The Dialogue of Justice* (1992).

5. See, for example, the campaign reform scheme advanced by Bruce Ackerman and Ian Ayres, *Voting with Dollars: A New Paradigm for Campaign Finance* (2002).

6. For background on this issue, see generally Bruce Ackerman and William Hassler, *Clean Coal, Dirty Air* (1981); for a recent update, see Douglas Jehl, "Subsidies for Clean Coal Miss Mark," *New York Times,* August 4, 2001.

7. Both quadrants III and IV can be considered instances of plebiscitary mass democracy because of their reliance on raw public opinion of the mass public—the first, via the proxy of random sampling, the second via the entire mass.

8. For a more extended argument along these lines, see James Fishkin, *Democracy and Deliberation* (1991).

9. For an overview, see generally Anna Coote and Jo Lenaghan, *Citizens' Juries: Theory into Practice* (1997).

10. See the coverage of the well-known citizens' jury conducted by the Jefferson Center on the Clinton health care plan. For example, Julie Rovner, "President Clinton's Health Care Plan on Trial Last Year," NPR radio broadcast, September 30, 1994.

11. The design would be strengthened with control groups so that one could know what changes are due to changes in the world (what Campbell and Stanley call "history") and what changes are due to the deliberations themselves. See Donald Campbell and Julian Stanley, *Experimental and Quasi-Experimental Designs for Research* (1963).

12. Consensus conferences originated in Denmark, primarily for public consultation on ethical issues pertaining to scientific and technical questions. Respondents are recruited via newspaper ads and then selected on the basis of diversity. The deliberations resemble those of citizens' juries. However, self-selection creates problems of representativeness. The universe of participants has already been limited to those who have some special interest in putting themselves forward. Efforts to ensure some demographic representativeness cannot fully compensate for the biases that have been introduced.

The consensus conference, like the citizens' jury, also lacks the secret ballot. By prescribing that the group reach a "consensus," it exposes the process of decision making to social pressure towards group conformity. The Deliberative Poll, by contrast, solicits opinions only in confidential questionnaires at the end of the weekend. Deliberation Day doesn't solicit candidate preferences in any way, with participants waiting until Election Day to cast their ballots.

Two other institutional strategies, Televote and the Choice Questionnaire, involve deliberation by many individuals who are in relative isolation from one another. In Televote, the respondents are given a survey on the phone and then sent materials on the issue. They are urged to discuss the topic in their homes, with friends and family. Then, at a later time, they are called back to see what their opinions are after further thought and discussion. Televote employs scientific random sampling rather than self-selection as in Consensus Conferences or the quota sampling typical of citizens' juries. A difficulty, however, is that the deliberation encouraged by the scheme is limited. Even respondents who are conscientious will usually discuss the issue only with like-minded friends and family. Perhaps for these reasons, the opinion changes recorded in Televote experiments are modest compared with those from Deliberative Polls and other microcosmic deliberations that require discussion with people from alternative viewpoints (through, say, assignment of random samples to small-group discussions). While Deliberation Day will take place in local communities, it will employ random assignment within convenient geographical areas in order to engage people in conversations beyond their normal interlocutors.

The Choice Questionnaire is another innovation that employs random sampling but with limited deliberation. Like Televote, it is meant to encourage thinking with more information. But unlike Televote, it attempts to provide further information within the survey instrument itself. And unlike Televote, the time for deliberation is limited to the time it takes the survey professional to ask the prescribed questions. For these reasons the deliberation provoked by the Choice Questionnaire is even more modest than in Televote. Its virtue, however, is that it provides a cost-effective way to investigate the effects of information on scientifically rigorous random samples and to incorporate control groups into experimental designs. See Peter Neijens and Vincent Price, "Opinion Quality in Public Opinion Research," 9 Int'l J. Pub. Opinion Res. 336 (1997); Peter Neijens, The Choice Questionnaire (1987).

13. See Peter Dienel and Ortwin Renn, "Planning Cells: A Gate to 'Fractal' Mediation," in Fairness and Competence in Citizen Participation: Evaluating Models for Environmental Discourse 117 (Ortwin Renn et al. eds., 1995). Selected local random samples do not add up to a random sample of an entire region. Nevertheless, if Planning Cells were conducted from a regional random sample, with respondents invited to decentralized assignments in local communities, then the process could offer the same kind of basis as a Deliberative Poll in representing counterfactual but informed opinion. Of course, with different events occurring in different places at different times, one would worry whether the process was sufficiently similar in each location for it to make sense to aggregate the results. Nevertheless, the method can be thought of as providing, or attempting to provide, a decentralized microcosm of the entire population, whose parts are gathered in different locations.

14. In the United States, this kind of activity has most notably been carried out by the National Issues Forums supported by the Kettering Foundation, the Study Circles Resource Network supported by the Topsfield Foundation, and the Great Decisions dialogue series supported by the Foreign Policy Association.

15. For an overview, see generally John Gastil, By Popular Demand 118–19 (2000).

16. See Chapter 6.

10. Alternative Futures

1. Merton describes how he was drawn into the evaluation of wartime radio broadcasts by his Columbia colleague Paul Lazarsfeld in Robert K. Merton et al., The Focused Interview: A Manual of Problems and Procedures xv–xvi (2d ed., 1990). Originally the focus group was the "focused group" interview because it was focused on shared group reactions to a particular stimulus. Later the spelling changed.

2. Id. at 13.

3. See id. at 61–62 for the gangster comparison and id. at 118 for Irish-American respondents' tepid reaction to stories about British heroism.

4. Leo Bogart, quoted in Merton, supra note 1, at xxv.

5. Id.

6. For a good overview of the wreckage, see Kathleen Hall Jamieson, *Dirty Politics: Deception, Distraction, and Democracy* (1992) (describing the strategic use of many ads derived from focus groups, including the infamous Willie Horton ad as well as debates over social security, defense, race, and crime).

7. Merton himself was a leading analyst of the phenomenon of multiple invention, and we share his caution against the romantic notion that individuals are uniquely capable of making particular discoveries. See Robert Merton, *On the Shoulders of Giants* (1965).

8. Annual focus group expenditures in the United States were estimated at $1.102 billion for 2001, rising at 5.2 percent a year. Hence the costs for four years would approach $5 billion. Total market research expenditures in the United States were estimated at $6.159 billion for 2001. Hence the four-year costs for market research efforts to better understand and alter the thinking and behavior of the mass public are more than $24 billion. See Laurence Gold, "U.S. MR Spend $6.2 Billion, Net Growth 1.2%," *Inside Res.*, May 2002, at 1–2.

9. Joseph A. Glick, "Focus Groups in Political Campaigns," in *The Manship Guide to Political Campaigns* 119 (David D. Perlmutter ed., 1999).

10. See the description of "products" on the web site of Greenberg, Quinlan, Rosner Research for a picture of how a successful political consulting firm uses focus groups in all three ways: http://www.greenbergresearch.com/campaigns_us/products.html.

11. The dial meter is reminiscent of the Lazarsfeld-Stanton program analyzer. Merton's launch of the focus group was in reaction to a session in which people pushed buttons of approval and disapproval in reaction to a broadcast. Those reactions were averaged on a primitive polygraph. Merton pioneered discussions that helped reveal the rationales behind the reactions. Now with the dial technology there is a return to aggregating mere approval and disapproval. However, these ratings can also be used to stimulate further discussions. See Merton, supra note 1, at xvi for the original device.

12. Roger Ailes quoted in Frank Luntz, "The Voices of Victory," part 2, *The Polling Report,* May 30, 1994, available at http://www.pollingreport.com/focus.htm.

13. Luntz, supra note 12.

14. For more on the strategic uses of negative ads, see Jamieson, supra note 6.

15. *Face the Nation* (CBS television broadcast, April 21, 1996) (transcript obtained via Burrell's Information Services). The CBS interviewers were Phil Jones and Bob Schieffer.

16. See e.g., Dan Balz, "A Picture of Trust, Taken Out of Focus," *Washington Post,* April 26, 1996; Calvin Woodward, "The Candidate as Father Figure," *Bergen Record,* April 28, 1996.

17. See Chapter 3.

18. See Stephen Ansolabehere and Shanto Iyengar, *Going Negative: How Political Advertisements Shrink and Polarize the Electorate* 55 (1995).

19. See id. at 99, 105. While we are persuaded by the demobilization thesis, it remains controversial. See Stephen Ansolabehere, Shanto Iyengar, and Adam Simon, "Replicating Experiments Using Aggregate and Survey Data: The Case of Negative Advertising and Turnout," 93 *American Political Science Review* 901 (1999) (presenting further analyses in response to critics, supporting the same basic conclusions).

For an overview of current research, see Lee Sigelman and Mark Kugler, "Why Is Research on the Effects of Negative Campaigning So Inconclusive? Understanding Citizens' Perceptions of Negativity," 65 *J. Pol.* 142 (2003). A mature assessment should also recognize that all negative ads are not alike. Some researchers have found a difference between irresponsible "mudslinging" and ads containing useful negative information. See Kim Fridkin Kahn and Patrick J. Kenney, "Do Negative Campaigns Mobilize or Suppress Turnout? Clarifying the Relationship Between Negativity and Participation," 93 *Am. Pol. Sci. Rev.* 877 (1999).

20. See our discussion in Chapter 3.

21. See Robert Luskin and James Fishkin, "Deliberation and 'Better Citizens,'" Presentation at the Annual Joint Sessions of Workshops of the European Consortium for Political Research (March 2002) (unpublished manuscript, on file with authors).

Appendix A. Estimated Costs for Deliberation Day

1. Office of Personnel Management, Federal Employment Statistics Fact Book 14 (Trend of Civilian Compensation and Benefits) (2002), http://www.opm.gov/feddata/02factbk.pdf.

2. Over the past decade the total expenditure on benefits for federal employees has been approximately 30 percent of base salary. Id. at 6.

3. The Federal Election Commission, for example, budgets a similar nonlabor vs. labor expenditure ratio. *Federal Election Commission Budget Request for FY 2001* (table 2), http://www.fec.gov/pages/fc2001just.html.

4. We are indebted to Gregory Huber for assistance with this estimate.

5. For example, of the telephone calls made to the Social Security Administration in 2001, 30 percent were handled entirely by IVR and 70 percent were handled by a live operator. Telephone interview with Roy Snyder, deputy associate commissioner for the Office of Telephone Services, Social Security Administration, and Dick Couture, Division of Integrated Telecommunications Management, Social Security Administration (August 29, 2002). These proportions are approximately reversed in the banking industry. Telephone interview with John Anton, director of the Center for Consumer Driven Quality, Purdue University (October 19, 2002).

6. Anton, supra note 5. Due to the impressive economies of scale that exist with regard to online processing, we do not expect that the costs of setting up the system would rise under the fifty million– and seventy million–participant scenarios. The main additional expense would be added server capacity, which we assume to be included in the increased costs of running a larger Deliberation Day Authority.

7. Id. More than 2,500 private call center companies of varying size exist in the

United States, the largest of which employ more than fifteen thousand people, so there is available private capacity to handle a job of this magnitude.

8. Id. Most government agencies run phone center systems at more than 95 percent efficiency, but a short-term diversion of some capacity may well be feasible without undue disruption of other operations. See also telephone interview with Maureen Allen, director, communications and liaison, Wage and Investment Division, Internal Revenue Service (October 5, 2002). The average cost per telephone inquiry at the IRS (handled in house by a combined IVR/live operator system) is estimated to be between $5 and $8. This is higher than the commercial rates because of the technical nature of taxation inquiries, requiring longer calls and additional knowledge.

9. Anton, supra note 5.

10. Telephone interview with Steve Jost, associate director of communications, Census 2000 (January 8, 2003); telephone interview with Paulette Lichtman-Panzer, supervisory management analyst, Office of Communications External Liaison Branch, Bureau of the Census (January 30, 2003).

11. Id. The Census Bureau spent approximately $67 million per year in 1999 and 2000 on the partnership outreach program described above.

12. A $20 million media advertising budget is about half of the advertising budgets of the leading candidates during the 2000 elections—Al Gore spent $36.7 million, George W. Bush $46 million. Anthony Carrado, "Financing the 2000 Presidential Election," in *Financing the 2000 Elections* 90 (David Magleby ed., 2002).

13. E-mail from Kurt Czarnowski, Boston regional communications director, Social Security Administration (October 7, 2002). A feasible proposal for reducing costs would be to appropriate the SSA's or some other agency's currently existing distribution system, as Deliberation Day payments would be sent out only once every two or four years. One expense that this figure does not include is auditing, although we can assume that this auditing would be covered by the expense outlay for the Federal Deliberation Day Authority.

14. Id.

15. U.S. Department of Labor, Bureau of Labor Statistics, Occupational Employment Statistics Website, *2000 National Occupational Employment and Wage Statistics,* http://www.bls.gov/oes/2000/oes119032.htm (figures converted to 2001 dollars).

16. The first shift would be from 7 A.M. to 1 P.M., the second from noon to 6 P.M.

17. U.S. Department of Labor, Bureau of Labor Statistics, Occupational Employment Statistics Website, *2000 National Occupational Employment and Wage Statistics,* http://www.bls.gov/oes/2000/oes252031.htm (figures converted to 2001 dollars).

18. U.S. Dep't Education, National Center for Education Statistics, *Internet Access in U.S. Public Schools and Classrooms: 1994–2001,* http://nces.ed.gov/pubs2002/internet/3.asp.

19. Id., http://nces.ed.gov/pubs2002/internet/4.asp.

20. Joe Agron, "That Sinking Feeling: American School and University 31st Annual M & O Cost Study," *American School and University,* April 2002, at 26–33.

21. U.S. Department of Education, National Center for Education Statistics, supra note 18.

22. A survey of online distributors reveals that metal folding chairs can be bought for $8.74 each (converted to 2001 dollars). *Folding Tables and Chairs, Metal Folding Chairs,* at http://www.folding-tables-chairs.com/metal-folding-chairs-NPS.html?mgi-Token=HHG51FI1AD9G7GFG14I9 (last viewed on August 22, 2003). We suspect that the government can obtain large quantity discounts for such a large order, but to be conservative, we are assuming a price of eight dollars per chair.

23. U.S. Department of Education, National Center for Educational Statistics, *Statistics in Brief: Overview of Public Elementary and Secondary Schools and Districts, 1997-98,* at http://nces.ed.gov/pubs99/1999322 (last viewed on May 15, 2003).

24. U.S. Department of Labor, Bureau of Labor Statistics, Occupational Employment Statistics Website, *2000 National Occupational Employment and Wage Statistics,* http://www.bls.gov/oes/2000/oes372011.htm (figures converted to 2001 dollars).

25. U.S. Department of Labor, Bureau of Labor Statistics, Occupational Employment Statistics Website, *2000 National Occupational Employment and Wage Statistics,* http://www.bls.gov/oes/2000/oes333051.htm (figures converted to 2001 dollars). Local governments typically charge only for labor costs when police are contracted for state or federal government purposes. Interview with Public Information Office, Los Angeles Police Department (September 4, 2002).

26. U.S. General Accounting Office, Briefing Report to Congressional Requesters, *Food Assistance: Information on Meal Costs in the National School Lunch Program,* GAO/RCED-94-32BR National School Lunch Program.

27. U.S. Department. of Education, National Center for Education Statistics, *Digest of Education Statistics, 2001* (table 51: Public School Pupils Transported at Public Expense and Current Expenditures for Transportation: 1929–30 to 1998–99), http://nces.ed.gov/pubs2002/digest2001/tables/dt051.asp.

INDEX

advertising, commercial, 145, 206–10
advertising, political: advertising for
    DDay, 222–23, 227 (table); before
    Congress Day, 102; before DDay,
    24; focus groups used, 207, 209, 211,
    215–16 (*see also* focus groups); and ini-
    tiatives, 162; length of ads, 10, 15, 24,
    86–87, 93; negative advertising, 93,
    215, 216, 245n8, 267n19; niche adver-
    tising, 82; positive effects of DDay
    on, 94, 95, 245n8; 2000 budgets,
    268n12. *See also* campaigns and cam-
    paigning; sound bites
age: and the digital divide, 142; of
    Iowa caucus participants, 251n17; and
    party leanings, 251n17; and voter/
    DDay participation, 93, 129, 243n14,
    244n15, 252n22
Ailes, Roger, 210
Andersen, Vibeke Normann, 239n12
Ansolabehere, Stephen, 216
anticipated reaction, law of, 76–77, 85,
    105, 127–29
approval voting, 237n14
Aristotle, 149
Arrow, Kenneth, 57
Australia: compulsory voting, 133,
    256n33; Deliberative Polls, 45, 49, 54,
    113, 171, 239n15, 243n10

balloting. *See* elections
Bartels, Larry, 60
Becker, Gary, 137–38
Birdsell, David S., 42
Bishop, George, 7
Bogart, Leo, 207
Bonner, Rebekka, x
Bradburn, Norman, x, 239n12
Brady, David, x
Brady, Henry, x
Brody, Richard, x
Brown, Jerry, 249–50n10
Bryce, James, Lord, 40
Bush, George H. W. (1989–1993),
    232(table), 250n10
Bush, George W. (2001–present),
    233(table), 268n12. *See also* Bush v.
    Gore election
Bush v. Gore election (2000), 6, 41–
    42, 145–46, 232–33(table), 234n9,
    268n12

campaign finance: campaign finance re-
    form, 10, 100, 146; campaign spend-
    ing, 145, 268n12; Feingold's pledge,
    86; and inequality, 190
campaigns and campaigning: current
    media coverage, 91, 243n11 (*see also*
    television); DDay's effect on strat-